A Worthy Girl's Guide to Life

One Day at a Time

Carla G. Harper

Veritas Conquistor Publishing

GREENSBORO, NORTH CAROLINA

Copyright © 2019 by **Carla G. Harper**

All rights reserved. No part of this publication may be reproduced, distributed or transmitted in any form or by any means, without prior written permission.

Veritas Conquistor Publishing
North Carolina
www.carlagharper.com

Book Layout © 2017 BookDesignTemplates.com

A Worthy Girl's Guide to Life/Carla G. Harper. -- 1st ed.
ISBN: 978-0-9971907-3-1

For Maggie

Who's a Worthy Girl?

You are a Worthy Girl, at any age.

God custom designed you to fulfill specific plans. He wants every girl to...

- Love, even when she does not feel like it
- Seek truth and hate lies
- Know that she's valuable, no matter who or what she's encountered in the world
- Act to protect herself and others from lies, excesses, abuse, and injustice
- Believe Christ died for her freedom
- Choose to be responsible for her actions and attitudes
- Live by percentages with her money and time so she's never too busy or too broke
- Work at every task as a service to him
- Take care of her mind, body, and spirit
- Enjoy life and relationships

What does a Worthy Girl want?

All girls want the same things: peace, love, happiness, freedom, health, meaning. A successful life is not random nor is the path to all these things free of challenges and hard decisions. The secrets are not complex, but you must first understand a basic set of principles that God set in motion.

The principles apply to all people, regardless of beliefs, age, status, color, or any other factor.

Life makes more sense and can be dealt with effectively when you understand the principles. Success is much more probable when following principles. Challenges come to all, but those who have applied the principles and made good choices are likely to enjoy life more and weather the storms better.

When you couple respect for immutable principles with trusting God, you have a recipe for a phenomenal life.

It's like investing money, the sooner you start the faster the investment will grow.

However, there are no fool proof formulas. Not every batch of cookies comes out the same, even when you follow the recipe. The fact that God will not follow a formula presents a tension as well as hope.

How can you have hope when things might not work out the way you want?

If there was an exact formula that applied to every single person, some people would give up prematurely. A person who made foolish decisions as a youngster would have no hope of getting their life on track. Dreams would be useless. It would eliminate the need for redemption.

Formulas that never varied would make arrogant, ungrateful people out of some and despairing wrecks out of others. God cares about every single individual. He has a unique plan for each.

Every plan contains good times and bad times because he cares most about your character. For those who believe in Jesus, the son of God, there's another level of life that exceeds what any person can imagine. This is the Christian life. It is available to any person, and everything you need to know about it can be found in the Bible (God's Word).

You might ask, "What if I was born into abuse or poverty, what if I have no education, etc." Don't disqualify hope with "what if" questions.

Jesus said, "But small is the gate and narrow the road that leads to life, and only a few find it" (Matthew 7:14).

The only thing that can prevent you from the road that leads to life is your choice.

HOW THIS BOOK IS ORGANIZED

This daily devotional book attempts to explain God's principles and promises in simple terms that are relevant to girls and women. The principles God placed in motion are applicable to all people. God's promises are for every person who claims Christ as their savior.

Around the 3rd grade, you likely got serious about multiplication, thanks to a teacher. Then you moved on to fractions and eventually Algebra, Geometry, and perhaps even beyond. Geometry would have confused and frustrated you in 3rd grade. Keep that in mind as you study the Word and concepts of God. Don't get confused and frustrated with deep theology before you master the basics. Like math, understanding God and his will for your life forms through building blocks. One concept opens the mind to the next concept.

This book is not written for a 3rd grader, but it does attempt to provide foundational concepts of truth in simple terms. "The journey of a 1,000 miles begins with a single step," said Lao-Tzu the Chinese philosopher.

If you will seek him, God will blow you away over and over with revelations and amazing experiences. Once you begin to see how God works, you will become addicted to those experiences. Don't give up when you find they cannot be controlled. God is not "on demand." You only play on his terms. Follow his principles and rules of engagement, and you will never cease to be amazed. Go ahead. What have you got to lose?

Regardless of your age, the desires of your heart and the things you grapple with don't change much. You either mature and graduate to bigger challenges and deeper levels of understanding, or you get stuck some place. God in his love and mercy will keep you on a lesson until you get it.

How to make the most out of this guide and study of the Bible

1. Acquire and use a copy of the NIV (New International Version) Life Application Study Bible 2000 or earlier edition. All scripture and references in this book are from the NIV Life Application Study Bible 1991 edition.
2. Read the foot notes for verses in the NIV.
3. Every verse, story, lesson in the Bible has at least three contextual meanings: a) historical, b) instructional for all Christians, c) a personal message for you potentially revealed by the Holy Spirit

Acknowledgments

Marcia Sinkovitz, Director of Leading Inmates in Faith and Education, and Mollie Williams served as invaluable editors. We all need a trusted editor.

I've been influenced, and quote where appropriate, by a number of great teachers. You too will find that there's a teacher for every season of life.

- My godly grandparents on both sides
- My loving parents, who did the best they could with a restless, prodigal child
- C.S. Lewis
- Dr. Charles Stanley
- Joyce Meyer
- Stephen Covey
- Henry Cloud and John Townsend
- Dr. Jordan Peterson

All Biblical references are sourced from The Life Application Study Bible, New International Version edition, 1991, published jointly by Tyndale House Publishers, Inc., and Zondervan. Life Application Study Bible copyright © 1988, 1989, 1990, 1991, 1993, 1996, 2004, 2005 by Tyndale House Publishers, Inc., Wheaton, IL 60189. All rights reserved.

DAY ONE

Who is God and where did he come from?
Genesis 1 - 2, Exodus 3:14, Revelation 1:8

As a child you may have wondered, "If God created the universe, who created God?" You may still be pondering this question.

In this life, you will never see God nor get the answer to questions about his origins. But you can know him. He very much desires a relationship with you, even though he knows every little detail about you - past, present, and future.

God is sovereign, the creator, and Lord of all. He always was and always will be. He is not bound by time. He is beyond your human comprehension, like counting the stars or sand on the beach. He spoke the world into being and chose to create humans and make himself knowable to us.

When Moses asked what he should tell the Israelites about who was sending him to free them from the Egyptians, "God said to Moses, 'I am who I am. This is what you are to say to the Israelites: 'I am has sent me to you'" (Exodus 3:14).

God is an enigma. Your inability to understand what he's up to or why, or his origins does not make him nonexistent. Don't break yourself on this.

His love is perfect. It never fails. It never ends.

The presence of God is everywhere. You will find his essence in interactions with others, nature, great architecture, and even in the darkest depths of your personal pain and suffering.

Once you exert even the smallest amount of trust in him and sincerely ask that he reveal himself, he will appear. Just like he did in the beginning when he created the heavens and earth and his Spirit hovered over the waters (Genesis 1: 1 - 2). The Psalms are a good place to seek descriptions of God's character.

Psalm + Description of God
All knowing and ever present   139

Beautiful and desirable	27, 36, 45
Creator	8, 104, 148
Good and generous	34, 81, 107
Great and sovereign	33, 89, 96
Holy	66, 99, 145
Loving and faithful	23, 42, 51
Merciful and forgiving	32, 111, 130
Powerful	76, 89, 93
Willing to reveal his will, law, and direction	1, 19, 119
Righteous and just	71, 97, 113
Spirit	104, 139, 143

Start your journey to find God right now. Ask him in your heart or out loud to reveal himself and his will for your life.

DAY TWO

Blood is life
Genesis 3:21, Leviticus 17:11

Your blood is vital. Without blood, life leaves the body.

God tells the people in Leviticus 17:11, "For the life of a creature is in the blood, and I have given it to you to make atonement for yourselves on the altar; it is the blood that makes atonement for one's life."

From the first sin committed by Adam and Eve in the Garden of Eden, God required that life, represented by blood, be taken to cover sin. In Genesis 3:21, God takes the life of an animal and uses the skins to clothe Adam and Eve.

God demands that all sin be addressed and covered over with blood. His justice means all sin is treated equally. In God's eyes, murder is the same as lying. Sin is sin.

This understanding of the power of blood pointed to Jesus and his role as the final blood sacrifice. With the coming of Jesus, sacrifice through blood shed takes on a whole new meaning. His blood covered the sin of all - past, present, and future.

People talk of an ancestral blood line. You have traces of the DNA present in the blood that flowed through your grandparent's blood. These traces of DNA run through the bloodlines of all humans going all the way back to the first man and woman, which is how we are all related within the human race regardless of skin color, national origin, or any other differentiator.

Think about what that means in terms of how we judge each other.

DAY THREE

How Jesus became the last blood sacrifice
Romans 3:25, 1 John 1:7

God's companion, his son, has existed since before time. God sent him to earth for three purposes and he willingly came:

1. To cover sin with blood once and for all as the ultimate sacrifice for all humans - past, present, and future
2. To give all humans a true understanding of God's character and his desire for how to live life
3. To bring the Holy Spirit permanently to people. The Holy Spirit opens the door for anyone - young or old, rich or poor, any skin color - to reach God through prayer at any time and to guide all seekers of God

Jesus is coming again. Get to know him.

DAY FOUR

Jesus - man and God
Matthew 1: 20 - 23

Be clear on this – Jesus is God. Jesus, God, and the Holy Spirit are one but operate across space and time as separate entities among the human and spirit world.

God came to earth around 5 BC in the form of a Jewish man called Jesus (the name Jesus means God with us). He was born, just like you. He had a mother and father. Mary, his mother, became pregnant through the spirit of God. She really was a virgin, meaning she had not had sex with anyone. Jesus grew up in Nazareth and became a carpenter.

During Jesus' life he never left the region of Judea, which was ruled by the Romans. Judea today consists of Israel, Palestine, and Jordan. The vast Roman Empire stretched across two million square miles, encompassing much of Europe and the Middle East.

Jesus' ministry lasted only three years. He was 33 when the Jewish leaders of the day had him crucified. They demanded that Pontius Pilate, the Roman governor of Judea, execute him for stating that he was God.

After three days, he rose from the dead and lived among his disciples in the flesh for 40 days. With his departure back to heaven, he left behind a counselor, the spirit of God, known to us as the Holy Spirit.

It would take nearly 300 years for Christianity to gain acceptance. The Roman Emperor Constantine encountered Jesus in a vision before the great battle at Milvian Bridge where he defeated Maxentius. He saw a burning cross and was led to go into battle with the symbol of the cross, promising that if he won, he'd convert to Christianity.

Jesus' impact was so great that time and civilization are marked by his death - BC (Avanti Christo or Before Christ) and AD (Anno Domini or Year of our Lord). He came to provide a way for eternal life to all people by offering up himself as the final blood sacrifice. He opened the way for us to gain direct access to God, the Father. Jesus was entirely human and God. He had the same authority and power as God. His persecution and crucifixion on a cross were not an accident. He chose to allow himself to be sacrificed.

DAY FIVE

Who is the Holy Spirit?
John 14:26, John 15:26 - 27, John 16: 7 - 15, John 20: 22, John 3: 5 - 8, Acts 1 - 2, Romans 8

The Holy Spirit existed with God and Jesus in the beginning (Genesis 1: 1). As the third part of the Trinity, he is a being just like Jesus and God. The Holy Spirit brings the spirit of truth to people and he counsels those who put faith in God. He helps, encourages, strengthens, comforts, and teaches you.

It's the Holy Spirit that convicts you of right and wrong. He often speaks to your conscience or initiates a "gut feeling." He reveals to the world God's standards and judgment against the dark forces of the enemy.

In the Old Testament (prior to Jesus), the Spirit would come to people when sent by God to reveal a message or provide help. The indication is that the he came and went from among men at God's command.

Jesus entered history later and said, "I have much more to say to you, more than you can now bear. But when he, the Spirit of truth, comes, he will guide you into all the truth. He will not speak on his own; he will speak only what he hears, and he will tell you what is yet to come. He will glorify me because it is from me that he will receive what he will make known to you. All that belongs to the Father is mine. That is why I said the Spirit will receive from me what he will make known to you" (John 16: 12 - 17).

After his crucifixtion, Jesus rose three days later. He remained among the living for 40 days. He told his disciples, "For John baptized with water, but in a few days you will be baptized with the Holy Spirit" (Acts 1:5). "You will receive power when the Holy Spirit comes on you; and you will be my witnesses in Jerusalem, and in all Judea and Samaria, and to the ends of the earth" (Acts 1:8).

Pentecost is the day that the Holy Spirit came to earth to live among us (Acts 1). Anyone who calls Jesus their Lord and Savior can also call on the Holy Spirit for guidance and help. He is everywhere and always available. He intercedes on your behalf to God, at times even crafting prayers on your behalf when you are at a loss for words.

DAY SIX

The personality of Jesus Christ
John 8: 3 - 11

A Christian is a Christ-follower. Who are you following? Today, we follow people on YouTube, Instagram, Twitter, and a host of other virtual places.

Jesus always exhibited four main qualities: Love, Humility, Truth, and Service (Romans 13:10).

The authors of the Gospels (documentation of Jesus' life and teachings) revealed much about his personality and character. For example, Jesus...

- Answered misguided and mundane questions, without impatience
- Never said, "what about me"
- Responded to criticism, and even hate, calmly
- Told the truth, even when it threatened the status quo
- Got angry when he saw injustice and expressed it with tough words and actions, not violence or hate
- Helped all who came to him looking for help but often not in a way they expected
- Showed concern and care for every individual he met
- Let all be free to choose their response to his invitation for eternal life
- Accepted every person as they were but urged them to be better
- Never let fear control him
- Rejected worry over anything

Matthew, Mark, Luke, and John record Jesus' life and ministry on earth. All four Gospels tell mostly the same stories, but they are written by different people with varied perspectives. Matthew and John were disciples of Jesus. The authors of Luke and Mark are often disputed but both wrote with authority.

Revelation, written by John, tells of Jesus' second coming in the future. Close study of the New Testament reveals much about Jesus' personality.

DAY SEVEN

Decide what you will do with Jesus
John 3: 16 - 18, John 1:18

What you personally believe in your heart about Jesus may not be clear. You owe it to yourself to decide what you will do with Jesus. Don't just say you are a Christian because someone took you to church on occasion. Don't just reject Jesus because someone says the Bible is made up of myths or too hard.

Historical evidence verifies that he lived and was crucified by the Romans at the request of the Jewish leaders of the time. He claimed boldly to be God in flesh and that belief in him as savior is the only way for a person to gain eternal life in heaven. Central to Christian faith is the deity of Christ. He is all the following:

- God
- A human reflection of God for all people
- Lord of all people and things
- Completely holy
- Judge of the world
- Supreme over all creation, including spirit world

C.S. Lewis wrote in *Mere Christianity*:
"I am trying here to prevent anyone saying the really foolish thing that people often say about Him: I'm ready to accept Jesus as a great moral teacher, but I don't accept his claim to be God. That is the one thing we must not say. A man who was merely a man and said the sort of things Jesus said would not be a great moral teacher. He would either be a lunatic — on the level with the man who says he is a poached egg — or else he would be the devil of Hell.

You must make your choice. Either this man was, and is, the Son of God, or else a madman or something worse. You can shut him up for a fool, you can spit at him and kill him as a demon or you can fall at his feet and call him Lord and God, but let us not come with any patronizing nonsense about his being a great human teacher. He has not left that open to us. He did not intend to."

Philippians 2:6, John 10: 30, 12:45, John 1:18, 14:9, Romans 9:5, 10:11, Revelation 1:5; 17:14, Heb. 7: 26, 1 Peter 1:19; 2:22, 1 John 3:5, Rom. 2:16, 2 Corinthians 5:10, 2 Timothy 4:1

DAY EIGHT

Keep trying to do what's right
Romans 7: 7 - 25

Christ tells you to keep trying and never give up (Luke 9:23). At the same time, he says to give the burden over to him (Matthew 11:30). "Well, which is it," you ask. It is both, and that is part of the mystery of being a true Christ-follower.

God's laws work like a reflection in water or a mirror.

The Apostle Paul says, "I would not have known what sin was had it not been for the law. For I would not have known what coveting really was if the law had not said, 'You shall not covet'" (Romans: 7:7).

The thing you promise not to do but do anyway is evidence that you've seen the reflection of God's rules, i.e., "law" for humans.

The enemy (Satan) wants you to quit in exasperation or go about in self-loathing. Either way, you are useless to God.

Don't pretend to know when you have tried as hard as you can. Just keep trying and keep praying. You will find Jesus shows up when you need him the most.

Who was Paul, the Apostle?

St. Paul the Apostle, original name Saul of Tarsus was born around 4 B.C. in what is now Turkey, died 64 A.D. in Rome. He was a Jew that persecuted Christians then became a key leader of the first-generation Christians. Read Acts 9:1 -31 to learn more about Paul.

DAY NINE

The purpose of law
Romans 7: 4 - 6

Without laws (or rules) how would you know what is okay to do or not do, the difference between right and wrong?

A common example uses "No Swimming" signs on a beach to illustrate the usefulness of rules and law. Let's say the sign is in place because the water is infested with sharks or stinging jelly fish, but you didn't see the sign or chose to ignore it. Your day could be more than ruined. Do you blame the sign, i.e., the rule?

The warning sign, rules, or law provides direction, but they do not remove the "sharks."

Beginning with Eve in the Garden of Eden, Satan (the enemy) deceives people by drawing their attention to the restrictions and away from all the freedom. Don't lie, covet, or steal. These "laws" translate to don't hurt yourself or others.

God loves you. That may be hard to accept, if parents or others in authority have broken your trust. Perhaps they made up rules arbitrarily or didn't follow their own rules. When you get a hold of the fact that God loves you and that his laws are there to build you up, you begin to live and serve not due to fear of consequences but out of a love for and trust in God.

DAY TEN

Christ brought a new kind of "law"
James 3: 5 - 7

The Christian has enormous power available but rarely uses it to a full potential. The reason is a lack of willingness to submit to self-discipline and God's principles. We want to do it our way, bend the rules just for us, but it simply does not work that way. It's a mirage when you see people "having it all" without consequence or not paying the price to get what they have. You only see the tip of the iceberg. No one escapes the principles God set in motion.

A day of reckoning will come for all, the Christian and the non-Christian. Judgment will come based on what you did with your time on earth, how you lived. How much you acquired or even how many hours you worked will not be a factor. With God, it's not about the external but the internal.

It will all come down to how you treated people, what you did with the gifts and talents God gave you, and ultimately, what you did with Jesus: accept him or reject him.

Accepting him means you acknowledge an inborn sin nature and inability to overcome it in your own strength. You see the need for a savior and reach out to the one God offered - his son, Jesus Christ.
A simple accept or not is the basic pass to eternal life in heaven versus eternal life in hell. They are both real places. Your state of affairs and what you will be doing in either place will be determined by how you lived life on earth.

Why does God let horrible people squeak by at the 11th hour?

God is the all-powerful creator of the universe. He can't be fooled or manipulated. It is foolish to think that you can live as you please and then in a dying moment quickly say, "I believe."

God's perfect justice makes provision for all regardless of type, shape, or duration of sin based on heart attitude. Your enemy and God's enemy, the first fallen creature known by many names including Lucifer, Satan, the devil, and Beelzebub wants to trick you into thinking that rebellion means fun and doing what you want, and submission means a boring and restrictive life. His game has not changed since the Garden of Eden.

The place where all those who reject God will remain for eternity with Satan does not involve partying with friends forever or anything else anyone has known on earth, not even the most brutal abuses. It is a place of utter darkness and separation from anyone or anything for eternity.

Why do so many take their chances and bet that hell is not so bad?

DAY ELEVEN

Understanding the Bible and Christian principles
Hebrews 4:12

The Bible contains sixty-six books written by forty men over a 1500-year time span.

Many people reject what they think are Christian principles and statements from the Bible because they seem harsh, old fashioned, or just don't make sense. Yet, often people have never read or studied the Bible in context, with foot notes, and an open heart. The Word of God has endured for thousands of years because it contains the stories and principles that have shaped humanity from the beginning of time. The Bible is also the guide to understanding love and truth.

When reading the Bible to understand what it means from an academic and/or personal standpoint use a Study Bible (this book relies on the NIV Life Application Study Bible, 1991 edition), and read the foot notes for each verse(s).

Everything in the Bible has context and meaning.

Historical context: The people described in the Bible existed, from Adam, Eve and their offspring through Jesus, his disciples and others to follow. All the New Testament was written during the days of the Roman Empire. To understand many of the passages, especially from Paul, you must understand Greek and Roman historical context as well as Jewish culture and conditions of the times. The laws and philosophy of America are heavily influenced by the Greeks, Romans, and Hebrews. Study history to have a grasp on the way people lived in the region and in those times.

Instruction for all Christians: Within the Old and New Testament lies God's instructions for how to live. But you will struggle to apply it to your life now, if you don't understand something about the historical context in which instruction and events take place.

A message for you personally: The Holy Spirit works to reveal God to each individual in many ways, especially through God's Word. If you will approach God's Word with sincerity and reverence, he will help you understand everything God wants you to know and do.

DAY TWELVE

Understanding "end times" and Jesus' return
Matthew 24: 26 - 27, 1 Thessalonians 4: 15 - 18

The best stories involve struggles between good and evil. The endings we love involve the good guys winning. The good guys win at the end of history. The book of Revelation spells out how the world as we know it ends.

Christ returns to lead the battle of all battles. Satan is put away once and for all into the lake of burning sulfur. Jesus takes his throne and judges the living and the dead. The earth is burned up, making way for the new heaven and earth. God will live among those who chose to repent and accept Christ forever.

Remember that time from God's perspective is not linear, like ours. To him a day can be like a thousand years, from the formation of the earth to the last days (2 Peter 3:8). Jesus' teachings and instruction on the end times are found in Matthew 24 and Mark 13. It is natural for people to wonder about what will happen and when.

Why does God not tell us an exact date?

If we knew the date, we would put off doing the work he's called us to do. Jesus said to spend time taking care of his people inside and outside the church. He said to focus on him and preparation for his coming versus looking for special signs and worrying about the end.

His point is to not wait to do the work he's called you to do. Like the coming of the rain in Noah's day, the exact time was not known, but Noah knew what to expect. It is the same with the end. You have been told how to prepare and what to expect but not a date.

The choice you have already made will determine your eternity.

Don't be fooled into thinking that the end is near by what people say, wars, natural disasters, or anything else. When he comes back there will be no mistaking it because he's coming in on the clouds with a lot of noise. Jesus says in Matthew 24:26 - 27 that his return will be visible just like lightning in the sky.

Paul summarizes Jesus' return in 1 Thessalonians 4: 15 - 18. Christians alive at the time will be taken up into the clouds (away from earth) to meet their king. They will be spared the final battle. The second coming will be swift. There will not be a chance for rethinking or doing anything over.

Jesus tells us what will happen to those who are faithful to the end and to those who have not accepted his teaching and salvation. The people who have lived according to God's ways and done their best to complete work they were given will be rewarded. Those who ignored or rejected God's message and offer of salvation will be put in "a place with the hypocrites, where there will be weeping and gnashing of teeth" (Matthew 24:51).

DAY THIRTEEN

Four things that will happen before the end of time
Revelation 20 & 21, Matthew 24: 26 - 27,
1 Thessalonians 4: 15 - 18

If you are a Christian, you will be persecuted in some form or fashion.

The persecution of Christians has gone on since Jesus walked the streets of Judea, and it continues today. As the end does draw near, it will become more and more difficult for Christians. Many Christians have and will be persecuted, hated, and even put to death. Some will not be able to withstand the pressure and reject their faith and Christ. But those who stand firm to the end of their time on earth will be saved. Are you committed to Christ or is your faith negotiable based on threat or promise of riches?

All nations and people groups will be exposed to the truth about Christ.

Before Jesus returns and the end of this world as we know it, the truth about Jesus and the gospel of his kingdom will be preached to the entire world; no people group anywhere will be left out.

Bible Translation Statistics as of 2016 According to Wycliffe.Net

Number of Languages in the World	7,097
Languages w/o translation (and needing one):	3,874
Total World Population:	6,506M
Number of people with no translation:	253M

*Language with the most speakers worldwide is Mandarin Chinese.

(http://resources.wycliffe.net/statistics/Wycliffe%20Global%20Alliance%20Statistics%202016%20FAQs_EN.pdf)

An abomination that causes desolation.

Daniel 9:27 and Matthew 24:15 address "the abomination that causes desolation" in the holy place (the temple in Jerusalem). No one knows what that will mean exactly in the future, but it will involve someone who has come to world power (referred to as the antichrist). This person will place his image on the alter within the temple and order all to worship the image.

An abomination that causes desolation is anything that mocks God in his place of worship. Two notable times in history this occurred include 168 BC when Antiochus Epiphanes sacrificed a pig to Zeus on the alter and again in AD 70 when Titus, after destroying Jerusalem, placed an idol on the temple alter.

An end to the earth as we know it.

Jesus says, "Immediately after the distress of those days the sun will be darkened, and the moon will not give its light; the stars will fall from the sky, and the heavenly bodies will be shaken" (Matthew 24:29).

Judgment will come. Jesus will return.

After the clash of world powers and the rule of the antichrist, Jesus will come back "on the clouds" (Matthew 24:26 - 27). This is when he will gather all Christians - those still on earth and those perhaps waiting in the heavens or already in heaven. His words indicate that Christians, living and dead, will be gathered together with him.

Matthew 24: 30 - 31 says, "Then will appear the sign of the Son of Man in heaven. And then all the peoples of the earth will mourn when they see the Son of Man coming on the clouds of heaven, with power and great glory. And he will send his angels with a loud trumpet call, and they will gather his elect from the four winds, from one end of the heavens to the other."

DAY FOURTEEN

Consequences
Luke 19: 11 - 16

Your actions are within your control. But your consequences are not under your control.

You are one of a kind and designed to do special things with your life. But you are not exempt from the Law of the Harvest.

God set the Law of the Harvest in motion. This law is sometimes referred to as reaping what you sow or karma. Every world religion has some way of describing this universal principle.

The Law of the Harvest illustrates how consequences work.

Your words and actions are just like seeds. The seeds you plant, or do not plant, along with how the seeds are tended determines what will come up at some later point. The harvest (consequences) is impacted by numerous factors, including weather, how much fertilizer is used, irrigation, insects or disease, and so forth.

The point is you have little control over what consequences will result from your actions exactly, but you do know that good actions eventually lead to desirable outcomes and bad actions eventually lead to undesirable outcomes.

What sort of seeds are you sowing today?

You will always reap what you sow. Hard consequences are not punishment. You are already forgiven, if you ask. However, you may have to live with unintended consequences that limit your opportunities, if you did not consider carefully seeds you sowed yesterday.

DAY FIFTEEN

Managing money
Malachi 3:8 - 12, Luke 16: 1 - 14

You can only do three things with money: spend, save, or give. God, as well as all good financial managers, says to live by percentages. Placing all money that comes to you into categories by percentage leads to a balanced life. A rule of thumb is 10% giving, 30% living, 30% saving, 30% enjoying.

Only in the giving of money (tithes) does God invite humans to test him.

"Bring the whole tithe into the storehouse, that there may be food in my house. Test me in this," says the Lord Almighty, "and see if I will not throw open the floodgates of heaven and pour out so much blessing that there will not be room enough to store it" (Malachi 3:10).

Jesus tells the Parable of the Shrewd Manager in Luke 16: 1 - 14 as a lesson in money. He summarizes in Luke 16: 10 -13 by saying, "Whoever can be trusted with very little can also be trusted with much, and whoever is dishonest with very little will also be dishonest with much. So, if you have not been trustworthy in handling worldly wealth, who will trust you with true riches? And if you have not been trustworthy with someone else's property, who will give you property of your own? No one can serve two masters. Either you will hate the one and love the other, or you will be devoted to the one and despise the other. You cannot serve both God and money."

Lessons on Money

- Everything belongs to God. He asks only for a portion
- Money is a medium of exchange that can only be given, saved, or spent
- Money generates power that can be used for good or evil
- Integrity with a little money leads to ability to manage a lot of money
- Don't let money be a master over your life. You cannot serve God and money

DAY SIXTEEN

Judgment versus judgmental
Matthew 25: 31 - 46

How you treat the people you encounter at work, school, or on the street and those in your life will determine your eternal future. This is a hard teaching to accept and understand. Jesus did not mince words in explaining what he expects from those who know him and have accepted his free gift of salvation.

In Matthew 25: 31 - 46, Jesus teaches three key things about life.

1. All people will be judged by the same criteria. There is no difference for gender, color, nationality, or any other distinction.
2. He will divide people into only two categories. Those who were kind to and served their fellow man and those who did the opposite. They will "go away into eternal punishment, but the righteous into eternal life" (25: 46).
3. Those who are meek, hungry, downtrodden, sick, in prisons of their mind or of steel due to their choices are the ones Christ expects you to be compassionate toward. Don't confuse compassion with enabling.

The point of this teaching is that you are responsible for your actions and attitudes. You are to judge situations and people wisely but not to be judgmental. We never enjoy the hard consequences that befall people but should also not intervene to play God in their lives.

For example, if you defy God's law or the civil laws, there should be a consequence you and others must live with.

DAY SEVENTEEN

Like school, the tests get harder, but there's no deadline
Job 23:10

God is the perfect teacher. He provides opportunities to learn by doing. There's always a test and like school they get harder as you move up.

In God's school of life, age does not determine level and you keep taking the same tests until you get them. Sometimes you get stuck on one particular test. God patiently gives you repeated opportunities to practice.

God's tests are character based. He's concerned about your attitude and how you handle what he gives you. He does this because he wants to bless you and use you in work he needs done here on earth. Like a coach, he doesn't want to send a player into the game unprepared. It will not go well for the game, and it will harm the player, either literally or in his or her sense of self-worth.

God never sets you up to fail. He won't throw you in the deep end, unless he knows you really can swim.
For example, honesty is a big one with God. If you are dishonest with yourself or others about little things, he knows you will be dishonest about big things. People may promote you based on raw talent or your ability to manipulate the truth and situations, but God never will do that.

If you want to enjoy the peace that accompanies being right where God has put you, in his timing, accomplishing his plan for your life, accept the trials and challenges (tests) that come your way with patience and diligence.

DAY EIGHTEEN

The strength to do anything God asks
Psalm 28: 7

We each have a mind, body, and spirit/soul. Christians also have within them the "spirit of God," also called the Holy Spirit. Jesus left him behind after his resurrection to help us.

If you will trust him, the Spirit will give you strength to do what he's asked of you.

In your own strength, there's no way to sustain anything you want. Everything you take or attempt outside of God's will is always doomed to fail. This can lead you to believe you are a failure. The truth is you are God's own creation and he loves you.

You can do anything God leads you to do because he gives you power to achieve, ability to love, and a will to self-discipline yourself as needed.

DAY NINETEEN

The tension between choices, principles, and a sovereign God
Deuteronomy 1

Choices set the course for your life. One choice, like choosing to drink and drive, can dramatically change a life in an instant. Who you choose to marry sets a course for your life. The college you attend has great influence. Trying recreational drugs can set a course.

The nature of choice (free will), consequences (principles), and a sovereign God can be confusing. You have a choice to accept the tension between the three or not. Consequences are not God's punishment. He's already forgiven you, if you accepted Jesus' sacrifice on your behalf.

1. Choice or free will has to do with what you have control over in life. Your attitude and reactions or actions are the only things you ultimately control. God created you in his image. Therefore, you are free to make a choice regarding how you will handle yourself. Each day you make a million choices. The more you understand and respect principles and God, the better your choices will be.
2. Consequences (principles) are rules set in motion by God. They apply to everyone, regardless of belief or values. Physics, the study of matter and energy and how they interact, reveals principles. For example, the law of gravity as first explained by Sir Isaac Newton, which in the simplest of terms means that if you drop an egg from the roof it will fall till it meets with a surface (matter). The law of the harvest is another example. There's Newton's Third Law of Motion: For every action, there is an equal and opposite reaction of some sort. The Ten Commandments given by God through Moses are principles too. Cecil B. Demille, the famous movie producer, said, "We cannot break the ten commandments, only break ourselves on them."
3. God is sovereign over all, in control of everything. While he can and has at times suspended the laws of nature, those laws apply to everyone. This means that you should not assume you are different and attempt to defy principles. But you have the right, and should exercise it daily, to pray to God for anything, including miracles of healing and restoration of all manner.

DAY TWENTY

The tension between choices, principles, and a sovereign God
Exodus

God's unique plan for each life allows for people to survive accidents, illnesses, and addictions. He often uses horrible experiences to turn lives into opportunities to teach or touch others.

Your life will include turning point opportunities. Choices you make at the turning points can change the course and timing of God's plan. In Exodus we see God's people freed from many years of slavery at the hands of the Egyptians. God's plan is to give them a "promised land." It is a real place, about an eleven-day journey by foot from Egypt. It took them forty years to get there.

They made bad choices and kept falling back into a bad attitude. God does not suspend free will to work out his plan for you. He is patient. Many of the Israelites died in that desert; never saw the promised land.
God is loving, holy, and just. He can redeem anything you turn over to him, but some of the opportunities he places before you have an expiration date. In most cases, where individual choices defy the basic ground rules God has given for how humans should live well, people and those around them suffer.

For many, an "eleven-day journey" becomes years of desert time where God works with them to mature and develop character.

The best chances for living a life of peace and for living up to your potential is to accept that God is sovereign, that he loves you, and his rules are in place to protect you and keep order in the universe.

*Read all of Exodus for full account of the Israelites journey from slavery to freedom.

DAY TWENTY-ONE

Understanding submission
Ephesians 5:21 - 33, Colossians 3:15 - 25, 1 Peter 3:1 - 5

In Ephesians 5:21, the Apostle Paul says, "Submit to one another out of reverence for Christ."

Submission is a tough concept for the modern woman. It has been defined culturally as subjugation, being less, enduring mistreatment or discrimination. Confusing a woman's understanding of submission and obedience is the devil's oldest trick.

It goes like this: "Why would God, who "supposedly" loves you, deny you..."

God has designed an order to things. Order leads to harmony. The first element of God's order is submission of yourself to him. It must be an act of free will. You will never fully submit to God if you do not believe with all your heart that he loves you, he is in control of everything that happens, you belong to him, and he's designed a unique plan for your life.

Submitting to God is the stumbling block for most. If you get stuck here, you will not enjoy the peace and harmony that comes from God's order of things or the leading of the Holy Spirit in your life.

DAY TWENTY-TWO

Submission and Love
Ephesians 5:22- 33, 1 Peter 3: 1 - 7

Submission is a misunderstood concept. Submission does not mean domination or control. In marriage, wives are called to submit to the husband's leadership. Husbands are asked to set aside their own interests to care for their wife as well as love and respect her.

Marriage, as designed by God, is the most sublime of human relationships. It is God's perfect gift to us. Marriage between a man and woman is symbolic of Christ and the church. A man is the head of his wife and household. Christ is the head of the church.

Willing submission acknowledges roles and a division of labor, the other's value, and mutual cooperation. Marital submission is about concern for each other's happiness, and between two mature people, it increases love and creates harmony.

Wives and husbands who do not follow this formula will have a great deal of trouble, especially when children are involved.

As Paul reminds us in Ephesians 5:21, "Submit to one another out of reverence for Christ."

If, in a household or any organization, everyone seeks to help each other with whatever chore or burden exists, things will run smoothly.

The *NIV Life Application Study Bible 1991 edition* describes four types of submission:

Functional	distinguishing of our roles and the work we are called to do
Relational	a loving acknowledgment of another's value as a person
Reciprocal	A mutual, humble cooperation with one another
Universal	An acknowledgment by the church of the all-encompassing lordship of Jesus Christ

Pray for a husband that understands mutual submission, love, and respect. Pray that you will be a wife who understands these things.

DAY TWENTY-THREE

Submission and Freedom
1 Peter 2: 13 - 25

Living under authority cannot be escaped - parents, teachers, employer, police, government regulation and taxation, etc. You will serve someone. Your master may be kind or cruel. Some masters you can choose; others are chosen for you. It is very hard to live under the authority of someone you do not respect.

An ability to submit to external authority while maintaining your individual freedom is possible only with understanding of how submission works in God's economy.

Christ possessed all power within the universe, yet he submitted to death on our behalf. He modeled submission throughout his life. He was able to submit to the corrupt Jewish leaders of the time and the harsh Roman rule because he submitted first to God's control of everything.

If you do everything as if working for God, you will find peace while submitting to even the most ridiculous authority. You will also know clearly when the time comes to throw off certain authority. You will never be called by God to defy his commands. His moral law trumps all manmade law or authority. You may have decided that those in positions of authority over you do not deserve your respect or submission. You have probably reached this conclusion based on solid evidence, which serves to vindicate any attitude or behavior, in your mind.

Be careful to not reject the authority God has placed you under. Satan is standing by to provide an authority of his choosing. The ones he chooses are always prisons reached by an alluring path. It looks at first as if you are exercising the freedom to do what you want, but soon you will find "it" or "them" becoming a burden.

First, respect yourself. Practice living under the submission of a desire to be a healthy, productive person with goals. If you will submit to the day-to-day commitment it takes to be a good student, athlete, artist, friend, or whatever is important to you, an understanding of the benefits of submission will begin to develop within you.

To gain the rewards of a life submitted to Christ, to those you must live and work with, and to the principles of nature, you must press through the innate human tendency to just do what feels easy.

DAY TWENTY-FOUR

Renew your mind daily
Romans 12:2

In Romans 12:2, Paul urges you to "be transformed by the renewing of your mind."

Renewing the mind is like rebooting a computer when it hangs up or needs to update a program. Sometimes a computer gets corrupted and needs to be reprogramed. Your brain is like a computer. It runs on whatever program you install (or others install). You can reboot or reprogram your brain, but it takes conscious effort.

Time with God each day is similar to rebooting. It allows you to unload the cares of each day and seek his guidance. In turn, the Holy Spirit renews your mind by speaking to you through scripture or to your heart about things. This is how you can come to know God's will.

It's important to acknowledge reality - the things that have happened or are happening. But don't dwell on the happenings, good or bad. Your brain believes what you tell it - truth or fiction. George Orwell wrote that the most dangerous times for societies are when people willfully choose to believe lies.

Your brain believes, "I'm a loser and everybody hates me," just as readily as "That hurt, but I'm gonna be okay."

Each day brings a full range of encounters from pleasant to downright harsh. God will help you refresh or restart your mind each day to function best in the world.

DAY TWENTY-FIVE

Submit and Resist
James 4: 7 - 10

Don't downplay the power of the devil in your life. Equally, don't forget the powerful tool you have to fight him off. Your enemy is real. He uses every trick in the book to keep you away from God's will. As a matter of fact, he made up those tricks. They are as old as dirt and you can avoid them, but you must be proactive.

James 4: 7 minces no words: "Submit yourselves, then, to God. Resist the devil, and he will flee from you."

It's a simple formula but requires action on your part. First, submit yourself to God - know his commands for all people. They are repeated over and over throughout the New Testament and are quite simple. Let God direct your life toward the unique plan he's made. Second, resist the devil's many schemes and efforts to distract you. When you use your power to tell him to go away, he must flee. He can't do anything you or God don't allow.

He can only tempt you. And don't think he's not tempting you every single day. Here's a simple analogy. My little dog has a fenced in yard. Within that area, she's safe. I protect her, feed her, and let her in and out of the house.

Sometimes she's enticed by something outside the fence and will dig her way out. Once outside the fence, she's on her own. There are hundreds of places her nose can take her. They may not all be bad, but once she's given in to the first temptation, it's much easier to give into the next and the next.

God's commands are the fence. It's not a prison but protection. He wants you to fence your mind off from the enemy. Put on your armor (Ephesians 6:10 - 13).

Taking the bait of temptation and going outside the fence is the devil's way of making you vulnerable to sin. If he can get you to take one step outside the fence, he's much more likely to lure you to the next and the next steps.

Resist him from the beginning when he comes lurking around your fence. Literally say, "Get away from me," and he must obey your command.

DAY TWENTY-SIX

"Shake the dust off your feet"
Matthew 10: 9 - 14

Jesus sent his disciples out without money or a suitcase to spread his message among the Jewish towns and villages. He basically told them to go to each place with an open heart and mind. If the people were receptive and treated them well, they would stick around and share their good news. If the people were not welcoming and didn't want to listen to their words, Jesus told them to leave and "shake the dust off your feet" (10: 9 - 14).

The saying, shake the dust off your feet, means to not stick around and beg people to accept what you have to offer as well as don't be upset when your message is rejected or forceful with giving your gifts.

Jesus' message is the same for you right now. He's given you a set of spiritual gifts as well as talents. If you are breathing, there's a place for you to serve. However, the current church, school, organization, or group you are offering those gifts and talents to may not be interested.

Sometimes God uses a lack of "favor" with people as a way to shut one door and direct you to another. If "they" do not want you, don't get too upset. Check your heart, but don't linger.

Shake the dust off your feet and either seek God's leading for a new place or bide your time until the term you are serving is finished. If you pray for his leading, you will know what to do. The main thing is to not waste time fretting over the people who don't see a place for you.

DAY TWENTY-SEVEN

Choices of maturity
Hebrews 5: 11 - 14

You want to be mature because it means more freedom, an ability to do what you want. The Apostle Paul boils maturity down to an ability to distinguish good from evil, right from wrong. Until you are willing to admit that there are right and wrong choices and submit your own choices to God, you will remain a child.

Once you have been taught the basics of faith, your responsibility is to mature by practicing what you know and help others in maturing as well. You will always need the Holy Spirit to help you continue maturing, but you get to make the choice regarding the desire.

The NIV Life Application Study Bible 1991 edition lists ways to distinguish maturity from immaturity:

Mature Choices	Immature Choices
Avoid attitudes, habits, actions that go against God's teaching	Be like everyone else
Teaching others	Only being taught
Developing depth of understanding	Struggling with the basics
Self-evaluation	self-criticism
Seeking unity	Promoting disunity
Active faith	Cautious apathy and doubt
Confidence	Fear

If you find yourself acting out of the right-hand column still but want to make mature choices, ask God to help you mature.

DAY TWENTY-EIGHT

The Gift of Chastity (Purity)
Psalm 119: 1 - 16

Psalm 119:9 asks, "How can a young person stay on the path of purity?"

The answer = "By living according to God's Word."

The enemy has convinced us that purity in people is a joke. Yet the world still values purity in things like gold, diamonds, and drugs. Something with claims of purity is highly valued.

Many give up on purity at a young age because their sense of self is weak due to negative messages or they've been fooled into thinking they are entitled to satisfying any desire, any time.

Seeking purity is not an attempt to be perfect. It is living with a belief that you are not your own; you belong to God (1 Corinthians 6: 19 - 20).

God asks a lot of his people, beginning at a young age, because he has much to give you. He can't give you everything he's planned, if you are polluted with confusion about yourself and his nature.

God commands that you refrain entirely from certain things and wait for others. Remain pure and you will be rewarded greatly later, much like the way an athlete is rewarded with muscle and endurance or an engineer with the ability to imagine and construct increasingly complex machines.

The key word is later. Gratification must be delayed to get God's best.

You won't be able to delay attempting to get what you want unless you trust that God has stored up for you every good thing you need. Dr. Charles Stanley's Life Principle #2 sums this up. "Trust God and leave all the consequences to him."

DAY TWENTY-NINE

Your power begins at home
Philippians 1:6-11

Take a moment and look through your mind's eye at the space you occupy. Imagine going in as if seeing it for the first time. Is there order or disorder? Would you feel comfortable having a guest into this place?

Joyce Meyer says, "Once rested, get up and work. You can't take authority over your life if you don't have authority over a sink full of dirty dishes or a messy garage. If you want to grow in ministry to others, the Word says you must get your own house in order first (1 Timothy 3:5)."

Your walk as a woman of faith, powerful in all you do, begins at home. We're not talking perfection. But a clean, orderly life is a reflection of a similar mind and heart. Your surroundings do have an impact on your psyche.

If you tell yourself that picking up clothes, making a bed, cooking, doing dishes and laundry is beneath you, there's a good chance you have a problem with obedience to God, and if you have a husband, submission to him.

What you will find, when you get a hold of Christ and the profound nature of salvation is that you use your freedom to keep your life and home in order or serve your family. You will humbly and gratefully take care of them and your home because, as Paul indicates in Philippians 1: 9-10, as knowledge and depth of insight increase so will your ability to discern what is best.

DAY THIRTY

Consider carefully what you hide
Psalm 125

God sees everything you do. He loves you no matter what and understands when you struggle. Hiding things from people is a form of bondage. We hide things out of fear of losing them or out of shame, disobedience, or selfishness.

You are free, if you choose to be. Imagine holding nothing tightly because you trusted God to provide for all your needs. Imagine never lying to hide the truth or worrying about being caught.

This is an element of the peace that surpasses all understanding. Think of the energy you could save for something else, if you hid nothing.

DAY THIRTY-ONE

Seeking your own "noble character"
Proverbs 31: 10 - 31

The book of Proverbs ends with a description of "The Wife of Noble Character." You may read it with dismay, or it may inspire you. The Proverbs 31 woman reveals character qualities for success.

You won't get all of these character traits right all the time or even some of the time. Seek to practice the qualities of this woman. You are already "worth far more than rubies" in God's eyes (31:10). As C.S. Lewis says, "God is easy to please but hard to satisfy." He wants the best for you.

Noble Character Traits

- Respects the Lord
- Considers the well-being of her family before acting or speaking
- Conducts herself with dignity and modesty
- Avoids being idle
- Works diligently at household chores
- Uses her gifts and skills to earn money or barter
- Saves money and invests it
- Gives time and resources to the poor and needy
- Takes care of her own
- Takes care of herself
- Speaks wisely, controls her tongue

DAY THIRTY-TWO

Am I good enough?
Galatians 5: 22 - 26

You want to be good. We all do. When you act reckless or hateful or with disrespect it is usually rooted in disappointment. You tried to be good and failed in your own eyes or someone else's.

God is never surprised or disappointed when you struggle with being good. He has no measuring stick for when good is good enough. He's never comparing you to someone else. God is the author of fairness. He set up principles that apply to everyone and they never change. God made up a unique plan for your life, but the rules for what it takes to enjoy your life and grow in character don't vary.

The Apostle Paul lays out nine simple verbs that describe how to be "good." He says, "Against such things there is no law" (5:22). Never has there been a law against love, joy, peace, forbearance, kindness, goodness, faithfulness, gentleness and self-control.

God knows that your "passions and desires" will make it hard at times to live out these virtues (5:24). Notice Paul calls them "fruit of the Spirit" (5:22). The Spirit (also called Counselor) is the guide Jesus gave us when he left earth to go back to heaven.

It is the Spirit that will fill you with "fruit." You cannot conjure them alone. You get to choose if you will seek these fruits. You are always free, no matter what your circumstances, to make the choice about how you will act.

DAY THIRTY-THREE

Am I bad?
Galatians 5: 16 - 21

Sometimes you don't care if you are good or bad. Being bad has a wide range of definitions. God gave you a conscience so you could know right from wrong, but he also gave you freedom to choose.

Jesus never called anyone bad. At times he spoke to people about leaving sin behind. Sin technically means to miss the mark. The mark is God's best for your life. When he says don't do something, it means don't hurt yourself, don't limit the ways he can work in your life, don't numb yourself to his voice.

The Apostle Paul refers to harmful things as "acts of the flesh" (5:19). He says they are obvious and include sexual immorality, impurity and debauchery, idolatry and witchcraft, hatred, discord, jealousy, fits of rage, selfish ambition, dissensions, factions and envy, drunkenness, orgies, and the like (5: 20 -21).

If you refuse to allow those things into your life, what might you lose or gain?

DAY THIRTY-FOUR

I know that was wrong
2 Samuel 11 & 12

If you are honest, you know when you've done real wrong. At times you may offend someone without knowing, and that can be more their problem than yours, but if you want to be in relationship, you sincerely say, "I'm sorry."

A willingness to admit wrong and restore relationship, where one has been bruised or fractured, is a vital step toward maturity. You will never be promoted by God, unless you develop a heart that is sensitive to your own mistakes and willingness to be corrected.

King David wrote many of the Psalms. He's a great model for relationship with God. After he had cheated with Bathsheba and then had her husband killed to ensure he could go on being with her, the Holy Spirit convicted David's heart in a big way (2 Samuel 12).

When you know you have done wrong go to God with this prayer: "God, forgive me, restore me, bless me."

After you pray with a sincere heart, trust him and wait.

DAY THIRTY-FIVE

Hope
John 10:10

G.K. Chesterton, English writer and poet, said, "When people stop believing in God, they don't believe in nothing, they'll believe anything."

Central to a belief in God is hope. When people let go of hope they give in to despair and self-indulgence.

Your enemy, the devil, is hard at work killing your hope. He tempts you to do the wrong thing and then condemns you when you give in. A vicious cycle begins. He whispers things like, "How could a loving God allow this (fill in the blank) in your life?"

Refuse to stop hoping. Believe that Christ came not just so you can live eternally, but so you might have a good life here on earth. Never give up.

John 10:10 says, "The thief comes only to steal and kill and destroy. I came that they may have life and have it abundantly."

Ponder those words from Christ.

"Those that hope little cannot grow much."

-George MacDonald

DAY THIRTY-SIX

There will be giants in your personal promised land
Numbers 13:1-33

You can achieve about anything you want, if you are willing to sacrifice for it. Sacrifice hurts. It costs you. Fear of failure keeps many from ever trying.

What opportunity is God offering that you are missing because of fear?

God had promised the Israelites that he would give them a land of their own; a land flowing with milk and honey. It took them a very long time to get there because they kept getting off track and defying God. Finally, they reached the gateway to the promised land.

Scouts from among the people were sent out to assess what the land contained. They found giants, such as the Amalekites, Hittites, and many other fearsome people. They also found fruit unlike anything imaginable including enormous grape clusters, pomegranates, and figs.

The beauty and bounty of the land did not outweigh their fear of the giants. All but two of the scouts told the people it was too dangerous, impossible. As a result, all of the people, except the two who wanted to press on, died in the desert just outside the promised land.

This story offers powerful lessons for you. The giants represent your fears. The fruit represents your potential. "Harvesting" your fruit comes with a price. There will be giants. But if God has called you, he will go with you.

DAY THIRTY-SEVEN

Don't get off track unnecessarily
Luke 9:62

There will be times when you mess up out of ignorance. There will be times when you throw caution to the wind. Your goal in life should be to limit both and focus on the day-by-day plan God has for your service.

Jesus told those who said they wanted to follow him, "No one who puts a hand to the plow and looks back is fit for service in the kingdom of God" (9:62). The hand plow is no longer in use, but it is a fitting analogy. Before the technological innovation called the tractor, people had to plow fields with a mule. A farmer had to hold on to the plow handles tightly. Looking to the side or behind, or anywhere but straight ahead led to uneven rows and inefficient use of land for crops.

The farmer who didn't pay attention to plowing straight lines created more work and less output from the field. When you look back at your failures or successes or to the side for pleasures or distractions, you too will get off course.

God does not lay a trap for you or want to make life hard. He's sensitive to your human nature, past hurts, and desires. This is why he gives you work to do, your own row to plow. He wants your attention on preparing for the plan he has or getting the tasks done for his plan.

Don't miss God's opportunities for you because you've taken your hand from the plow. The costs are too high.

DAY THIRTY-EIGHT

You are powerful
Acts 1:8

You may not feel powerful, but you are. Power is available to you. It is inside of you waiting to be tapped. The reason you do not live daily in the power Christ offers is that you let the enemy steal it.

Power is stolen when you are tempted to do something you know is bad for you. After you've given in, the enemy condemns. You feel defeated.

Remaining in the power Christ died for you to have requires renewing your mind daily and taking captive all negative thoughts.

Remember, no one can take your power unless you allow them to. Teachers can take your grade. Parents can take your privileges. Friends can tell your secrets. Guys can reject you. But only you decide how you react. The giving away of power comes when you let the hurtful or unkind things people do shape your self-image.

Examples of how you give power away:

Bad grade = I'm stupid
Punishment from parent = They don't love me
Secret revealed = Nobody likes me
Rejection = I'm ugly

Keep your eyes on Christ. You are powerful when you submit to letting him work through you. Don't give your power away.

DAY THIRTY-NINE

Hope actively
Psalm 25:10

A person with hope does not give up, does not do the opposite of what they hope for while hoping for something good to happen. Hope is expressed in words and actions. The two must not contradict.

The woman who says, "I hope to marry a man who loves and respects me," but proceeds to date men who do not respect her and who press her to compromise her morals is contradicting words with actions.

In Psalm 25:10 King David prayed, "May integrity and uprightness protect me, because my hope, Lord, is in you."

Integrity means whole, undivided. "Integrity is the quality of being honest and having strong moral principles," according to Webster's Dictionary.

Uprightness means unchanging principles, genuineness, honorable, trustworthy, righteousness.

The part you must do while waiting for the Lord's answer to the things you hope will come to pass is maintain your integrity and uprightness. This is how you will be "protected" as you hope in the truth of God's Word.

DAY FORTY

Investing my time, abilities, and money
Matthew 25: 14 - 30

Capitalism is the term used to describe an economic system where individuals own the factories, stores, fields, and other places where production takes place. Countries where Capitalism is allowed enable a "free market." This means you decide if and how you trade your time, abilities, and money with others.

Notable economist and George Mason University Professor Walter Williams uses this simple example: If I mow yards and convince you to allow me to mow yours, and then you pay me $20, I've just served you. In turn, you have rewarded me with currency.

With my time and abilities, I've earned money. That money allows me to go and buy other goods and services.

In Matthew 25, Jesus tells a parable about a man who gives several of his workers different amounts of money based on their abilities. The story relates how each worker responded to what was given to him. Some invested the money and made more money, but one dug a hole and buried his money.

When the man returned, he was happy with those who had invested the money and angry with the one who had buried his money.

This story reflects the choice we all have with the freedom God has given us. While we are not all equally talented, we all have the same measure of time. What will you do with your time and talent?

Many are tempted to say, "Well, I'm not very talented, so why bother."

Each day you get to choose whether or not you will invest your time in things that build your mind and body, such as helping others, reading a book, practicing an instrument or sport. Think about what you spend your time doing.

Are you investing your talents or burying them?

DAY FORTY-ONE

How to confront people you care about
(Breaking passive aggressive patterns)
2 Corinthians 7 and 10

There's nothing more important in this life than relationships. If you have a relationship with Christ, you will never be alone or without guidance. Much of what your life is about involves relating to the various people the Lord puts in your path. Sometimes that means confronting difficult topics or situations.

Passive aggressive behavior involves masking hurt or anger with sarcasm, silently not doing what is asked of you, or pretending all is okay when it's not.

The people you encounter, whether short or long-term, are there for you to practice love. When something feels not right, confrontation may not feel loving, but it is necessary. Practice the following steps to deal with issues and honor relationships:

- Stick to facts about yourself and a situation
- Don't be afraid to speak truth and be firm without anger or aggression
- Affirm the good in the person
- Reflect Christ's teachings in your words and actions regarding the situation
- Follow-up after a confrontation to keep communication open

What happens when none of that works?

See entry one hundred & eight on boundaries. Sometimes you must temporarily or permanently pull away from a person to protect yourself. This is a very hard subject.

DAY FORTY-TWO

The spheres of friendship
Proverbs 12:26 and 17:17

True friendship is something everyone craves. To be a good friend demands a willingness to spend time as well as to be honest and vulnerable. You are called to love everyone (your neighbor), but you are not called to be friends with everyone, i.e., spend time with everyone, give of your time and resources to everyone.

Throughout your life many people will come and go. Some will become like a thread running through your life. Others come only for a season. You will instantly feel attracted to some. Others will initially repel you.

The requirements of life only leave a limited amount of time for intimate relationships. You and your time are very valuable. Treat potential friendships the same way you would an investment of money.

A few commonsense friendship considerations:

- When you first meet someone, go slow. Observe how they treat you and others. Don't rush to intimacy. Protect your secrets, i.e., your deepest dreams and vulnerabilities.
- Is the person honest about themselves and other things? Are they willing to hear about what's on your mind and heart as well as share what's on theirs?
- Are they real? Are they themselves regardless of who's around, not putting on a show for people in authority or considered elite?
- Most importantly, for a serious friend, do they share your values, beliefs, and respect for God? As the old saying goes, "Birds of a feather flock together."

You will get hurt and disappointed by even the best of friends, and that is part of growing as a person. But you can lower the risks of getting entangled with people who will lead you astray by asking God to send you good friends and by using good judgment.

Pray for discernment as you meet people.

DAY FORTY-THREE

The symbolism of marriage
Genesis 2:19-25

Marriage symbolizes the desire of every human soul - to have a partner, lover, advocate, best friend, a "better half," a soul mate. Marriage is something almost everyone wants for their life, often without understanding fully what it means and symbolizes.

God said, "That is why a man leaves his father and mother and is united to his wife, and they become one flesh" (Genesis 2: 24). Marriage is sacred for many reasons, but the two becoming one flesh represents an alchemy hard to grasp.

God is talking about the vulnerability that comes with submitting yourself entirely to another person within the confines of commitment - the good, the bad, and the ugly. There's nothing more powerful and frightening to some than being fully known.

Don't play games with God's plan for what it means for two to become one flesh. Sometimes you will practice at love without being prepared for the necessary time to get "real" and "undress" your heart.

Sometimes people want marriage to be like a salad bar. They'll pick and choose the parts they like, leaving the rest behind. But marriage is more like a diamond or an ocean or a sonnet than a salad.

Those words - diamond, ocean, sonnet - describe something specific. They can be mimicked and look a lot like the real thing, but the imposter will never be the same as the real thing. A cubic zirconia, from a distance, looks like a diamond. Yet, a real diamond only comes from immense pressure. You can call Lake Champlain an ocean, but it lacks the salt and depth of an ocean. You can write poems all day long, but you've not got a Sonnet without fourteen-lines written in iambic pentameter.

Marriage means something specific.

Imagine a world where nothing had a fixed meaning, and everything was subjective. Agreeing to fixed meanings does not limit creativity or freedom. It enables it. The artist is not prevented from expression by the name blue for a color that resembles the sky or water or a baby's eyes.

Marriage is a creation of God. It is the union of one man and one woman. Marriage is meant to be a permanent commitment. This is necessary for the depth of spiritual, emotional, intellectual, and physical intimacy God intended for a man and woman to experience through marriage.

Faithfulness is also integral to the marriage foundation. Marriage endures when love is practiced, not necessarily felt. Who you choose to marry is second only in importance to your acceptance of Christ as your Savior.

Like the tree of good and evil from the beginning, God has given us the ability for not just union but ecstasy and passion. This is why marriage is a covenant of great seriousness.

DAY FORTY-FOUR

Instruction in "keeping it real"
Ephesians 4:11-32

In Ephesians 4, Paul lays out what it looks like to live as a Christian. One aspect of this life is to "speak the truth in love." Being someone who speaks up for truth with individuals and for community and society takes enormous humility, commitment, and rigorous prayer for wisdom and discernment.

Just as you can't give love if you don't have it for yourself, you cannot speak truth if you don't understand it. Several factors make being a truth teller exceedingly difficult.

1. Our society has accepted a "politically correct" attitude. This means saying things that affirm God's Word and contradict permissive, undisciplined lifestyles. America was the first country to give citizens the "freedom of speech." The First Amendment to the U.S. Constitution explicitly gives a right to speak, worship, and petition the government freely, without fear of punishment.
2. Human nature is to resist being convicted of wrong, whether it is through contrast of other people, a societal law, God's Word, direct confrontation, etc. Most people don't consciously set out to be wrong. They've rationalized behavior or simply aren't aware.
3. It is easy to come across as self-righteous and judging. When you understand that someone around you is doing wrong, it usually comes out whether words are spoken or not. Be humble. Ask God for guidance. Take all things into consideration - timing, the individual, the situation, God's Word on the subject - before you act.

Why bother with "speaking the truth" if it is so tricky and risky?

Look at the components of what a Christian life entails according to Paul's instructions:

- Be alert to false ideas, teachings, and those who promote wrong schemes
- Don't be willing to give yourself over to sensuality and indulgence in impurity and greed
- Be honest in dealings and never steal
- Be a worker seeking ways to contribute to community and society
- Don't be someone who rants and raves, allowing a disagreement or anger to linger

DAY FORTY-FIVE

Ideas have consequences
Exodus 18

All actions are preceded by ideas. All ideas are inspired by beliefs.

America became a great country based on ideas that were translated into habits of living. The same is true for Nazism in Germany, Marxism in Russia, Socialism in the United Kingdom.

The America Declaration of Independence and Constitution are documents based on a belief that there is a God of the universe who is in control of everything. That same God created people with a right to be free to make their own choices (see the preamble to the Declaration of Independence in entry one hundred & sixteen). These beliefs in God and how he set up the order of things, informed the American founder's notion that government should serve the purpose of protecting people's right to exercise freedom of thought, worship, how they would work, and so on. The government was also seen as an umpire in the affairs of communities and business versus a master or overlord. The "isms" force individuals, communities, and businesses to be controlled by government or a powerful few in some form or fashion.

Oftentimes the danger in ideas is hidden by nice sounding words. There are "red flags" to look for when listening to the ideas of a movement, a politician, a leader, and your friends.

Be careful of ideas that promote the following:

- Others outside of yourself taking responsibility for your welfare or actions
- Making special rules that apply to one group but not another
- Racial, religious, or any segregation imposed by leaders
- Money taken from one group and given to another by compulsion
- Removing national borders
- Currency without ties to a country or forms of tracking
- Excusing or overlooking bad behavior in some individuals or groups yet blaming or criticizing others for the same things

How to govern and live well is all laid out in the Bible. Check everything you hear and learn against God's Word.

DAY FORTY-SIX

The kind of government God gave people
Genesis 1:26 – 30, 1 Kings 16:28 - 22:40

God made people in his image with the ability to govern themselves. But as sin entered the world and people multiplied, there had to be methods for resolving conflict, protecting the weak and powerless, and restitution for crime.

Government is intended to protect people's rights to their life and property. What a person produces with their labor is their property as well as what they buy with money earned from their labor. The closer government is to the people it protects, the better. Self-governing people chose leaders from their communities to take turns protecting their interests.

At the root of bad governance is the desire for power over people. Power seekers come in all forms. Some wear the mantle of religion, others come as dictators, and still others come claiming democracy and freedom.

Be wary of those who seek to hold office for life or make great profits from their positions as leaders in government.

DAY FORTY-SEVEN

How Jesus defined government
Matthew 22:15-22

Jesus Christ changed everything when he entered history, including the philosophy of government that formed America.

Two-thousand years ago when the Romans ruled the world and Jesus walked the earth, people had never known government designed to protect their freedom. While great Greek and Roman thinkers, such as Cicero, Seneca, and Socrates, had acknowledged natural law and some higher authority, they had not made it real for the common person. Political authority was absolute. Only a few powerful and wealthy had real rights.

One day in hopes of setting a trap, the Jewish religious leaders asked Jesus if the Jewish people should pay tax to Rome. Caesar was the ruler of Rome. Jesus amazed the crowd when he asked whose face was on the money. Of course, they answered, "Caesar."

Jesus said, "So give back to Caesar what is Caesar's, and to God what is God's" (Matthew 22:21).

Lord Acton, famous British law maker, academic and historian (1832 - 1909), pointed out that with those words, Jesus gave to the civil power, under the protection of conscience, a sacredness it had never enjoyed and bounds it had never acknowledged.

Jesus captured in that one statement God's plan for government.

Government is important for civil society, but it has no right to every aspect of a person's life and business. Give to Caesar (government) a share so it can function. But reserve an individual's freedom to serve God and others.

Jesus represented freedom of the individual. With his message and life, he gave to liberty a meaning and a value it had not possessed in the philosophy or in the constitution of Greece or Rome or any other before that point. It took over 1,700 years for the fullness of Jesus' political message to emerge for a people.

Americans established the first government in all of history based upon the freedom and natural rights God gives to all humans. None since have replicated entirely the unique constitutional republic the founders devised.

DAY FORTY-EIGHT

Is America still a Christian nation?
Acts 10:42

A lot has been said by powerful people about whether or not America is a Christian nation. America was founded as a Christian nation and remains one in form. Much evidence portrays this truth - the symbols woven into the halls of government, In God We Trust on money, the underpinnings of our laws, and many of the habits our culture practices.

But the most important fact revealing America as a Christian nation is the value we still place on the individual. Only Jews and Christians (Judeo-Christian), place inherent value in the individual, from conception to death, above the collective or state (political system). One way Christians grew in stature while living as a minor sect of Jews in the Roman empire was a habit of saving living infants thrown into the trash heaps because they were female or in some way physically less than perfect.

A belief that all individuals, regardless of health, color, age, etc., have a right to life and protection under law is the beauty of Jesus Christ's message. No country before or since America has created laws and a culture with this appreciation for individuals.

True freedom is only possible in a society willing to live under laws that encourage a love for the humanity of all individuals, even though it means some will slip through the criminal justice system and some will do bad things with their freedom.

Our society has been confused about how this works by those who are uninformed or intent on undoing America. People (society) cannot be ultimate judges of individuals. Christ himself will be the judge of "the living and the dead" at the end of time (Acts 10:42).

We are called to create and enforce laws that protect the individual. To truly let everyone just do what they feel like is called anarchy (absence of government). When there are no laws or laws are not enforced by those in power, those hurt most are the weak, the minority, and the powerless.

If the law is unpredictable or based on the preferences of the elected officials in power at a given time, no one is safe. Your group may be favored today, but tomorrow another group could come to power that has a different set of beliefs and values.

DAY FORTY-NINE

Can a society respect individual freedom and uphold morality?
Galatians 5: 7-22

Respect for individual freedom and morality are necessary for a truly free society to endure. An experiment in holding the tension between both has only occurred in America, beginning well before the Revolution in 1776.

The founders understood and accepted the wisdom of Judeo-Christian teaching. They did not question basic principles of morality. Through common sense they knew that written and unwritten laws to protect children, women, elderly, and property must be in place or else society would decline and return to the condition all people, with the exception of a privileged few, had experienced throughout history.

Paul's message to the Galatians in 5:17-22 remains true today regarding freedom. "Do not use your freedom to indulge the flesh...For the flesh desires what is contrary to the Spirit, and the Spirit what is contrary to the flesh. They are in conflict with each other so that you are not to do whatever you want. But if you are led by the Spirit, you are not under the law. The acts of the flesh are obvious: sexual immorality, impurity and debauchery; idolatry and witchcraft; hatred, discord, jealousy, fits of rage, selfish ambition, dissensions, factions and envy; drunkenness, orgies, and the like..."

To "inherit the kingdom of God" has a double meaning. There is the eternal kingdom called heaven where those who have believed in Christ will remain forever. There is also an idea of a kingdom on earth. In this earthly kingdom, you get to serve your fellowman, use your gifts and talents to prosper, have children or not, build cities or grow crops. America embodies this idea of a kingdom on earth. It did not mean a place without toil or hardship. It was the idea of a place where all people could experience the God-given right to live free regardless of skin color, religion, or opinions.

Ending slavery was written into the U.S. Constitution but ignored. America fought a bloody war to end it. No other nation on earth has ever fought to end slavery.

America is one-of-a-kind. She cannot exist for a society of people unwilling to accept that there is right and wrong, and that civil society must hold up right as the desired goal, all the while knowing none of us will get "it right" all the time. Written and unwritten laws are intended to preserve prosperity and a civilized society. They point people toward what is right.

DAY FIFTY

Is America worth keeping?
Nehemiah 9:13-15

A country, just like your home, school, or church, is an idea container. All of these examples are much more than brick and mortar or lines on a map. America as a country has not always done the right thing. Because it is a country ruled by the people versus rulers over people, we are responsible for the wrong and the right actions.

America was the first and only country based on freedom, not conquest. Yet, we allowed leaders to break treaties with Native Americans and force their people onto reservations in some cases.

America was one of the few countries to end slavery and the slave trade. Yet, our leaders allowed slavery to continue past the deadline set by the Constitution of 1808. The first Republican president, Abraham Lincoln, oversaw the worst war in American history in order to stop slavery in 1864.

Our government, even today, continues to do wrong things. Even when we aspire as individuals and a country to be good and do the right thing, we will always fall short. We strive for perfection yet live in human bodies with a nature prone to imperfection.

Living as a free person, responsible for your actions and the condition of your country, is difficult at times. You will falter. Christ's life, death, and resurrection are the model and answer for how we continue to believe and not give up.

He shows us that we will never be perfect yet points us to perfection. He offers to help us in our effort to be like him and promises to never give up on us.

Don't give up on America. Don't give up on yourself. Keep hoping and doing your part daily.

DAY FIFTY-ONE

Why is "In God We Trust" on U.S. currency?
Isaiah 25:9

On April 11, 1864, Congress authorized two-cent coins with the motto "In God We Trust" inscribed.

The motto was removed from new gold coins issued in 1907. Americans protested so fiercely that in May 1908 Congress made "In God We Trust" mandatory on all the coins that previously had the motto in place.

In 1955, the law expanded to include all coins and paper currency. Congress soon after made "In God We Trust" the national motto of the United States.

In 2010, the appearance of "In God We Trust" on our money was challenged by atheists in the federal courts. The challenge was rejected by the lower federal courts, and the Supreme Court of the United States declined to review the case.

How you get and use money is an important indicator of your faith. Having the American motto of "In God We Trust" on our money is a powerful statement.

DAY FIFTY-TWO

Why study history?
Acts 17:25-27

What actually happened in the past helps you evaluate the present and predict the future.

It is important to distinguish between interpretation of the past versus exact historical facts, and the words as written by people who lived through particular times.

Pray to know the history of your family, community, church, and country. Go and seek the true history of all by reading multiple sources. Ask people who lived through certain times to tell you what really happened and what it was like then.

Because human nature has not changed, nor will it ever change, you will find good and bad people throughout history. No one is without faults and weaknesses. Be careful that you don't allow someone's personal struggles to overshadow their accomplishments and role in history. Look to understand the principles behind what certain groups of people did throughout history and what outcomes they experienced.

God has a role for you to play in history. Equip yourself with the truth about those who went before you. Ask God to give you wisdom and understanding to put that truth to work today.

DAY FIFTY-THREE

Make your own 7-7-10 plan for life balance
Matthew 6:25-34

We all get the same 24-hour span each day. Taking a thoughtful look at the realities of your days can help with making realistic commitments to yourself and others. Jesus encourages us to seek him first (Matthew 6:33) and to "... not worry about tomorrow, for tomorrow will worry about itself. Each day has enough trouble of its own" (6:34).

This is not a call to do nothing, but one of setting priorities based on what God is leading you to do. There are some things you don't need to ponder. Everyone is called to care for their bodies through food, rest, and cleanliness. Everyone is called to work, to serve, to seek God. The details of how God wants you personally to carry out each task comes via the Holy Spirit as you pray for direction.

Your equation may vary in division, but the total is always the same. In this example, 7 hours of sleep, 7 hours of work or school, and 10 hours for everything else is the break down.

The point is everyone must balance multiple demands. In order to maintain peace and good health, you'vee got to accept a day with only 24 hours and certain non-negotiable needs. When you try to load too much into each day, the joy goes away and stress enters. You are not meant to live that way.

DAY FIFTY-FOUR

Working for God
Matthew 9:35-38

Jesus asks those who believe in him to give their lives to him. Many won't do it. They fear it will be too hard or limit their opportunity and freedom to do what they want. If you've ever worked for anything, you know that anything worthwhile requires a lot of work.

Working for God means submitting to him like a boss, teacher, or parent and trusting that whatever he asks you to do is important and deserves your best. It requires you to set aside judgment of the task's value. It will test your faith in the promise that he will work all things for your good, if you love him (Romans 8:28).

Volunteers in the U.S. Military have a good sense of what working for God is like. They sign a blank check with their lives, submit to an authority often unseen and not understood, give the job everything they have without surety of promotion or even survival.

Why would so many of the very best American men and women freely sign up for such a life?

On a very deep level they believe that the freedom America represents is worth laying down their life to preserve. Jesus Christ represents freedom in this life and for all of eternity. Can you think of anything more worthy of your energy and dedication?

DAY FIFTY-FIVE

Carry on with the great project God has given you
Nehemiah 6:2-4

There will be times in your life when you must stick with a job long past what you think is fair or reasonable. When faced with tough, long jobs your character will be built, for better or worse. In God's economy being a janitor is not lowly nor is being a CEO high and mighty. He has a job for you right now.

The job you are fulfilling right now might be a drudgery. Motherhood is often a challenging job because to do it right you must set aside many of your own desires. You really can't have it all. And, honestly, it's not "all good."

What is your attitude toward a thankless, tiresome job?

Nehemiah is an Old Testament character who illustrates the right attitude toward work that is difficult and long. God called him to lead the rebuilding of the wall around the city of Jerusalem. It was a huge job, and many people either didn't care about the wall or saw its completion as a threat.

When some men who wanted to see the work stop kept attempting to distract Nehemiah and get him sidetracked, he said, "I am carrying on a great project and cannot go down. Why should the work stop while I leave it and go down to you" (6:3)?

Where God has you working right now is important: school, motherhood, training, tough marriage, menial job, etc. You may have to endure disappointment or even anger from those who attempt to distract you. Some of them are well meaning and simply don't want you to suffer. Some feel convicted by your hard work while they are not doing the work God has given them.

Working for God means you are at his service without judgment of the task or time. He may ask you to do some pretty nasty jobs, without praise from people. He may take you from a place of plenty to one of little. He's your creator and gets to do that. He's building your character, preparing you for eternity.

Your time on this earth is just a blip. The average life span of an American woman is 86 years if born in 2000. Go to the Social Security Administrations Life Expectancy Calculator to learn more. https://www.ssa.gov/oact/population/longevity.html

DAY FIFTY-SIX

You can choose freedom or slavery
Galatians 5:1-12

The defining question of this time in history and for your life is this: Will you choose freedom or give in to slavery?

Freedom is costly, not just for you but for many you will never know. Slavery is cheap. It is the path of least resistance. It does not take a literal prison or chains to enslave you. Freedom begins in your own mind and the choices you make. A million things seek to enslave you - people, habits, philosophies, bad laws, etc.

Get a hold of the truth about your right to freedom paid for by the life and death of Christ. It is not found in rejecting rules and the boundaries of society or in having no responsibility for yourself or others. Neither will you find it when you let your emotions run wild or another person dictate how you should feel and what you must say.

You have a purpose designed by God.

He gave you freedom to choose his way or not. He did this because robots are not teachers or artists or engineers or soldiers. When you understand the amazing nature of this freedom you have, it will humble you.

Americans received a greater level of political and economic freedom after the Revolution of 1776. Never before in human history had a people enjoyed a government designed to protect their God-given right to life, liberty, and the pursuit of happiness.

Protections that allow you to come and go as you please, pursue a career, or any passion openly is just the beginning stage. The deepest, most meaningful freedom defies status, political boundaries, geography, color, age, anything.

Viktor Frankl, an Austrian-born neurologist, psychiatrist, and Holocaust survivor, captured in his writings about life as a Nazi prisoner the essence of freedom:

"We who lived in concentration camps can remember the men who walked through the huts comforting others, giving away their last piece of bread. They may have been few in number, but they offer sufficient proof that everything can be taken from a man but one thing: the last of the human freedoms -- to choose one's attitude in any given set of circumstances, to choose one's own way."

Frankl determined that for every human, "Between stimulus and response, there is a space. In that space is our power to choose our response. In our response lies our growth and our freedom."

The promise of Christ is that your freedom from the sin nature, shared by every human, has already been bought and paid for. All you must do is accept it and reject any thought or words that contradict that truth.

Paul's words in Galatians 5:1 jump off the page like a command: "It is for freedom that Christ has set us free. Stand firm, then, and do not let yourselves be burdened again by a yoke of slavery."

Become protective of the freedom Christ made possible and wait eagerly for God's call each day.

DAY FIFTY-SEVEN

Doing what you want is not freedom
Galatians 5:13-18

Freedom is not self-indulgence. True freedom is an ability to resist doing what feels easy or good now in order to work toward or wait for what you really want. Freedom enables you to share gifts and talents to serve others.

You, like everyone, have some weakness that, if not kept in check, will slow you down and limit your potential. You know what it is in your gut. You can ignore your conscience and make up excuses or not.

Some will blame laws (either God's or man-made) for making it hard to do what they feel like doing. Others will seek to rewrite or make up new laws to confirm what they feel like doing.

DAY FIFTY-EIGHT

Truth is costly
Matthew 10:26-39

Truth convicts people. Truth confronts prejudice, manipulation, hateful words, lies, stealing, immorality. Truth calls people to action. They will either listen or they will reject it and remove the messenger.

There's a difference between truth and honesty. You can be honest about your feelings and opinions. Your feelings and opinions can be wrong. Truth is a representation of reality that is accurate. A lie is when you knowingly present an inaccurate portrayal of reality. If you present something false unknowingly, you are being honest but untruthful.

Jesus warned his disciples that following his teachings and being a speaking the truth about him would not be easy. In Matthew 10:34 he says, "Do not think that I have come to bring peace to the earth. I have not come to bring peace, but a sword."

His message then and now upsets the order of power. It brings light into dark places and demands justice. The sword is both literal and figurative. In Hebrews 4:12, God's Word is called sharper than a double-edged sword, able to penetrate and divide soul and spirit, and judge thoughts and attitudes of the heart. Words have power, and they can heal or kill.

Choosing truth will cost more than you ever thought possible. Seeking the truth and God's path for your life will include tears and strain, many chances to give up because it's just too hard.

Don't give up on finding and understanding the truth. Jesus promises in John 8:32 that the truth will set you free. This is always the case, even though it may feel scary or even hurt initially.

DAY FIFTY-NINE

When things just keep getting worse
Mark 5:21-36

There will be times when you've done everything you know to do, but things continue to get worse. It will seem like your whole world is coming undone. You are weakest in these moments, most susceptible to a wrong voice calling you to take matters into your own hands or to give up.

Jesus encountered a woman one day who had unimaginable problems. She had suffered for twelve years with some form of bleeding disorder, perhaps endometriosis. She risked her life to simply touch Jesus' cloak. Touching a strange man could have gotten her stoned to death.

Jesus said to her, "Daughter, your faith has healed you. Go in peace and be freed from your suffering" (Matthew 5:34).

Women in the first century were highly protected and constrained, sometimes even to an extreme. They were not allowed to speak to men outside of the family, let alone touch a man. When menstruating they were considered "unclean" and could not be around men nor go into the temple.

Many women from Middle Eastern and African countries still live under this type of system. It's taken a step further in these cultures. Women must keep their faces and entire bodies covered in public.

This woman with a bleeding problem exhibited the kind of faith that activates the power of God. This kind of faith does not calculate risk or cost. It believes whole heartedly that Jesus is God and capable of healing any wound, winning any battle, changing any heart.

DAY SIXTY

Don't be afraid; just believe
Matthew 5:36

Fear can rule your life, own you. Think of all the things you are afraid of right now. Make a quick list.

The list might include failing, being alone, not finding a job, illness, crime, and on it goes. Jesus often told people to not fear. In Matthew 5:36 he said, "Don't be afraid; just believe."

What a simplistic, almost insulting thing for Jesus to say in the midst of the devastating mess you face.

Yet, if you think about it, fear is not useful beyond a momentary call to action. Fear, like anger, is intended to get your attention so you will act. Those emotions elicit the fight or flight response that can save your life.

If you feel fear and don't act, it's the equivalent of holding your foot on the gas pedal while the car is in park. Just believing, as Jesus says, is the first step toward action in your life. If you believe, you will pray when afraid. The act of prayer opens you to guidance from the Holy Spirit, which is how you will know what step to take next.

Look over your list of fears. Think about what's the worst-case scenario for each of those fears. Facing fears is a step toward overcoming them.

DAY SIXTY-ONE

Wielding your power, love, and self-control
2 Timothy 1:7

In 2 Timothy 1:7, Paul advises Timothy saying, "God did not give us a spirit of timidity but a spirit of power and love and self-control."

Power, love, and self-control are like key ingredients in a cake. You must have a measure of all three or the cake will not come out as intended. Being timid, i.e., afraid or wimpy, usually comes from not understanding how the three gifts of power, love, and self-control are to be managed.

Power without love or self-control is destructive. Love without power or self-control leads to mistreatment. Self-control without power and love is meaningless. What you will usually encounter are people who have more of one ingredient than the other. The result is people who dominate or even bully others to get their needs met, people who are overly submissive and passive, or people who are obsessive about controlling details in their own lives and other's.

If you have not learned the importance of embracing the power, love, and self-control God intends for your life, you will live a limited life. Mature people have learned these ingredients and the importance of balance.

Here's an example of how a mature person acts: Two friends have a plan to go someplace. One of the friends shows up with someone else, unannounced to the other. She feels disappointed and not so special, because the plan was just the two of them. But she goes ahead and enjoys the outing.

The next time they talk she says, "Hey, I liked the show. Did you? Joe seems to really be into you. I felt a little awkward when he came along. I thought the plan was for just us to go. Let's talk next time in advance if others are coming, okay?"

Be powerful = speak the truth
Be loving = put yourself in their shoes; don't judge
Have self-control = wait for the right time to speak or act

DAY SIXTY-TWO

In case of trouble, use this
Psalm 23

Some sort of trouble will find you, somewhere along the way. It may be disappointment or life threatening danger. Some trouble may last a few moments. Some may last many years. Psalm 23 is one of the most commonly known scriptures because it has calming power.

If you will choose to believe that God is sovereign over all, including good and bad times, peace is always available to you. Commit the words of King David to memory. Say them as you walk around, as you lay down at night, and when trouble confronts you in any form.

Psalm 23

The Lord is my shepherd, I lack nothing.
He makes me lie down in green pastures,
he leads me beside quiet waters, he refreshes my soul.
He guides me along the right paths for his name's sake.
Even though I walk through the darkest valley, I will fear no evil,
for you are with me; your rod and your staff, they comfort me.
You prepare a table before me in the presence of my enemies.
You anoint my head with oil; my cup overflows.
Surely your goodness and love will follow me all the days of my life,
and I will dwell in the house of the Lord forever.

DAY SIXTY-THREE

When Jesus delays
John 11:3-6, Isaiah 55:8-9

Nothing will test your faith and strength more than waiting for the answer to a prayer with an expiration date.

In the story of Lazarus' death and resurrection, sisters Martha and Mary trusted Jesus without reservation. When he became very ill, they sent a simple message to Jesus: "He whom you love is sick" (John 11:4).

Jesus delayed. By the time he arrived, Lazarus had died and been buried for four days. The time for action had passed in their minds. Lazarus was dead, and Jesus had let them down.

They thought that either Jesus didn't care or didn't have the power.

You might face that same dilemma when the sincere, serious, and reasonable prayer offered to God seems to go unanswered. The person died. The job is taken. He married someone else. Your application is rejected. You lost the game.

The very human conclusion is to assume God didn't care or that he wouldn't or couldn't answer. That is small faith thinking. Big faith looks back at all the times Jesus has shown up on time in both big and small ways. Big faith remembers that His ways are higher than your ways.

When Jesus finally arrived at the home of Martha and Mary, he performed a miracle. He brought Lazarus back to life.

Do you have a "Lazarus" - a hope, dream - that now feels dead and buried because Jesus delayed?

With Jesus, it is never too late. He has a plan. He sees what you cannot see. His purposes are higher and encompass all of time. You know your faith is getting big when you continue to believe and say, "Your will not mine" when Jesus delays in coming to answer your prayer.

DAY SIXTY-FOUR

Making room for Martha and Mary
Luke 10:38-42

Martha and Mary were the sisters of Lazarus, the man Jesus brought back to life. Martha was a Type A planner with a sense of responsibility. She was self-directed. No one needed to tell her step-by-step what to do. All she needed was the vision cast by a leader, an outcome defined, budget limits identified, human resources available. It would get done.

Mary was a bit dreamy, a Type B. She too could get things done but didn't mind being told what to do and when. Mary liked to just hang out. She had no issue with not knowing the end goal. She would just as happily put rocks in boots as prepare a meal or build a wall.

Martha was a natural leader. Mary was more of a follower.

But under the right circumstances they could switch roles. You likely have a tendency toward being a leader or a follower. The world needs Marthas and Marys. Remember that you see the world as you are not as it is. If you are a Martha, give Mary a break. Speak her language sometimes. Mary you do the same for Martha.

DAY SIXTY-FIVE

Crabs in the bucket syndrome
Luke 11:37 - 12:12

If you're ever on the Atlantic coast at night, get a flashlight, net, and bucket and go out crab hunting. Place a bunch of crabs in the bucket, and you will notice that as one attempts to crawl out of the bucket, another pulls her down. They climb on top of each other attempting to get out. Instead of cooperating, they ensure all endure the same fate - stuck in the bucket.

This same tragedy occurs too often in your school, neighborhood, friendships, church, club, etc. Someone begins to excel or gets a new idea. But rather than cheer the person on or cooperate for mutual benefit, the group or the one in charge sabotages the person.

For example, a 4th grade girl liked math. She and a handful of others in the class excelled and got all the concepts at the beginning of the year. The teacher didn't want any of the students to fail or perceive themselves as not smart. She stuck with the same concepts all year long, holding out for the last student to get it. In the end, 20 students were denied learning while the one student struggled to get the first concept.

The teacher set up a crab in the bucket environment in her classroom. None succeeded because not all could succeed.

DAY SIXTY-SIX

"Then you will know the truth, and the truth will set you free"
John 8:31-32

Truth always comes with a cost. The truth requires something of you. In John 8: 31 - 32, Jesus said, "If you hold to my teaching, you are really my disciples. Then you will know the truth, and the truth will set you free."

Sometimes it means accepting that the person telling you the truth loves you enough to risk making you angry or sad.

Telling the truth can cost you friends, reputation, a good grade, a promotion or even your job.

Standing for and telling the truth has cost many great people their lives: Jesus, our savior; Cicero, a Roman Senator; Socrates, a Greek philosopher; Martin Luther King, an American pastor and civil rights leader. There are many more throughout history.

If you seek the truth, you will find it. Knowing and accepting the truth is the only way to be free as an individual human.

DAY SIXTY-SEVEN

Tricky lies
John 8:48-51, John 14:6

Your enemy is a liar, unable to tell the truth. His goal and the many demons under his employment are hard at work luring you away from truth and into a web of lies. If they can keep you content with lies, they own you eternally.

They plant stubbornness, pride, and prejudice to keep you from believing the truth. They use hatred, power craving, and murderous intentions to trap people into carrying out their work.

When Jesus lived on earth, the leaders among his own people hated him. They accused and scrutinized him but could never find a single sin. He was convicted and crucified for telling the truth about who he was - the Son of God.

Jesus embodied truth because he is truth. He never shied away from challenging questions. He welcomed those who asked hard questions then, and he still does today.

Many fail to find him and the truth that leads to peace in this life and eternally. Some never accept his challenge to check him out. Others hear and experience the truth but reject it because they fear the personal cost.

The truth is expensive. Lies are cheap.

DAY SIXTY-EIGHT

God reflects the perfect father, husband, priest, leader
Ruth 4:13-16

Your experience with key male figures in your life will influence how you view and relate to God. For example, if you grew up with a father that didn't love, cherish, and support you, it will be harder to see God as a heavenly father that will do those things.

You can be blessed with a father or husband that seeks to reflect a Godly attitude or maybe you will not have that experience. Either way, God cares for and supports you perfectly. Seek relationships that model care and support, knowing none on earth will be perfect.

God values you. Don't let your experience with a father or husband that fell short discourage you.

Pray for good relationships and let them begin with you.

DAY SIXTY-NINE

Eager to find him
John 20:1-18

On the third day after Jesus was crucified, Mary Magdalene went to the tomb and found it empty. She went straight to Peter and John, two of Jesus' inner circle disciples, and told them that Jesus' body was gone. They ran to the tomb, eager to find him.

They were eager because the body missing meant one of two things. Either someone had stolen the body, or Jesus' promises of coming back from the dead were true. The first meant they had given up their lives for a lie. If Jesus had in fact risen from the dead, everything had truly changed forever.

Notice in the story that only Mary Magdalene lingers at the tomb. The men run back home, perhaps to tell others and begin the search, or maybe they were afraid whoever took Jesus' body would be coming for them.

Mary encounters two angels and Jesus. They dispel her anguish and confirm that it is true; Jesus is alive. He conquered death. Finding Jesus requires lingering with a hopeful expectation. It is hard to believe from a worldly standpoint that he is God, yet he is, and he came as a humble servant and was murdered in the most horrible way imaginable.

All of those that knew Jesus gave their lives to spread the truth about the events of the past. Today, we have everything because a few wrote the story down and shared it with others.

DAY SEVENTY

Making straight paths
Proverbs 3:5-6, Matthew 7:13-14, Isaiah 45:2

In Matthew 7:13-14, Jesus says that straight is the gate, and narrow is the way to life, but few find it. Proverbs 3 gives three ingredients for successfully finding the straight path.

1. Trust the Lord with all your heart. All of your heart means everything, no doubt.
2. Don't lean on or bet on what you understand. At best, you only have a very limited view of the big picture. If you trust God with all your heart, you won't lean on what you think.
3. In everything you say and do, acknowledge God. This means to think about what God would have you do and pray for guidance.

Finding the straight path for your life should be a daily prayer. Even if you get the average 70 years, life is short. Don't miss the things God has planned for you on the straight path.

DAY SEVENTY-ONE

How to live right
Ephesians 5:1-20

Once you know the truth about something, you become responsible for it. You cannot go back or claim, "I didn't know."

In God's perfection and sense of justice, he set the principles of the universe in motion so that they apply to all people the same, regardless of whether they understand them or not. Think about gravity or the law of the harvest. What goes up must come down, and what is sown will eventually come up.

Paul's letters to the early churches simplify God's principles for living. They remain relevant today. We too live in a society unfriendly to the things of God and his nature. Yet, as a Christian you don't answer to this world's standards but to those of God.

Here's a summary of Paul's advice on how to live in the world as a Christian:

1. Don't practice sexual immorality, don't be greedy or use obscene language or hateful talk of any sort toward people
2. Be thankful in your heart and in expression of words
3. Listen closely to people's comments in the media, classroom, or in person and evaluate the information in light of what you know God says so you won't be fooled by empty words and lies
4. Love all humankind but don't partner in marriage, business, or politics with foolish people who scheme to hurt others, lie, or mislead
5. Seek to be a good person and tell the truth
6. Be careful about how you live. Be wise. Seek the Lord's will. Make the most of opportunities that come your way to be kind, gentle, or helpful
7. Don't get drunk because it leads to debauchery
8. Let the Spirit of God fill you up
9. Always give thanks to God the Father for everything, in the name of our Lord Jesus Christ

DAY SEVENTY-TWO

Everything you need to travel through hell
Philippians 4:10-19

The things God calls you to endure or accomplish will never be easy. A misunderstanding of God's ways and purposes causes many to develop a bad attitude or give up. God's Word is filled with promises and reminders that he's got you. He's in control and will take care of your needs. Maybe you've never really known what it's like to do without. But you've likely experienced some anxiety around wanting something and not getting it or having to wait for it.

In speaking to the Philippians, Paul reflects the attitude and understanding of God that you need to embrace.

Paul thanks this fledgling church for sending him money. Woven into his words are reminders that his life is tough, very tough. He's been through hell, yet he's on the mission Jesus gave him.

Until you've felt what it is to be in need and what it is to have plenty, you will be unable to learn the secret of being content in any and every situation, whether well fed or hungry, whether living in plenty or in want (4:12).

You can get through anything Jesus calls you to because you have access to his strength. His provisions and strength allow you to have peace during challenging times (4:13). But you won't until your attitude and perception change from focusing on what you want to one of accepting his provision and power, no matter what happens.

Everything you need to accomplish the task God has given will be supplied by God because he is the owner of all and in control of everything. You don't need to worry about who, what, or where the resources will come from. You just need to set about doing the thing God has led you to do.

The Christ-follower, like Paul, will experience plenty and want, smooth seas and stormy seas, feeling loved and lonely. These times should never surprise you nor make you think they will go on forever. Few get to a place and say as Paul did, "I have learned to be content whatever the circumstances" (4:11). However, God calls us to strive for that kind of trust. When we seek it and strive for it, the Holy Spirit comes along with us to help.

DAY SEVENTY-THREE

The trial of waiting
Psalm 39 and 40

"Often blessings cannot be received unless we go through the trial of waiting," says the NIV Life Application Study Bible 1991 edition notes from Psalm 40:1-4. In that same Psalm, King David rejoiced after he'd "waited patiently for the Lord" (40:1). He talks about being lifted up from "the slimy pit, out of the mud and mire" (40:2). He's got a "new song," and "a hymn of praise to our God" (40:3).

But what about when you are still wallowing in that slimy pit, enduring the trial?

Psalm 39 tells the story of David's suffering. He'd determined to stay silent. "I will put a muzzle on my mouth as long as the wicked are in my presence" (39:1).

He could not stay silent. His heart "grew hot within" him. He didn't go to his friends or "the wicked" (unbelievers) (39:3). He went to God and complained. He models the right steps for taking your anguish and disappointment to God.

1. Acknowledge God's authority to discipline all people and the short-lived, fragile nature of a life.
2. Ask God to hear your prayers for help and to take pity on you.
3. Wait. Wait patiently and actively do your work.

You must wait even in the midst of unbearable circumstances for God's timing. If you've prayed like David, God is at work. He's heard you.

Will you trust, and keep your mouth from saying that God cannot or will not take care of you and the situation?

DAY SEVENTY-FOUR

Hard times require strength
Psalm 40:12-13

Life's troubles seem to come in clusters. One leads to another often. It's like when you are tired and worn down, your immune system is low, and sickness finds you.

Real trouble cannot be helped by friends or family beyond a certain point. It's good to talk to people and even seek assistance for many issues. Prayer about situations should be part of daily life, but when serious trouble finds you there's an inexplicable, desperate need for God.

King David reveals this need and how to get through soul crushing times of trouble throughout the Psalms.

He always goes to God naming his problems, and he owns them. He never makes excuses or blames God for the way he feels or what's happened to him.

He describes how everything is affecting him. Sometimes finding words to describe your pain and heartache is a relief in and of itself. Sometimes those words are too personal to share with anyone but God.

Without fail, David pleads with God to help or save him, to come quickly, to forgive, to deal with his enemies. Real trouble means we have exhausted all human means at our disposal to fix it. Only God can turn it around. If the situation gets better at this point, there will be no confusing who did the rescuing. It will be God.

It may seem hard to accept this level of submission and sheer dependency on God, but it's reality. You can't change it. You can rail against it, but God is still God and he will allow you to know blinding trouble in order to show you that he is a merciful, loving, and just God.

DAY SEVENTY-FIVE

Entering your promised land
Deuteronomy 10 - 11

Life is lived mostly in the flat desert lands in between mountain top experiences. Much of the Old Testament gives an account of how God's people historically made their own journey from slavery and bondage in Egypt to possessing the most abundant, rich land on the earth at the time. Those stories are full of principles that apply to your life.

When you reach points, like the Israelites, where God is about to take you to the next level, give you something bigger than you've yet experienced (graduation, marriage, new job), it is vital to stop and read Deuteronomy 10 - 11. Moses words and those he brings from God are just as relevant to you today as they were to those weary Israelites. It had been 40 years and finally they were about to see the "promised land."

To paraphrase, God is saying, I've used the desert to shape and strengthen you. I'm giving this next level opportunity to you, but it comes with a few stipulations.

Respect me. Follow me. Love me. Serve me. Obey me.

In Deuteronomy 11:26 - 32, he could not make it more clear: "I'm setting before you a blessing and a curse (11:26)."

Graduating to the "promised land" can make or break people. Don't let it go to your head. Remember where you came from, those days of perseverance, loneliness, fear, and wondering if you'd ever make it to the next level.

God needs you to continue the same formula of "respect, follow, love, serve, and obey" no matter what your position in life, regardless of whether you are in the valley or the mountain top. If you will continue to stay committed to those commands, he will take you to increasingly higher places in life and do incredible things with your life, things you could never even dream.

DAY SEVENTY-SIX

Will you finish strong
2 Timothy 4:7-8

"Begin with the end in mind" is Stephen Covey's advise for people who want to be effective. Covey was a leadership guru who wrote *The Seven Habits of Highly Effective People.* To begin with the end means to think carefully about what your final product or outcome will look like, whether in a class, job, sport, or life itself.

A good life rarely happens by accident. There's always a high cost to achieving anything of value. You will be confronted with many opportunities but only able to truly accomplish a few things. God will equip you to accomplish everything he intends for you. But you must choose to do your part.

Therefore, take on nothing without first beginning with the end in mind. If you discern that achieving that end is right and feasible for you, commit to it. Courage is vital to staying the course in life.

Paul's life is a study in finishing strong. He went from presiding over the killing of Christians to becoming the foremost teacher of faith in Christ. Don't dwell on whatever mistakes or bad experiences lie in your past. Start with today, close your eyes, and imagine your ending. What does it look like, who's around you and what are they saying?

DAY SEVENTY-SEVEN

Self-Discipline
1 Corinthians 9:24-27

The most important, elemental thing you should learn is self-discipline. So, few people reach their full potential because they never learn this simple, basic skill, available to each and every person regardless of background or education.

Self-discipline is doing that which will eventually result in reaching a goal or some desired outcome when no one is looking or telling you to do it.

For example, brushing your teeth twice a day, shutting off the technology and going to sleep at a decent hour, saying no to drugs, alcohol or whatever else might diminish you, practicing piano (whatever your thing might be).

People don't self-discipline for a number of reasons. Some never get the chance to experience the benefits of delaying gratification. Some are just lazy. Others sense it would help them achieve what they desire and try to stay on course for a while, but when the inevitable distractions or obstacles emerge, they give up.

Self-discipline is one of the "secret" ingredients to life. You must first decide you are willing to submit to discipline. Second, you must lean into God for help. From there, you must be courageous and refuse to give up.

A disciplined life is a lot like learning an instrument or ball sport (tennis, golf, basketball, etc.). You will mess up a million times before you become expert. And even at expert level, you will still make mistakes.

Make a choice to practice self-discipline and then pray for help from God to stick with it, especially after you fail.

DAY SEVENTY-EIGHT

Discernment
James 4:11-12, Genesis 9:6, II Timothy 4:2, I Peter 4:14

You are called to use good judgment but not to judge an individual's heart or soul. Often Christians confuse the difference between judging others and using good judgment. Actions (words and deeds) are the way to form the basis for using your good judgment.

God established laws and principles to keep an order to the universe and individual lives as well as to provide a lighted path for people. In Deuteronomy 11: 26 - 36, God explains that following his order leads to blessings. Ignoring the order leads to curses.

You have a responsibility to protect the order of things in your life, home, community, and country. This means that turning a blind eye to activity and ideas that contradicts good order is wrong. Righting wrongs is not your job alone, but you must use judgment based on God's teachings.

You do not have a right to judge individuals, even your own family. God is the judge. He will convict hearts, work circumstances and consequences together for the good of each person.

The tension between responsibility to use judgment and getting along in society is great. Our society as a whole has allowed for things we know are wrong. It feels judgmental to speak against them even though we know good judgment would not condone them in our own lives.

Discernment is required in these areas that have become land mines of controversy, often dividing family and neighbors. Make up your mind to uphold truth and God's order in your life and home. When confronted with questions about God's order, do not be afraid to speak truth or work for it to be upheld in the laws and social mores of your community and country.

God will judge you on how you responded to opportunities to stand up for truth as well as the measure of compassion and mercy you showed individuals. Your imperfection does not negate your responsibility to speak up for God's laws and principles.

DAY SEVENTY-NINE

Getting what you want
James 4:1-3

Think of ten things you actively want right now, from a manicure to a husband. It's hard to acknowledge reasons why we don't get things desired. Often, it's a lack of maturity or timing.

Unfulfilled wants often lead to jealousy and discontent. It takes energy to be upset. James 4:2 says, "You do not have because you do not ask God."

Use your energy to ask God for what you want and to do whatever work he's given you right now. Ask boldly and clearly in your prayers. Confess that you are not getting everything right. Always end a prayer with "Lord, your will be done."

God is like a good parent. He wants you to have everything but will not give anything harmful. If you ask and trust that he will provide anything you want in due time, if it is for your greater good, it will be done. Then there's no need for discontent. You can go on about life and focus on what you already have from God.

But remember that anything you take outside of God's will eventually turns to ashes.

Most of your desires are normal, legitimate things that in good time God will provide in your life. But there's a catch.

If you want the desires of your heart, in a lasting way, you must wait, do your part, and trust God with every aspect of your life. And accept that many times the answer to a prayer is not what you had in mind.

James says your fights and quarrels come out of wanting something and not getting it. He adds, "You do not have because you do not ask God. When you ask, you do not receive, because you ask with wrong motives, that you may spend what you get on your pleasures" (4:2-3).

God will not leave you in your self-pity and guilt. He draws you toward higher standards and does not indulge your every desire immediately because he wants to shape your character. You may feel like a horrible failure at times. Seek God's mercy and grace.

DAY EIGHTY

The motivation to succeed long term
Deuteronomy 7:9, Colossians 3:23

You do many things because someone tells you to do them. Most tasks are associated with a paycheck, grade, or some form of external approval. Other things you do simply gratify a desire. However, if you seek to know God, you will also do the right thing out of love and gratitude toward Christ.

Which motivator is based on freedom: being directed by someone else, being directed by your desires, or being motivated by love and gratitude?

Some people will spend their entire life attempting to please others, themselves, or even God through a check list of rules, performance indicators, or accolades. They will make their own prison of these things and hate God for it.

Christ made freedom of the mind possible, even for the slave or poorest person. We are all like children of a king with full inheritance rights. We did nothing to earn it. Christ removed all obstacles to God, except one. Knowing him requires an individual choice. When you grasp this truth, you want to become more like Christ. You serve him out of love and gratitude freely.

Do not look at others for acceptance or even your own performance as a measure. The Holy Spirit will guide you if your heart is willing in all pursuits.

DAY EIGHTY-ONE

The gift of time
Luke 11:5-8

God is about relationship. He wants to be in relationship with you, and the desire for relationship is hardwired into your soul. The primary ingredient for relationship is time. Without making time for someone, you will never enjoy real relationship.

The greatest gift you can give is time.

Reading about Jesus' ministry from a time management perspective reveals a wonderful model for your life. While he had no job, home, spouse, children, or any real worldly responsibility, he kept a schedule. Within that schedule he provided lots of room to pause and give his time to the people he encountered as well as his friends.

Jesus' time translated to all sorts of transformations in people. He listened and gave them what they needed.

With your relationships, it's not so much about the amount of time you give but the quality of time spent and attitude you bring with the time. Nothing hurts you more than to sense that someone has checked you off a list after calling or visiting, multi-tasking while spending time with you, or over-emphasizing the short window of time they have for you.

You cannot spend time with everyone, every day. However, you are called to provide a slice of quality time to those God has called you into relationship with, whether the family under your roof, stranger on the street, or estranged friend that keeps texting.

The secret is to first listen to God's leading. He will guide you toward those he wants you to spend time with.

DAY EIGHTY-TWO

Tested faith
Genesis 22:1-14

Faith can be summed up as a belief that between the three aspects of God – Father, Son, and Holy Spirit – you are covered. Nothing can or will happen to you outside of God's permission. You may not always understand it, and you have free will.

The story of Abraham's reaction to God's request that he sacrifice his only son Isaac illustrates raw faith. God made what on face value seemed like a ridiculous request of Abraham. In response, Abraham began getting ready for a journey. He chopped wood and saddled his donkey. He asked no questions and set immediately about the work required to do what was asked.

As they approached the mountain, Isaac became curious. "The fire and wood are here," Isaac said, "but where is the lamb for the burnt offering"(22:7)?

Abraham answered, "God himself will provide the lamb for the burnt offering, my son" (22:8).

God did provide the lamb that day. Many years later Jesus came as the ultimate lamb in sacrifice for us all.

God will test your heart and faith. He will ask that you sacrifice everything that is dear to you – yourself, your children, your family. It must be this way for you to grow up.

Will you chop wood and saddle your donkey? That's the practical part you must do, all the while not knowing what God will do, but trusting he has a plan.

You will only have the sort of faith that enables action when God calls, versus only feelings and questions, if you trust that God is all seeing, all powerful, righteous in his judgment, and the embodiment of love and mercy.

This is the kind of faith Daniel exhibited in the lion's den as well as Peter when Jesus called him to put his fishing nets back out when it didn't make sense. You must act when God urges or confronts you with a situation, even though you don't understand. You must wait when the hour seems late. If you refuse, the outcome will be far less than what God had planned for you.

DAY EIGHTY-THREE

Habits of the good and the evil
Psalm 37:5-7

From beginning to end, the Bible contrasts good and evil. The many stories, Psalms, and Proverbs show the behaviors and consequences of each. One path is narrow and slow but leads to peace. The other is wide and fast but leads to weeping and pain.

Whatever you really want in your heart of hearts will come only with diligence, patience, waiting on God, trusting God, doing the right thing over and over and over. This is a reflection of what it takes to enjoy eternity with God in peace. You can't see it today. You must trust it is out there.

The "righteous" trust, commit, delight, wait, are blameless, turn from evil, take refuge.

The "wicked" fret, envy, are angry, show wrath, plot against others.

To follow the way of a righteous person often seems slow and without excitement, but it leads to peace. God will honor and care for the Christian who seeks to do good and right, as well as their children.

DAY EIGHTY-FOUR

The danger of extreme disappointment
Matthew 26, Proverbs 13:12

Extreme disappointment can lead you to drastic measures.

Judas Iscariot was one of the twelve disciples picked by Jesus. For 30 pieces of silver he betrayed Jesus and gave him over to the Jewish leaders by the dark of night. After realizing what a tragic mistake he'd made, Judas took his own life.

Jesus' disciples believed he was going to lead a revolution and become a king of the Jews in the tradition of the great King David. When Jesus made it clear that the kingdom he was bringing to earth at that point was in the hearts of mankind and that he would conquer death not Caesar, it crushed them. They had given up everything in hopes of landing a spot in the new king's court.

When you've "given up everything" to achieve a dream or get something or somewhere, and it passes you by, disappointment can turn to anger. In anger you can determine to take matters into your own hands. Do you find yourself often telling yourself or others that you are not angry? If so, you probably are quite angry inside.

Anything you decide to "take into your own hands" will turn to ashes.

Judas had an idea about how a revolutionary and future king should act. Jesus didn't comply. Judas possibly believed that he could force Jesus to accelerate the revolution by facilitating the confrontation of the Jewish leaders and Jesus during the Passover festival. Jesus didn't fight.

Judas saw his hopes of fame and a Jewish revolution unraveling. There would be no revolt against Rome led by Jesus. He would die in the most horrible, humiliating fashion - nailed to a cross.

It was not necessary for Judas to commit suicide. Jesus would have forgiven him, like he did Peter and all the others.

Whatever you desire, ask the Lord. Wait patiently for the answer. If you get frustrated while waiting and attempt to take matters into your own hands, stop and ask for forgiveness. Jesus will forgive you. He'll give you what is best for you.

DAY EIGHTY-FIVE

Keeping rebellion at bay
Exodus 34:6-8

Rebellion lies within you. It is a part of human nature. Right now, rebellion may be dormant, active, or stirring within you. God does not reward the rebellious Christian. Your life is expanding or contracting in direct correlation to how willing you are to deny sin and follow God's leading in your life.

You rationalize that just a little of this won't hurt. You get in a hurry. God delays. Worry sets in. Guilt from the past haunts you. You believe, "Why bother. It's futile."

Make no mistake. Sin that you condone and refuse to turn away from will destroy you and likely those you love in some form or fashion.

God in his holiness cannot reward sin, but in his mercy provides the power to resist. He forgives you when you fail. Overcoming whatever sin plagues you begins with an attitude of humility. Trusting God to help you and that his forgiveness is unlimited is vital. You see, anything less is proclaiming God a liar.

Get with God every day to pray and meditate. Ask him to show you his best for every decision throughout every day.

DAY EIGHTY-SIX

Using your freedom to obey
Romans 6

If you boil the concept of Christ down, you get a simple equation: His death and resurrection = your freedom.

You have the freedom to choose your master every day. No matter what kind of circumstances you endure, you can give yourself completely to God. We make ourselves slaves to many things such as emotions, handicaps, relationships, authority, philosophies, substances, and so on.

Make God your master.

Get up every day and go to bed every night praying, "God, help me. I work for you."

You will still slip, fall, and cry. You will still face challenge and tragedy. But you will get back up. You will persevere. "...The peace of God, which transcends all understanding, will guard your hearts and your minds in Christ Jesus" (Phillipians 4:7).

Commit yourself to obeying Christ with your freedom.

DAY EIGHTY-SEVEN

God rewards according to what you have done
Psalm 62:12, Revelation 22:12

Everything you say and do has a reward. It might come immediately or later, but your reward will come. This is the Law of the Harvest, reaping what you sow. God placed this law in effect for all people. It does not discriminate between Christians or non-Christians, color, nationality, wealth, or anything else.

People will make decisions about you based on behavior. Your basic mental and physical health is largely tied to behavior.

God will ultimately judge you by what you did with the opportunities, gifts, and responsibilities placed before you. The outcome of your final judgment is connected to attitude and action based on what God called you to do as an individual and as a Christian in general.

Don't give yourself a pass because of what's happened to you or what you lack. Regardless of your appearance, you can act pretty. Even "dumb" people can study to do their best. Average athletes or artists can become good ones with diligence.

Everyone can practice kindness, patience, generosity, love, gentleness, and self-control.

What are you doing today with your opportunities, gifts, and responsibilities? The answers will determine your tomorrow here and in eternity.

DAY EIGHTY-EIGHT

It's not the sin but the attitude that matters
1 Corinthians 6:9-11

All can spend eternity in a place called heaven, but not all will get to go. Entry requires one simple thing, yet many find the cost too high.

Sin is not what keeps people out of heaven. God does not rank sin. He groups the murderer with the liar and the sexually immoral. He will forgive all equally. God knows you've tried to stop lying, stealing, or whatever. You just can't do it on your own.

This is exactly why God must treat all sin the same, and why we require a savior. Jesus came as God in flesh and gave up his self so all sin could be covered. It's not the perfection of the individual that opens the gates of heaven but the heart attitude.

The price for living this life fully and entry into an eternal life with God is admitting that you cannot be "good enough." You need Jesus.

DAY EIGHTY-NINE

Four human endowments that give you power
Romans 2:12-15

Stephen Covey described four human endowments wired into us by God in his book *First Things First*. These endowments distinguish us from the animal world and, as Covey writes, "Create our ultimate human freedom: the power to choose, to respond, to change."

Self-awareness
Self-awareness is the capacity to look at your thinking, motives, history, scripts, actions, habits and tendencies and make choices.

Conscience
Conscience is the sense of morality built into human nature. With rare exception, people are born with a sense of right and wrong. Covey writes, "Conscience connects us with the wisdom of the ages and wisdom of the heart."

Independent Will
Your power to act for change or status quo, for good or evil is uniquely human. Covey writes, "We're not victims. We're not the product of our past. We are the product of our choices."

Creative Imagination
Imagination enables you to envision and create a future in your mind. According to Covey, everything has two births. First in the mind and second in reality.

DAY NINETY

A tendency to turn back when it gets hard
Exodus 13:17 - 14:31, Luke 14:28

Whatever has enslaved you will not let go easily. Much of the battle involved in breaking bad habits, leaving abusive relationships, pressing through to a goal involves your willingness to keep fighting.

"When Pharaoh let the people go, God did not lead them on the road through the Philistine country, though that was shorter. For God said, "If they face war, they might change their minds and return to Egypt" (Exodus 13:17).

We all have a personal Egypt. It's whatever or whoever you've allowed to hold you back. When God opens a way for you to leave Egypt, you've got to trust the path he lays out. It might not be the shortest or most comfortable way.

He knows when you are ready for a battle. Too often you will change your mind and "return to Egypt" if you "face war." But you will eventually have to fight for freedom. It may mean that you keep moving ahead without looking back, or it may involve physical battle.

Leaving your personal Egypt behind and living in the freedom God intends for you will always entail an emotional and mental battle of choice. Don't give up and go back to where you started.

DAY NINETY-ONE

Deciding the size of your heaven or hell
John 14:1-4

In John 14:2, Jesus makes it clear that no one need ever be excluded from heaven. You get to decide whether your final home is heaven or hell.

He says, "My Father's house has many rooms; if that were not so, would I have told you that I'm going there to prepare a place for you" (14:2)?

The stumbling blocks to heaven are created by people, not God. For example, someone from church mistreated you, someone introduced you to drugs, someone abused you, someone in authority pushed you down, and on it goes.

Often, we reject Jesus' call to follow him on a path to heaven where there are many rooms that represent the many different types of people because of pride. Priest and writer, Richard Rohr says the more inclusive you are the bigger your heaven and the more exclusive you are the bigger your hell.

Don't get hung up on the rules or who did what to you. Just simply seek after Jesus, and he'll find the room for you on earth and in heaven.

DAY NINETY-TWO

All shall be well
Julian of Norwich
Jeremiah 22:15-17

Julian of Norwich lived in England from 1342 - 1416. She lived an isolated life in order to seek a deeper knowing of Jesus but is remembered today for writing about her "Showings" from God.

Julian wondered why God allowed sin to enter the world and allowed awful evils to continue. It's the perennial question of many serious and not so serious seekers: "How can a good God allow tragedy to befall so many good people?"

In her writings, she shares the answer Jesus offered.

"But Jesus, who in this vision informed me of all that is needed by me, answered with these words and said: 'It was necessary that there should be sin; but all shall be well, and all shall be well, and all manner of thing shall be well."

Without the freedom to do wrong, you are but a slave or robot. The rules and laws of God and society are necessary for you to have a choice. Think about what happens when there are no limits set for people. Chaos ensues.

Homes, businesses, and churches have doors that lock. Countries must have borders. Without locks, borders, fences, or boundaries, how do you know where to stop or how do you limit those who have no intentions of stopping? Setting up boundaries, fences, doors is the only way to create spaces where chaos does not overwhelm. You have a right to your personal boundary. Healthy societies extend rights to have fences and doors that lock and even boundaries for who can come into the society.

Read more at:
https://www.christianhistoryinstitute.org/incontext/article/julian/

DAY NINETY-THREE

Use your wounds to redeem the world around you
Richard Rohr
Isaiah 53:5, Psalm 139:16, Ephesians 5:16

There's just no way to live into adulthood without getting wounded in some form or fashion. It's part of God's plan for growing you up. Until you experience something less than the ideal, something other than getting your way, you can't be of any use to your fellowman or God.

Don't go seeking wounds. But don't try to hide behind the hurt that's left you unsure of yourself and your position in the world.

Writer and priest, Richard Rohr writes the following in his book, *Falling Upward*:

"It has been acceptable for some time in America to remain 'wound identified' (that is, using one's victimhood as one's identity, one's ticket to sympathy, and one's excuse for not serving), instead of using the wound to 'redeem the world,' as we see in Jesus and many people who turn their wounds into sacred wounds that liberate both themselves and others."

Your hurt and disappointment can be overcome. It's the you that remains after the overcoming that encourages and helps others.

Rohr also quotes Carl Jung. "Where you stumble and fall there you find pure gold."

DAY NINETY-FOUR

To be a real friend
Proverbs 17:17

Real friends are priceless.

They are there in good and bad times and speak truth to you in love. A friend accepts you, even if she doesn't always agree with you, and gives you freedom to be yourself.

The ability to be a real friend is not something you conjure up at will. You must have first practiced being a friend to yourself before you can give friendship away to others. If you are not honest with or accepting of yourself, you won't be honest with or accepting of others.

Stephen Covey called the type of people capable of real friendship "interdependent." They understand that there's a time to get help and work with others, and there's a time to be independent and rely on yourself.

You are free to be a friend or not. If you appreciate the freedom of spirit and mind that Christ died for every single person to have, you can extend true friendship and receive it.

DAY NINETY-FIVE

Acceptance versus Approval
Mark 2:8-11, John 8:11

If you question the behaviors and attitudes of someone you love, they might respond this way: "You don't accept me. Jesus accepted everyone. I'm living my life. Why don't you respect me?"

This is a cunning strategy of the enemy that keeps everyone confused and in turmoil, if allowed. No matter what, we can love and accept our children, parents, family, friends, and even strangers.

What you will have a hard time doing when destructive behavior is involved is approving of that behavior or condoning it by joining in or looking the other way. Approving may reduce conflict and enable you to be close to the person again. But that is not loving in the long term.

People following the world's path away from what they know is true will push away from the person that is calling out the behavior or attitude. They may even taunt and mock.

If you are not careful, you may get caught up in a battle that leads to sleepless nights and hard feelings. It's not a matter of education when someone who knows the difference between what is good and bad is running down life's wide path.

Jesus modeled how to navigate relationships of every sort with love and peace. The peace part is vital. If you are not careful, you'll lose your peace fretting over and fighting with the person you love that's off course.

- Jesus accepted and interacted with everyone he encountered
- He showed compassion and mercy to anyone who came in humility
- Jesus often healed people who were not coming in humility, but he didn't condone their bad behavior. He told the woman caught in adultery to "go and sin no more" (John 8:11). He told the cripple by the pool to "pick up your mat and go" (Mark 2: 8 – 11).
- He didn't chase after those who contradicted him or refused to accept his message or him
- Jesus never argued with anyone. He spoke truth either plain and simple or in parables, based on the situation.

- Jesus didn't evaluate whether or not individuals or communities deserved his gifts or would accept him in advance. He was on a mission to teach and help as many as he could on the way to Jerusalem where he would die. If he showed up and people rejected him, he left. If they welcomed him, he'd stay for a while teaching and healing.

When someone you love is in trouble, on the wrong path, you want to help them find the way back. With Jesus' manner and methods as a reference, keep loving them, but don't chase them or reward bad behavior. Most importantly, keep praying. Pray day and night. Ask others to pray with you. Fast for the sake of the one you love and then pray during the fast.

Only the Holy Spirit can get their attention. If they at some time in the past claimed Christ as savior, the Holy Spirit is in them. Pray that Jesus would release the creative power of the Holy Spirit in that person to reveal truth to them and bring them to understanding. Pray that for yourself too.

DAY NINETY-SIX

You can only control yourself
2 Corinthians 9:6-15

Control is a natural desire. It starts at a young age. You want to control your situation and often those around you to maximize your comfort and pleasure.

Stephen Covey wrote, "We're not in control of our lives principles are."

For example, it's a principle of life that for every action there's an equal or greater reaction. How you treat people will be reflected back to you in the form of their reactions to you. The state of your health will be directly impacted by what you eat as well as how much you sleep and exercise.

The only thing you control in life is your own actions. Covey writes that it is an illusion to think that you can get something for nothing or control things with desire, force, or wishing.

Part of the illusion is an appearance that you've gamed the system or gotten to the destination quicker with a short cut. Consequences resulting from your trade-offs will eventually emerge. As Dr. Charles Stanley says, "You always reap more than you sow, later than you sow." This is another way of saying "what goes around, comes around."

Focus on controlling yourself and accepting the principles built into life.

DAY NINETY-SEVEN

Humility is not a bad thing
Proverbs 11:2, Psalm 130

Humility is often equated with being humiliated, e.g., by a bully, an opponent, teacher, boyfriend, etc.

Humility means respect for principles, authority, natural order. A humble person considers the needs and sensitivities of others before their own and finds contentment and security in God's leading. In *Mere Christianity*, C.S. Lewis wrote, "True humility is not thinking less of yourself; it is thinking of yourself less."

Pride presents itself as an insatiable restlessness, a need for more no matter what or who you have. It overvalues the self and undervalues others.

Famous movie director Cecil B. Demille said, "We cannot break the ten commandments. We can only break ourselves on them."

Humility allows you to accept that there is a God who created the world and immutable principles to govern His world. Your dislike of those principles does not change them.

"When pride comes, then comes disgrace, but with humility comes wisdom."
(Proverbs 11:2)

DAY NINETY-EIGHT

Never ever compare yourself to others
Matthew 20:1-16

Never indulge in comparison or assumptions. It will always get you in trouble. When you compare yourself to another, you will always find yourself better or worse. If you perceive them as better, you will grow jealous and ask, "What about me?"

Jesus makes clear in the parable of the vineyard laborers that it is really none of our business who and how God chooses to pay (or bless) others. God is holy, loving, and just. He has a plan for every life much of which we cannot see or understand.

If you consider yourself better - prettier, smarter, richer, cooler - arrogance will set in and that's always followed by a loss of compassion.

Without compassion, you cease to see the other as human. Horrible crimes against humanity result from individuals and groups of people stumbling down this path, e.g., slavery, the Holocaust.

If you think yourself worse - uglier, dumber, poorer, uncool - self-pity will set in.

This leads to a loss of confidence and eventually self-hatred. You will not value yourself, so neither will others. A chain of self-fulfilling prophesies will unfold. You will miss God's best plan for your life because you will have come to see yourself as a victim, cheated of the good things in life. Horrible crimes against humanity result when people take this path, e.g., rape, genocide, bullying.

We are free to go to God and say, "I would like what they have for my life. Show me how to have that." But never develop an attitude of ingratitude toward God because you don't have what "they" have.

DAY NINETY-NINE

Vision and hope
Proverbs 21:21

If you have a vision and hope, it means you believe there's something good in your future.

You already have a vision for yourself. Maybe your vision does not extend past this week, a semester in school, or season in life. Many people's vision only involves one aspect of life, such as making money or excelling at a sport.

Stephen Covey wrote that a vision not fueled by focused actions ends up causing a person discouragement and disappointment.

He means that today determines tomorrow. If you want to be successful at something, the habits must be practiced today that foster the desired outcomes.

You may not yet understand the plan God has for your life, but there is a plan based on your unique combination of skills, gifts and life experiences. Take time to detect and ultimately accept your mission by thinking and praying about what you like to do and are good at doing.

Begin imagining yourself in twenty years. What does life look like? Who's around you? Put it on paper. Next, write a personal mission statement that describes who you are, what you do, how you do it, and who you do it for.

Writing down your vision and mission is the best way to begin detecting God's intentions for your life.

DAY ONE HUNDRED

How to speak the truth in love
Galatians 4:16

Truth is always the best. But sometimes speaking the truth at the wrong time, too forcefully, or too often can negate the good that is intended.

It's hard to separate out what is truth and what is nobody's business, your own "issue," or just a misunderstanding.

If you care about someone, telling the truth is a responsibility. It is also the only way to have a true relationship.

If you have lied to protect yourself from criticism or being found out, you may not be able to hear and accept truth right away. In fact, you may avoid being around people that you suspect know the truth about you or disagree with you in some way.

You may find yourself concocting reasons why that other person is not good and should be avoided all together.

Here are the steps to speaking truth in love:

- Establish a foundation of trust over time by aligning actions with words
- Check in with your heart before speaking. Never say anything that is really about your own need to be vindicated, apologized to, or made to look superior
- Confront the problem or concern with humility in a calm, non-accusing manner: "I'm concerned about you…," "I noticed that you…," or "It hurts me when you…"
- Avoid "preaching," condemning, or threatening
- Stay connected, even if you are mad or hurt
- Don't take back the truth in order to make the person happy again. The person who is told the truth in love may leave and not come back.

Being truthful is the foundation for a lasting, meaningful relationship.

DAY ONE HUNDRED & ONE

Forgive and set boundaries
Matthew 14:22 - 23, 23:27

The world is teaming with hurt people. To some extent we've all been hurt in some way. As Joyce Meyer says, "Hurt people, hurt people." You must forgive those who hurt you and others to model Jesus' teaching. Equally important is the next step, which is often not understood - set boundaries so the person cannot keep hurting you.

Sometimes the appropriate boundary is a prison or mental institute.

It makes no common nor biblical sense to allow forgiven people to continue hurting you or others. When you must continually forgive someone over and over, it wears you out. You will remain frustrated, hurt, and liable in some cases because often other people are affected by the situation.

In everyday life, you may be involved with someone who manipulates, overspends, abuses substances, can't control anger or other emotions, etc. You may only be vaguely aware of the problem until one day you see it. Your eyes are opened, and the pain of it crashes on to your heart.

Anger and sadness will alternate in you. This is the point at which you must get busy forgiving. Take all of this to the Lord, your part, their part - all of it. Get it off your soul. Don't hold onto unforgiveness.

You will feel better quickly. But you won't stay better unless you pray about and seek wise counsel on how to set the right boundaries so the person cannot keep hurting you and those you are responsible for leading and protecting.

Boundaries don't mean you always remove the person from your life, but it means you see the truth and act accordingly.

DAY ONE HUNDRED & TWO

God wants everything
Luke 10:26-28, II Corinthians 9:7

Everyone wants something from you, and it often seems more than you can give. God wants everything, every ounce of your mind, body, and soul.

In the Old Testament, he asked the people to give ten percent of everything to provide for the priests, the poor and sick. In the New Testament, Jesus comes along and asks for your entire life. He never mentions giving a percentage of your money.

God's audacity is grounded in what you get in return - salvation for eternity. Yet, he goes further. He pays for everything you need in this life too. The person willing to give up her right to make up her own rules and go it alone gets to work for God. He's the ultimate boss.

Few take the offer because the entry-level feels so small and boring. All the others are living it up, enjoying the perks of what looks like a much better deal. Don't be fooled. Take God's offer. No one who worked for God comes to the end of life and wishes they had refused his offer.

Ten percent of your money is a pittance. That's just a tithe. Giving begins when you go beyond the ten percent. Whatever you give, do so joyfully.

DAY ONE HUNDRED & THREE

God's waiting principle
Psalm 106:6-15

Waiting is part of life. Nothing of any real value will come quickly. Every good thing God has planned for you comes at the end of a wait.

God does not make you wait to watch you suffer. The waiting teaches you to trust him and protects you from things you can't handle.

The faithful spend a lot of time waiting. In fact, much of life for everyone is about waiting: for transportation, for the season to change, to get finished with something, to get married, to graduate, to pay off debt, to get a better job, to lose weight...

The duration of the wait correlates to the following points in varying degrees:

- Your attitude while waiting
- How you spend your time while waiting
- A strengthening of your faith
- Revealing and purifying of your motives
- Timing, i.e., are you ready, has God lined everything up

DAY ONE HUNDRED & FOUR

Why should you wait?
Isaiah 40:27-31, Psalm 27:13-14

You should wait because if you do, you will get so much more than expected and the benefits will be lasting.

Waiting is one of the hardest things for modern girls. Technology, social media, and the internet in general make everything instantly available. Gratification does not have to be delayed.

To wait implies expectation, hope. To rush things and be impatient implies a lack of trust and a scarcity mentality. God requires a waiting period before receiving anything you really want. Anything you take prematurely will crumble, burn up, or die. To fret over why or how long you must wait is futile.

Determine to wait and make good use of your time until the answer to your prayer arrives.

DAY ONE HUNDRED & FIVE

How do you wait?
Psalm 37:1-9, Psalm 40:1-4, Isaiah 64:4-5

How you wait reveals a great deal about your character and attitude toward God. Which of the words below best describe how you wait?

Nervous, impatient, questioning, irritated, miserable, quiet, patient, trusting, calm.

Waiting is integral to faith. When something delays, you may feel angry, disappointed, or discouraged.

You have three choices:

1. Take matters into your own hands and get what you want
2. Give up
3. Lean on your faith and God's Word

DAY ONE HUNDRED & SIX

It all begins in the mind
Mark 4:24

Your mind believes what you say. The things you repeat form your mindset. That mindset determines your behavior, words to others, goals, and accomplishments.

Where and how you were raised plays an important role in how you view the world and your thoughts proceed from that.

In Joyce Meyer's great book, *Battlefield of the Mind*, she writes, "For most of my life, I simply thought whatever fell into my head. Much of what was in my head was either lies Satan was telling me or just plain nonsense. The devil was controlling my life because he was controlling my thoughts."

Your thoughts stem from what's been said and taught to you. From beginning to end of the Bible, God loves and values people. That includes you and those you encounter. Refuse to believe that you or others are worthless.

Everything good or evil begins with an idea. Next come words and then actions. Test every thought and idea against God's Word. You can take responsibility for what you think or someone else will. You can avoid many mistakes (sin) by learning to think before you act or speak.

DAY ONE HUNDRED & SEVEN

Hearing God's voice
1 Corinthians 10:13, John 10:27

Do you know the voice of God?

The Holy Spirit of God will speak to your heart and lead you away from temptations, if you are listening. He's the intuition that something is just not right or leads you to what you seek. If you pray often and ask for his direction, there's nothing he won't help you with for your greater good, the greater good of those around you, and his glory.

The Holy Spirit will never encourage you to humiliate someone, cheat, lie, overeat, get drunk, take drugs, or anything else that harms you or others. As a matter of fact, when you do things unkind or harmful, it causes the Holy Spirt to move away, like a butterfly or dove.

If you reason that telling a lie is okay because it will benefit you, that's not the Holy Spirit.

If you develop a practice of praying and reading God's Word, discernment will develop. You will learn how to distinguish between God's voice and the many other voices that compete for your attention.

DAY ONE HUNDRED & EIGHT

Establishing boundaries
Mark 3:20-34

You will not live the productive, peaceful life God intends without personal boundaries.

Jesus modeled the meaning of personal boundaries in everything he did, from getting up early to pray alone to rejecting anything people said or did that contradicted what God called him to do.

Dr. Henry Cloud, in his book *Changes that Heal*, says, "When we think of relationships we think of love. When we think of boundaries we think of limits. Boundaries give us a sense of what is a part of us and what is not a part of us, what we will allow and what we won't, what we will choose to do and what we will choose not to do."

In relationships with those you love, sometimes a sense of responsibility for others' actions and feelings can develop. You are not that powerful. You cannot make someone mad, make them happy, make them do anything, etc.

Dr. Cloud describes the person without good boundaries as someone who feels responsible for someone else's feelings yet out of control of their own.

God will help you determine what is right and wrong for you, where your responsibility begins and ends. Pray. Trust the Holy Spirit's leading when he urges you to say no or yes. Remember that you can only control your own thoughts and actions; no one else's.

Also, no one owns you - not a parent, boyfriend, friend, employer. Only God owns you. He bought and paid for you. The reason he did this was so you could be free to serve him and have eternal life, if you choose.

"This is the essence of boundaries: where do I end and where does someone else begin," says Dr. Cloud.

DAY ONE HUNDRED & NINE

Protection comes from hope in God
Psalm 25:1-15

God knows everything about you, but he wants to hear from you. God wants you to humble your heart and speak to him.

You will face challenges and experience trouble in life. Things in life not going well will always lead to your growth and greater opportunity, if you seek God and trust him, no matter what.

Many of the Psalms are places of great comfort and encouragement when times are tough. King David endured challenges beyond what most can comprehend. He knew God had a plan for him to be King of Israel, but for many years he had to hide like a fugitive and endure the hatred of King Saul.

He reminded himself often through his writings and songs that God would care for him. He placed his complete trust in God. Here's a prayer based on David's words in Psalm 25:

> I trust you, Lord. Let integrity and uprightness protect me because my hope is in you. Show me your ways. Teach me your paths.
>
> Forget all of my sins from the past. Remember your mercy and love. You instruct sinners and guide the humble because you are loving and faithful toward those who seek your ways.
>
> Those who revere you will be instructed by you in how they should go.
>
> God, I'm so scared and lonely, and it seems many hate me. Be near me, forgive me, relieve me from my anguish and fear. Please don't let me be put to shame.
>
> Amen.

DAY ONE HUNDRED & TEN

What God says about sex
I Corinthians 6:18-20

God put his essential rules for living into the Ten Commandments. If it's in the top ten, he's serious about it. "Thou shalt not commit adultery" means sex with anyone not your spouse is forbidden (Exodus 20:14).

God is clear in his Word from Genesis to Revelation that he created sex for pleasure and procreation between one man and one woman within a marriage. Sex is a beautiful, powerful gift given by God. "That is why a man leaves his father and mother and is united to his wife, and they become one flesh. Adam and his wife were both naked, and they felt no shame (Genesis 2:24-25)."

Many people are confused about what constitutes sex and confuse intimate sexual acts with entertainment. Sex means performing or receiving acts that involve the genitals of a man or woman for some form of sexual gratification. If you are receiving someone's sexual body parts into any part of your body outside of marriage, you are misusing your body and sex as intended by God.

God knows that used improperly or prematurely, sex causes a lot of suffering and harm. If you believe that sex is something you can do with whomever, however, or whenever you feel like, you are dishonoring God and yourself.

God created sex for 3 purposes intended to work together:
1. Unite a man and woman in a bond of intimacy called marriage designed to create family with or without children
2. Give a man and woman pleasure
3. Enable the perpetuation of humans

Sex outside of marriage is a sin against God's will and law because sex outside of that context is a misuse of God's purpose and design. Ignoring God's design for sex will erode your integrity and your ability to love in his right way.

Honoring the fact that God has created sex for marriage between one man and one woman will not go unnoticed by God. Ignoring his rules will lead to unintended consequences every time. You can pick your actions but not your consequences (Genesis 39:11-18).

DAY ONE HUNDRED & ELEVEN

God is specific about how and when sex is okay
Leviticus 20:1-22, Deuteronomy 22:13–30

Leviticus 20:1 – 22 and Deuteronomy 22:13 - 30 contain information passed from Moses to the Israelites after they'd been taken out of slavery and spent forty years in the desert preparing for the Promised Land. What sounds harsh to our ears today is God making it clear to his people the seriousness of sin, especially sexual sin. While God does not condone sin, he always makes a way for repentance and forgiveness.

God says the following to expound on his rule that sex is for marriage:

- Sex before marriage diminishes the special relationship designed for couples
- Rape (forced sex) is wrong. It is sin. It is a form of murder.
- Women should be protected and honored
- Men should not leave a wife for frivolous reasons or vice versa
- No one should have sex with the same gender, animals, children, another person's spouse, or close relatives by blood or marriage

God gives special attention to women in rules about sex
God's rules emphasize the protection of women. Prior to very recent times women could not make their way in the world without the help and protection of a husband or male family members. In many ways, that's true today. No man, woman, or child thrives without the help of others. He also makes it clear that women should not take advantage of their protected position by seducing a man or claiming rape falsely.

Your body is not your own
You were uniquely created, "knitted together in the womb," and known personally by God (Psalm 139). He cares about the physical and spiritual aspects of every person. Your body is intended to be united with Christ. That is why your body is called a temple. The Holy Spirit lives inside of your body. You do not own your body. It is loaned to you for the purpose of honoring God. If you use your body sexually in ways not intended by God's design, it is a sin against God and dangerous to your health. (1 Thessalonians 4:1 - 8, 1 Corinthians 7:3 - 11, 6:13, 19 - 20).

You have the freedom to do many things, but if you choose to do things that God has forbidden, you will have trouble, often much later and in ways you cannot imagine now. Be careful and responsible with your desires (Matthew 5: 27 - 28).

DAY ONE HUNDRED & TWELVE

God cares about your pleasure and well-being
Revelation 2:23

God created sex for pleasure in his timing and circumstances. He cares and will satisfy your needs if you wait.

Your attitude toward sex reflects your relationship with and attitude toward God. When you go your own way, it hurts God. His rules are designed to protect you and to cultivate family and civil society.

Decide now what kind of character and faith a person that you will love should have. Most of the time you spend with a spouse is not sexual but focused on day-to-day life and problem-solving in the home. Give yourself time to get to know someone before committing to them. You may initially see only physical appearance or attraction to the idea of that person (Judges 16).

It feels as if being someone that is committed to purity prior to marriage is abnormal. The common refrain among Christians is "Everyone does it and God will forgive me. He understands."

It's true that defying God's commands does not lead to a loss of his love. It's true that he holds you accountable for what you know to be true.

His commands are there because he loves you. But God does not provide you a pass on rules he created for everyone. If you love God, you will not willfully disobey what he's said don't do and has explained at great length why it is harmful.

If you rationalize doing what you want with statements like "God loves me no matter what" or "everyone does it," you love yourself more than you love God, and that is pride. No sin does more damage to individuals, families, and society than pride.

Sex is no different than any other sin in terms of your choice to avoid the temptation or give into it. You strive for perfection in everything. When you fall short, you ask for forgiveness. The greater sin is to not try or tell yourself that you will just do it and get forgiveness later.

What does natural or "born this way" mean?

Desires for love and acceptance are part of every person's natural inclination. You may find yourself thinking about sexual matters with a member of the same sex or opposite sex at a young age. It is not wrong or sinful to have thoughts. If you allow your thoughts to become obsessions, they will become actions. Wrong things can happen, and you will find yourself going in directions and practicing activities and attitudes that limit your opportunities (Romans 1: 26 – 27).

Jesus has the last word about sexual immorality

In Revelation 2, Jesus talks about Christians tolerating Jezebel and her promotion of sexual immorality. Jezebel represents the prevailing culture which promotes all forms of sexual immorality and ridicules those who attempt to honor God's rules about sex.

Jesus says, "I will strike her children dead. Then all the churches will know that I am he who searches hearts and minds, and I will repay each of you according to your deeds" (Revelation 2:23).

Primary Verses Revealing What God Says About Sex
Genesis 2, 34: 27 - 29, 39:9
Exodus 20:14
Leviticus 20: 10 - 21
Judges 16
Deuteronomy 22: 5, 13 - 30, 23:17
Proverbs 2: 16 - 17, 5:3, 18 - 20, 6: 25 - 35, 7: 25 -27
Song of Songs 4
Matthew 5: 27 - 28
Mark 10: 5 - 9
Romans 1: 26 - 27
1 Corinthians 7: 3 - 11, 6:13, 19 - 20
1 Thessalonians 4: 1 - 8
Revelation 2:20

DAY ONE HUNDRED & THIRTEEN

Everyone matters, especially you
1 John 4:7-21

At its most elemental form, love is to simply appreciate all human life because God does. John gives us a simple measure for how to know we live as Christians - we love all, hate none. This love of all - even those who hate us and are different or ugly or diseased - is the natural response of the person who has accepted God's unconditional love.

Once you grasp God's love for you, no matter what, you will be humbled. The person aware of how much God gives in spite of how little they deserve, begins to love themselves and others without condition.

Loving without condition does not mean you allow others to mistreat you or condone bad or immoral behavior. In fact, loving is often refusing to allow mistreatment or speaking the truth about behavior. We love the person, not always the words and actions of a person.

"God is love. Whoever lives in love lives in God, and God in them. This is how love is made complete among us so that we will have confidence on the day of judgment: In this world we are like Jesus. There is no fear in love. But perfect love drives out fear, because fear has to do with punishment. The one who fears is not made perfect in love. We love because he first loved us. Whoever claims to love God yet hates a brother or sister is a liar. For whoever does not love their brother and sister, whom they have seen, cannot love God, whom they have not seen" (1 John 4:16 - 20).

DAY ONE HUNDRED & FOURTEEN

What sort of character are you?
Romans 5:3-5

Characters are engraved or stamped on coins or seals, often making up the branding mark or symbol of someone or something. People play characters on stage to tell stories about the human experience.

You were born with certain personality traits and propensities for coping with life. However, your character was formed by repetition. It is the way you are as a result of training, habits, beliefs, and relationships.

Good character traits include respectful, fair, trustworthy, responsible, etc.

Your character, good or bad, does not form overnight.

No matter what kind of circumstances you live in, you get to decide what sort of character will guide your life.

What character traits have you allowed to form within you?

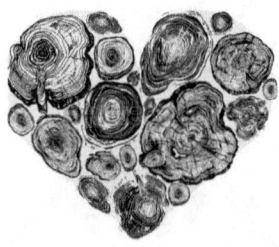

DAY ONE HUNDRED & FIFTEEN

Beware of the stinking thinking trap
James 1:2-8

Sometimes when you have a 'win' it is followed by a 'loss.' You get a promotion, and then the next day the car breaks down. You begin to feel good about your tight knit group of friends, and then somebody starts a drama.

The devil loves these situations because it sets the stage for stinking thinking. If he can get you on a course of negative thinking, he's got you. There's no chance you will enjoy your life or be powerful for God.

Too often we are programmed to think that when something is going well, we are good and when things go bad, we deserved it, or we will never have anything, etc.

God wants you to remain stable and trust him no matter what. If you can thank God and ask for his provision, protection, and will in all situations, it does not matter whether what's happening is a test from God or a temptation from the devil.

You will never reach a point of invulnerability. There's no amount of money, fitness planning, personal growth, relationship building, or anything else that will protect you from something going wrong. Use common sense - save money, eat well, exercise, work on yourself. But, never look at those measures as complete prevention against bad things. They are preventatives.

God is in control. Say this out loud - "God, I work for you. What are you going to do about this situation; what would you have me do?"

DAY ONE HUNDRED & SIXTEEN

Appeal to your human right
I Corinthians 10:23-33

God gives every person a right to her life. Another way of putting it is a right to herself. Until the American assertion to break from Great Britain in 1776, no government had formed to acknowledge and support that right.

This fact of nature was summed up beautifully in the Declaration of Independence. "We hold these truths to be self-evident, that all men are created equal, that they are endowed by their creator with certain unalienable rights, that among these are life, liberty and the pursuit of happiness."

This is not the right to live lawless or just do what you want. It means to not be constrained by the will of others, to be neither completely dependent nor independent. You need others. You need a society with laws and social standards that uphold decency.

George Washington understood this concept and emphasized it in his famous 1796 farewell address:
"Of all the dispositions and habits which lead to political prosperity, religion and morality are indispensable supports. In vain would that man claim the tribute of patriotism, who should labor to subvert these great pillars of human happiness, these firmest props of the duties of men and citizens."

"And let us with caution indulge the supposition that morality can be maintained without religion. Whatever may be conceded to the influence of refined education on minds of peculiar structure, reason and experience both forbid us to expect that national morality can prevail in exclusion of religious principle."

Washington and most of his contemporaries believed in allowing for a vast expression of religions but that morality in general was grounded in natural law and available to all for understanding. They didn't believe a free people should be told how to live but that all must live and let live. You don't need to be controlled by the dysfunction of others. Don't follow the script someone else has written for you.

The American leaders who dared to defy the most powerful ruler in the world in 1776 did so based on a belief that it was better to be free than ruled, regardless of the cost.

DAY ONE HUNDRED & SEVENTEEN

Human nature does not change
Ecclesiastes 4

Some believe that human nature is changeable, and that society can control the process of change. They imagine remaking people to be without war or want. Do not be fooled by these philosophies.

You are born, like all other humans, with the potential for great cruelty or compassion, for love or hate.

Throughout history those with the strongest will - good or bad - usually prevail. You can choose to use your power for betterment of yourself and others or to simply get what you want.

Whatever you choose, it will only come with effort and strain. Make up your mind to be the best person possible with an acceptance of human nature as an unchanging factor in the world.

DAY ONE HUNDRED & EIGHTEEN

Secrets to happiness
Proverbs 3

The third chapter of Proverbs is the starting point for understanding the secret to happiness. It provides a recipe for those who desire God's best. It's quite simple, yet hard to follow for most.

The final verse (35) sums up the outcome for those who stick with it: "The wise inherit honor, but fools get only shame."

Here's a summary of the Proverbs 3 wisdom:

- Be loving and faithful to yourself and those you encounter in life.
- Trust God with all of your heart, and don't think you understand anything without his help.
- Fear doing wrong and refuse to participate in evil with your words, time, or money.
- Give back to your church and community out of gratitude for all you have.
- Don't hate discipline from God or those in authority. Embrace the learning that comes from rebuke.
- Seek out wisdom and knowledge as if searching for silver and gold. They are of the highest value to you.
- Don't live in fear of what might happen.
- Do good whenever it is in your power without delay
- If someone asks for your help, offer it as soon as feasible; don't put them off as a way to avoid helping
- Never plot alone or with others to harm anyone
- Never make false accusations against someone
- Don't envy those who get what they want through violence, manipulation, or illegal means nor ever mimic those habits
- Do not mock others or be prideful about what you have.

Make up your mind. Who are you gonna be? Let nothing deter you.

DAY ONE HUNDRED & NINETEEN

Living by the flesh or in the spirit
Galatians 5:13-26

Paul tells us in Galatians 5:22 - 23 what the life of a person filled with the Holy Spirit will exhibit: love, joy, peace, forbearance, kindness, goodness, faithfulness, gentleness, and self-control.

These "fruits of the spirit," must be sought. They are mostly traits that do not "come natural." Human nature trends toward the ways of the world, which Paul warns against: sexual immorality, impurity and debauchery, idolatry and witchcraft, hatred, discord, jealousy, fits of rage, selfish ambition, dissensions, factions and envy, drunkenness, orgies, etc.

The fruitful ways are all focused on others. The flesh acts are selfish and rooted in getting what you want.

The *Law of the Harvest* is a universal principle God made applicable to all people, regardless of belief. For every seed planted, more comes up much later than the planting. The health and abundance of what comes up is directly linked to how the seed and growing plant was treated.

How a person speaks and acts is evidence of the "seeds" they've planted or what's been planted in them by those with influence over them. If the Holy Spirit is in your life, you will produce good "fruit."

It is not easy to live this way, but it is possible to try even when you don't feel like it.

DAY ONE HUNDRED & TWENTY

Speaking with wisdom
Proverbs 18:21, Proverbs 31:26, James 1:19-26

Proverbs says the tongue has the power of life and death. This is the case both literally and figuratively. Think of a time when someone's words made you smile or cry. With a word, wars have launched, heads have rolled, and hearts have broken.

The tongue is your smallest organ, but it can determine the course of your life. Do you ever think about what you say?

The blessed woman in Proverbs 31 speaks with wisdom and faithful instruction (31:26).

The things you say to yourself and others matter. Your words can lift up a stranger or tear down someone you love. Be thoughtful about what you say. Experiment with words of kindness and watch the results.

DAY ONE HUNDRED & TWENTY-ONE

American liberty
Isaiah 61:1

The American system of government is still valid. It is worth fighting for, but you must understand how it works because it only works when individuals do their part.

The American Founders made up a dream team of leaders, gathered in one place with an understanding of human nature, history, and government unlike any, ever.

Never before in history had a government been created to protect the liberty of individuals, literally to free them to enjoy God-given rights and pursue them as they wished.

America is not a Democracy (majority rules). America is a Republic (rule of law).

Remember the Pledge of Allegiance? "I pledge allegiance to the flag of the United States of America and to the Republic for which it stands, one nation under God, indivisible with liberty and justice for all."

American government is based on representative government. Representatives (Senate and Congress) and a President are democratically elected by the people to represent the people. All other governments throughout history, and many today, are based on "ruler's law." The people have rights only as determined by the ones in power.

Today, many proclaim that America's limited government is wrong. They want a form of ruler's law in this country where your rights come and go based on what the government says they should be. This kind of thinking is what led to the horrors of Nazi Germany, China's Chairman Mao, Pol Pot of Cambodia, and more.

"The state exists simply to promote and to protect the ordinary happiness of human beings in this life," wrote C.S. Lewis in Mere Christianity. When leaders begin to talk about taking away the rights laid out in the American Declaration of Independence and Constitution, it is a warning sign. Also, do not trust leaders who talk about making up new rights while taking the old ones.

Do you believe all people have a right to life, liberty and the pursuit of happiness given by God or do rights change based on the times and who's in charge?

DAY ONE HUNDRED & TWENTY-TWO

Civilization requires limited government
Deuteronomy 4

Winston Churchill, the United Kingdom's Prime Minister during World War II, once said, "Civilization is a society based on the opinions of civilians. It means that violence, the rule of warriors and despotic chiefs, the conditions of camps and warfare, of riot and tyranny, give way to parliaments [governments] where laws are made, and independent courts of justice in which over long periods those laws are maintained. That is Civilization—and in its soil grow continually freedom, comfort and culture."

Think about parts of the world that do not have freedom, comfort, and culture (arts, access to education, green space, etc.).

The American Founders understood that to create a civilization that would foster the best virtues and habits within people, a limited constitutional government is necessary.

Three branches of government were created to impose checks and balances: Executive, Legislative, and Judiciary. The Legislative is divided into a Senate and House.

The purpose of all this division is to ensure deliberation. Laws are meant to be slow in the making. Laws should only be made with the consent of the governed - the people. America's system of government was based on the rule of law (a republic) to protect the "life, liberty, and the pursuit of happiness" for all people. The Declaration of Independence acknowledges that these rights are God-given and should be protected in all citizens.

DAY ONE HUNDRED & TWENTY-THREE

Being respectful
1 Peter 3:8-17

To find out who you respect think of people that you listen to, want to imitate, or be around. Do those you respect treat others respectfully?

How you treat others regardless of their position in society reveals your character.

Peter reminds you that compassion, humility, and love should come from you, even in the face of insult or evil (8 - 9). He also calls you to be prepared to give an answer to any who ask you what your beliefs and values are (15).

If you seek Christ and his truth, you will often be confronted with situations and people that contradict your beliefs. Some will come smiling, others will come in anger intent on harming you. To use a modern way of speaking, Peter is telling you to remain "chill." Don't allow yourself to be pulled down into hateful arguments nor be afraid to speak honestly about what you know to be true.

Being respectful always wins the day.

DAY ONE HUNDRED & TWENTY-FOUR

God calls, you get to decide how to answer
John 6:44, John 14:27, Philippians 4:7, Romans 8

In John 6:44 Jesus says, "No one can come to me unless the Father who sent me draws them, and I will raise them up at the last day."

God is the initiator in relationships with people. A choice to believe in Christ is an affirmative response to God's urging through the Holy Spirit. You have freewill to choose or not.
When you encounter a call to accept Jesus' gift and authority, the choice is to ignore him because you don't like the demands of his message or invite him into your life. Once you invite him in, your salvation is sealed. But it's only the beginning of receiving the benefits he offers in this life.

Christ invites you to give up the right to do whatever you please. It's only through agreeing to this step that you gain an ability to live in Christ's power. Living in Christ's power is what allows for peace - the peace that "transcends all understanding" and guards your heart and your mind (Philippians 4:7).

Jesus promised – "Peace I leave with you; my peace I give you. I do not give to you as the world gives. Do not let your hearts be troubled and do not be afraid" (John 14:27).

It's hard not to get side-tracked by a desire to do it your way or by your weaknesses. Accepting Jesus is a one-time event. Following him is a commitment you must renew often with assistance from the Holy Spirit.

DAY ONE HUNDRED & TWENTY-FIVE

Open wounds won't heal
Job 5:18

Job was innocent yet God allowed him to be wounded. He had an amazing life with all the worldly accoutrements, and he was a man who loved and honored God. Suddenly he lost it all and was struck by all manner of physical ailments, but he lived to see complete healing and restoration.

Whatever wounding happens to you, whether of the heart or physical body, you will never completely heal if it remains open allowing insult and injury to keep the wound inflamed and raw. A healing time is required for you and perhaps your family and community or even country.

Job's story focuses on how he handles and talks about his wounding while surrounded by people who think they are being helpful but do not understand the nature of healing.

The details or time frame for healing vary with every people group and individual. Every healing process must ultimately lead to closing the wound. Healing includes an end to the cause of pain or conflict, forgiveness and letting go of blaming self, others, or God as well as a return to productive activity such as work, parenting, training, school, etc.

Sometimes it's hard or even impossible to close the wound if you keep repeating the act or belief that led you to the wound or if those responsible for the wounding are allowed to continue the hurt or harm. Too often individuals, communities, ethnic groups, or even entire countries remain wounded and unable to reach their full potential because others receive power from the wounds remaining open and raw.

Job suffered great harm. God could have stopped his suffering or prevented it from the beginning, but he did not. Yet Job never stopped honoring God's greatness. "For he wounds, but he also binds up; he injures but his hands also heal" (Job 5:18).

DAY ONE HUNDRED & TWENTY-SIX

Knowing what to do
Luke 18:23, Philippians 1:9-11, James 1:2-8

You are faced almost daily with choices. Many do not have a clear right or wrong answer. Wisdom and practical discernment are the source of ensuring every decision is the right one for you.

Step 1 = Sincerely ask God. He will answer no matter who or what you are.
Step 2 = Don't doubt that he will and can give you the wisdom for any situation or choice.
Step 3 = Take the path he leads you down, beginning with preparation steps he gives.

This final step is where we falter. You've asked God, and you believe in his power and perhaps even his sovereignty. The problem is we don't like the answer he often gives because it's not the one we desired.

Like the rich, young man in Luke 18:23 who went away from Jesus "very sorrowful, for he was rich" we go away hoping for another, more pleasing answer. Note that in the Luke 18 story where Jesus tells the man to sell all his possessions and follow him, this is not a commentary on wealth.

The man's wealth represents whatever stumbling block a person has that keeps them from taking the steps Jesus calls them to.

Be honest about what idea, habit, attitude, possession, relationship represents the thing you don't want Jesus to touch.

If you've asked for wisdom, God is doing his part. Are you doing your part?

If not, he'll continue to give the same answer in different ways and at varied times, but he will not pursue you and force you to take the step necessary to achieve your wisdom. That is yours alone to take. No one can do it for you. The first step leads to the second and so forth. God only gives the steps one at a time. He may give you a glimpse down the road but never the opportunity until you are ready.

You can take comfort in knowing that Jesus will not leave you alone in taking your steps. He'll stay close, if you ask him, and help you through it all.

DAY ONE HUNDRED & TWENTY-SEVEN

Don't break yourself searching for the meaning of life
Ecclesiastes 12:8 , Jeremiah 29:11

"Meaningless! Meaningless!" says the Teacher. "Everything is meaningless!" (Ecclesiastes 12:8)

Solomon, the wisest and richest man ever to live (even to this day), found himself wallowing in existential malaise. He had everything, literally. Yet, he kept finding himself confronted with the fact that wise or foolish, rich or poor, all people ultimately die.

All thinking people eventually come to this question: "What is the purpose of my life?"

Behind that question is a desire to see your life getting better, more fulfilling. God has a plan for your life, for every single life. He promises this in Jeremiah 29:11. God will give you opportunities to step into the plan for your life. Sometimes we miss the opportunities because they don't look fun or empowering.

Solomon finds that the answer to the meaninglessness of life is to simply enjoy the life God gives you and do the best you can. Don't hate your status in life or your unknown future. Love and allow yourself to be loved. That is the meaning of life.

DAY ONE HUNDRED & TWENTY-EIGHT

Know your enemy
Ephesians 6:10-16

It's hard to believe that you have an invisible enemy, but you do.

Your enemy works full-time in all manner of craftiness to keep you from living out God's plan for your life. In fact, there are two plans for you. One is designed by God uniquely for you. One is devised by Satan.

In Ephesians 6:12, Paul writes, "For our struggle is not against flesh and blood, but against the rulers, against the authorities, against the powers of this dark world and against the spiritual forces of evil in the heavenly realms."

Your enemy wants to keep you focused on people - flesh and blood.

The enemy works through people. You are only responsible for your behavior, not others. Only when you "put on the full armor of God" can you defeat your enemy and experience what God has planned for you.

God's armor is yours. It's available through his Word from the Bible, placing your faith in him, and commitment to living as he directs your steps.

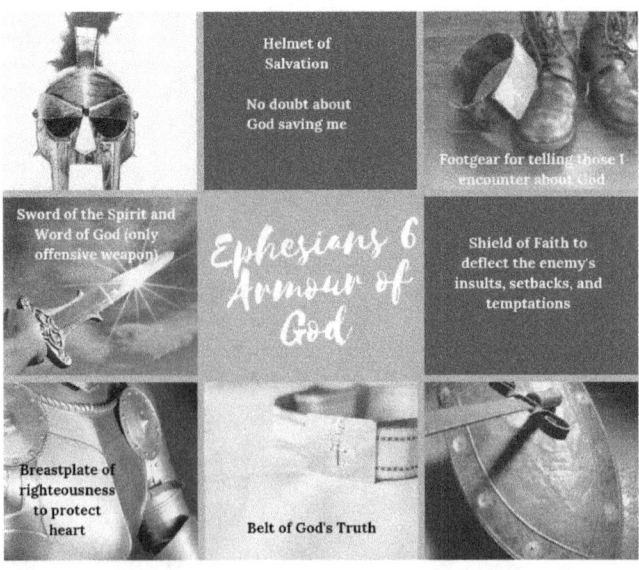

DAY ONE HUNDRED & TWENTY-NINE

Every seed must die to live
2 Timothy 4:5-7, Matthew 6:25-34

Nothing illustrates the alchemy of dying to live like the seed.

A speck of matter - a seed - seems dry and without consequence, but if buried in the ground it comes to life, eventually. God uses the very thing that contributes to sustaining our life to illustrate the key to life.

You must die to live.

You will literally one day die and be buried. But that comes later. Right now, you get to figuratively die like the seed to produce "fruit" in this life.

It's the very hardest thing, dying to self. For those who are beautiful, smart, popular, productive, wealthy, and ambitious, this seems like a pitiful waste.

Paul understood this well and wrote in 2 Timothy 4:6, "For I am already being poured out like a drink offering." In Paul's day, they poured precious wine on a rock as a symbolic offering to God. There was no way it could be salvaged or of any good to anyone.

This sacrifice is symbolic of surrendering your precious self to God for his use, regardless of how much of a waste it appears to be on the surface. While you sit "dying" like the seed or "poured out" like expensive wine, don't forget that God values you and knows every detail about you (Luke 12:5 - 7).

Surrender to the tension. Get up and go do whatever you can to make someone's day a little better. Stop thinking about yourself for a couple hours.

DAY ONE HUNDRED & THIRTY

Earthly riches, and your place in heaven
Matthew 19:16-30

Jesus spoke often about rich and poor. In Matthew 19:24, he says, "It is easier for a camel to go through the eye of a needle than for someone who is rich to enter the kingdom of God."

Some turn his parables and lessons into a theology of rich is bad, poor is good. Do you believe that your wealth and comfort on earth will be deducted from you in heaven?

The problem with this interpretation is much like attempting to please God by being good. How good is good enough? How poor is poor enough to be rich in heaven?

Jesus does not favor poor people over rich people or vice versa.

If you live in the Westernized world, you are rich beyond imagination compared to the rest of the world. The dilemma faced by the rich man in Matthew 19 is one many face. His possessions were a stumbling block to making himself available to God.

Jesus asks everything of us, and in return he gives back to us beyond our imagination. You must first be willing to put it all on the line, holding nothing back. Think all the way back to the story of Abraham and Isaac on the mountain. When God asked him to sacrifice his son, Abraham prepared to do so without question because he trusted God completely (See Genesis 22:1 – 14).

Don't focus on how you will acquire more or keep what you have. Keep your hands and heart open before God, and he will fill you with everything you need emotionally and materially.

DAY ONE HUNDRED & THIRTY-ONE

Lukewarm life
Revelation 3:15-21

Lukewarm is neither cold nor hot. A lukewarm life is comfortable. It has a culturally convenient level of faith.

In Revelation, Jesus calls out the people of the Laodicea church, one of the seven churches forming the root of Christianity, for being lukewarm.

He tells them, "I know your deeds, that you are neither cold nor hot. I wish you were either one or the other! So, because you are lukewarm—neither hot nor cold—I am about to spit you out of my mouth" (Revelation 3:15-16).

Jesus wants everything you have available to him on a moment's notice. He wants you to be ready each day, like a soldier, to grasp the opportunities coming your way.

He goes on to say in verses 19 - 20 that those he loves will be rebuked and disciplined. "So be earnest and repent," Jesus says (3:19).

Don't be lukewarm. Will you risk your reputation, time, and comfort to do whatever Jesus asks?

DAY ONE HUNDRED & THIRTY-TWO

With God, things happen in good time
Galatians 6:7-9

As you live and trust God, one day you will reflect on how he rewards those who wait. If you dream, pray, and seek something good for a long time, you might find it "suddenly" coming to pass.

It starts with a desire, dream, or vision. This leads to a time of preparation both visibly and invisibly. God almost always ties the lives of people together through fulfillment of needs or wants.

Take baby steps toward the things you desire. Then pause and pray - "God, I'm taking this step to do my part. But I trust you to work in your time. Open or close this door."

You will know when he's ready because things will come together. Doors will open, others will close. One day you will wake up and numerous pieces will have fallen into place, miraculously. God takes your faith, offering of resources, and skills to knit and stitch lives together and accomplish amazing things.

He works all things together for those who love him (Romans 8:28).

DAY ONE HUNDRED & THIRTY-THREE

About being part of the church
John 4:23-24, Ephesians 3:16-20

The church is not just a building to attend on Sunday morning. The people who follow Christ, i.e., Christian believers, are the literal church. He calls you as a living member of his church to come together to do the work he needs to have done in this world and as a gift to you that comes through fellowship. This can happen with two or many more when you gather in the name of Christ.

You cannot benefit from the full power of God without being part of a community of Christ-followers.

This does not mean you need a church to love God. Jesus told the Samaritan woman that "True worshipers will worship the Father in the Spirit and in truth. God is spirit, and his worshipers must worship in the Spirit and in truth" (4:23 - 24). Jesus ushered in a new era. His life and death made way for the Holy Spirit so anyone, any place could access God the Father by way of the Spirit.

An organization under a denomination or nondenominational meeting in a building or under a tree is not the ultimate purpose of Christ in calling for a church. When he calls you or any other person, there's a mission associated, and it is never easy. He calls you to love with your hands and feet, with your words and resources. The fulfillment of your mission requires connection to the family of believers in some form or fashion.

Keep asking God to lead you to the gathering of believers right for you. Don't isolate yourself from God's family. If you are attending a church already, see if there is a place to serve that fits your skills and current abilities.

In Ephesians 3:20 - 21, Paul writes of God's immeasurable ability to do more than we ask and even more than we can imagine through his power that works within us. We are able to do more together as God's people of all color and nationalities. That is the church.

DAY ONE HUNDRED & THIRTY-FOUR

How to move mountains with faith
Mark 11:22-26

One of the most amazing promises Jesus ever made was that if you have faith in God without doubt your prayers will be answered.

"Have faith in God," Jesus answered. Truly I tell you, if anyone says to this mountain, 'Go, throw yourself into the sea,' and does not doubt in their heart but believes that what they say will happen, it will be done for them" (Mark 11: 22 - 23).

A misunderstanding of Jesus and the larger context of this promise leads many to disappointment. They confuse his statement with stories about genies in bottles or a lucky rabbit's foot. Genies and good luck charms are imaginary servants to the person who possesses them. Jesus is your Lord and Savior. He modeled servanthood for us, but you are ultimately his servant.

Many pray for something and either do not get a quick answer or the answer is not what they had in mind. Maybe the thing you prayed for had an expiration date. The person you asked for got married to someone else. Someone you prayed would be healed has died.

If you've prayed a sincere mountain moving prayer, and it didn't come to pass, you probably started to feel a little embarrassed, maybe even foolish, and perhaps disappointed and a bit angry, especially if you shared this mountain moving prayer endeavor with others.

Believing that prayers went unanswered by God rather than believing in God causes many people to miss the opportunity for stability and peace. Come to God first with thanksgiving for what you have and forgiveness for others and yourself.

The kind of faith that moves mountains is rooted in a belief that God is all seeing and all powerful versus belief in your own desire. If you place all the emphasis on the thing you want and it is denied for reasons you cannot understand, you will be left with nothing but disappointment or despair.

God answers every prayer of a sincere Christian with a heart willing to forgive.

DAY ONE HUNDRED & THIRTY-FIVE

Seven lessons on getting things done right
Nehemiah 6:8-9

Nehemiah was a servant to King Artaxerxes around 445 BC. He'd been taken into captivity when the Babylonians invaded Jerusalem. His boldness and wisdom took him from being a captive servant to Governor of Jerusalem.

Nehemiah illustrated seven practices that lead to getting things done right, regardless of your position in life.

1. In-the-moment prayers that praise and thank God, repent of sin, ask for specifics, and commit to doing what God calls you to do
2. Once clear on the mission, ask for help boldly
3. Gather information, observe and assess the situation, confidently present a plan based on a realistic strategy
4. Ignore the detractors and distractors by staying focused on outcomes
5. Combine constant prayer with preparation, planning, and effort
6. Encourage yourself and the workers when discouragement and fatigue set in by remembering what God has called you to do, the goal, and that God protects work he's called you to
7. Look out for and love one another because it is people that will benefit and people that will get the job done

*Consider reading Nehemiah chapters 1 - 6.

DAY ONE HUNDRED & THIRTY-SIX

Doing even greater things in Jesus' name
John 14:9-14

Jesus accomplished everything needed to defeat the powers of darkness and evil. He overcame death for you. He has already won the battles you and everyone in the world fights each day. You have access to his authority as a Christian.

He left us with his name and the Holy Spirit as a helper to activate his authority.

He claimed that you will do even greater things than he did. This is feasible because he fulfilled his mission on earth and left behind the helper known as the Holy Spirit.

Whatever you ask in his name, he will do. All of your prayers should end like this: "In Jesus' Name, I/we pray."

Think about the implications of asking in Jesus' name. You would not willingly ask anything dishonoring of his name or contrary to the model he set. A person wielding the authority of Jesus can overcome the power of the enemy.

If you are not praying in Jesus' name and calling daily on the Holy Spirit, it is the equivalent of setting out on foot for a long journey when you have a Ferrari sitting in the garage.

DAY ONE HUNDRED & THIRTY-SEVEN

The fairness question never to ask God
Luke 15:11-32

The older brother of the Prodigal Son felt an indignation that seemed justified. His younger brother left home with a pocketful of their father's money and went on a wild binge. He came back broke and disgraced. Their father asks no questions and throws a huge welcome home party.

"The older brother became angry and refused to go in. So, his father went out and pleaded with him. But he answered his father, 'Look! All these years I've been slaving for you and never disobeyed your orders. Yet you never gave me even a young goat so I could celebrate with my friends. But when this son of yours who has squandered your property with prostitutes comes home, you kill the fattened calf for him" (Luke 15:28 - 30)!

Deep within us all is a fairness question for God. "Why do "they" get by with (x, y, or z) while I seem to suffer for every transgression?"

Don't entertain that question, even for a moment. Beat it back every time it rears up. The reason you strive to do your best, to do God's will, and never give up is because you don't know what he's got planned for you. Don't miss his opportunity for you.

"The horse is made ready for the day of battle, but victory rests with the Lord" (Proverbs 21:31).

The horse is a metaphor for you. The battle-ready horse is well-groomed, decked out in the gear, anxious, muscles toned, ready to run the race. The outcome of your personal challenges and life are in God's hands. Your job is to be ready for what he will send your way.

DAY ONE HUNDRED & THIRTY-EIGHT

To surrender is not natural
Luke 9:21 – 26, Jeremiah 33

Jesus asks that you surrender all rights to yourself to be part of him in this world. To give up your rights is counterintuitive. You have been taught that your rights to do whatever you want, whenever you want is what freedom is all about. Then Jesus comes into your life and wants you to give all that up.

"Whoever wants to be my disciple must deny themselves and take up their cross daily and follow me. For whoever wants to save their life will lose it, but whoever loses their life for me will save it" (Luke 9:23 - 24).

He's talking about dying to self - pride, discouragement, selfishness, etc. What great athlete, artist, soldier, scientist, or any other accomplished person didn't at some point deny all the things that did not contribute to the goal? They pressed on past a point of hurt and hopelessness.

There are many benefits to living a life surrendered to God, but the best one is peace, also called stability. Once you cross your personal Rubicon, there's a freedom words cannot describe. The woman who has put complete trust in Christ neither swells with pride when people love her nor sinks to self-loathing when they hate her.

Surrendering to Jesus' call frees you to be yourself moment-by-moment. If the God of the universe has truly counted every hair on your head, will really not give you a snake when you ask for bread, and is actively working everything out for your ultimate good, then you are able to do your best day-by-day.

The world is full of half-hearted, defeated Christians as well as people who've abandoned the faith all together. They could only see the cost of the moment, not the payoff way down the road.

Plan, hope, dream, but also wait and ask his will. He's a good and perfect father.

DAY ONE HUNDRED & THIRTY-NINE

Forgiveness is not optional
Matthew 5:23-24, 43-46

Has someone done something unforgivable to you? Do they "make you" feel bad?

People can be cruel. Life often seems unfair. But no one makes you do or feel anything. Forgiveness is one of those deal breakers for many when it comes to Jesus. He calls you to forgive everyone, even those who have done what seems like unforgivable things.

He goes so far as to say in Matthew 5:23 - 24 that making things right with someone who has something against you should come before you make any kind of offering. He calls you to put aside what may seem like a right to be mad and even pray for people who have done you wrong.

It may seem that Jesus is not concerned about your hurt. What you will find is that letting go of the offense is really about you. Hanging on to any injustice is, as Joyce Meyer once wrote, "like drinking poison and hoping someone else dies."

DAY ONE HUNDRED & FORTY

Lose the pride at all costs
Proverbs 8:12-15

Pride can be hard to see in yourself. It lurks within you though. God will go to great lengths to help you shed pride. Don't fight him. Don't nurse pride for a moment. If you find yourself lying about things, anything at all, there's probably pride behind the lie.

C.S. Lewis wrote in *Mere Christianity*, "It was through pride that the devil became the devil: Pride leads to every other vice: it is the complete anti-God state of mind…"

He draws an important distinction between pride and other sin such as greed, drunkenness, promiscuity, cheating, vanity, and so on. Those other sins come from your flesh. Pride, according to Lewis, comes straight from hell. And this is why it is such a dangerous trap. The devil loves nothing more than to see you comfortably "serving" God, all the while full of pride.

Don't confuse pride with affection or admiration. You can enjoy the sense of having "made your parents proud" (coach, boss, teacher) by working hard and doing the right thing.

Pride compares you to others. It looks down on others. Pride is never satisfied with a job well done or the things it has. Pride needs more. Pride must get the last word. Pride needs to be right, justified.

Wondering if there's pride in your life? Look closely at the people and things that irritate you the most.

DAY ONE HUNDRED & FORTY-ONE

What is sin?
Psalm 32:5, Jeremiah 16:10-12, Micha 6, and Malachi 3

In Old Testament Hebrew there are over twenty terms for sin. According to Jewishvirtuallibrary.org, the most commonly found terms that denote sin are ḥeṭ', pesha', and 'awon as they characterize a "failure," a "breach," or a "crooked" action as related to the covenant with God. So, sin can be seen as failure to meet God's expectations either by accident or intentionally.

The original writers of the New Testament used forms of Greek spoken and written at the time to translate Hebrew. The most common Greek word used for sin is hamartia – literal meaning is "to miss the mark." In Old English this word is associated with archery.

God repeats his expectations for people over and over throughout the Bible in many ways. The Word of God makes clear that humans know right from wrong. Micha 6:8 says, "He has shown you, O mortal, what is good. And what does the Lord require of you? To act justly and to love mercy and to walk humbly with your God."

Your proclivity to sin or not is directly correlated to your attitude toward God's right to your life. God created everything, including you. He has a good plan for you. But it requires surrender of the right to be in charge, the ability to always understand what's happening in your life.

If you refuse to surrender, you turn good into bad. All things harmful or hurtful in the world are good things God created that have been inverted, perverted, or pushed to excess.

Vengeance is perversion of justice. Lust is natural desire allowed to become excessive. You can think of a million examples where bad things started good. Overcoming your habits, handicaps, and excessive desires, requires help. You simply cannot do it alone for a sustained period of time.

If you want to avoid sin, you must surrender to the help God offers.

Jesus came to earth and sacrificed himself to cover any and all sin you ask to be forgiven for and turn away from. He sent the Holy Spirit to be your helper and counselor. You get to choose whether to accept Jesus as Savior and Holy Spirit as helper or not. But remember that as long as you retain rights to certain sins, God cannot accomplish what he has planned for you.

Prayers, even the most generous, cannot be heard by God when your heart is filled with an unwillingness to surrender.

https://www.jewishvirtuallibrary.org/sin

DAY ONE HUNDRED & FORTY-TWO

The desert between knowing and seeing
Exodus 2:11 - 3:11

The word desert when used in the Bible means a time of that which feels like nothingness, loneliness, testing. Think about Jesus tested by Satan, the Israelites' 40 years trying to get to the promised land, Moses' 40 years tending sheep after he killed the Egyptian. Many people spend what feels like most of their life in the "desert."

Truthfully, you can't be much use to God unless you've spent some time in the desert. It's there that we lose a since of individual purpose, bravado, and pride. It's not that you don't have a purpose. Usually it's the people with a very important purpose that end up spending long periods in the desert. They get a vision, a sense of God's calling and either run away or get excited and try to make things happen in their own timing.

You have a purpose. Your purpose may not be what you think it should be. God will direct you toward your purpose by creating opportunities for you to learn and grow. You may first need to become discouraged or even fail at something before the purpose of your life is fulfilled.

DAY ONE HUNDRED & FORTY-THREE

Avoiding timing temptations
Matthew 4:1-11

Before Jesus started his public mission, around the age of 30, he had to endure forty days in the desert wilderness without food while Satan taunted and tempted him. Eventually, you will endure a tough experience that must be faced alone. You will be faced with temptations.

Satan didn't tempt Jesus to murder, steal, or rape. He offered temptations that would have satisfied a natural need or desire - hunger, safety, popularity.

God created all of your desires and needs. There's a proper order and timing to fulfilling each of them. Your enemy wants you to take fulfillment into your own hands. When you do this, what is natural becomes a burden you must carry.

Don't be fooled by the tempter into putting trust in yourself instead of God. Do your part to be ready for blessings, but trust God to close the deal, even when he delays or allows a "wilderness" experience.

What desire or need have you taken into your own hands? Give it back to God. He will right the wrongs and fulfill you.

DAY ONE HUNDRED & FORTY-FOUR

Contending with People and God
Genesis 32:22–32

You've got to "grow teeth" or the world will ravage and eat you alive. Growing teeth is the same as getting a backbone. It means standing up for yourself, being wise about the world.

You are called to be morally upright, to do the right thing, be kind. Many will perceive your efforts to meet that calling as weakness, and they will take advantage of you.

Don't be mad at them or come to see everyone as a predator. You have the same tendency within yourself. Maybe you are aware of it or not. Depending on your personality and how you've coped with the tragedies of life, you will either approach the world in an aggressive or passive manner.

Jacob, who God renamed Israel, was quite a character. He stole his brother Esau's birthright and then later his blessing. He ran away to escape his brother's wrath. His karma caught up with him big time. All the bad seeds he sowed came up in his life. Eventually, Jacob took his entire family back home. He made things right with Esau.

On the way home, he wrestled with God (or an angel of God) one night alone by a river. He refused to let go of God until God agreed to bless him. He got a major blessing, but he also bore a limp the rest of his life. He and his family became the nation of Israel. The name means – he who wrestles with God.

DAY ONE HUNDRED & FORTY-FIVE

True friendship
1 Samuel 20:41-42, Proverbs 18:24

True friendship is invaluable but rare. A fulfilling life is not possible without at least one real friend. To be a friend will cost you.

Friendship costs time, patience, willingness to be vulnerable, and commitment to keeping it real. Friends give each other grace, acceptance, comfort, laughter, and encouragement.

Most people don't seek enduring friendships, but some form of relationship based on one of the following:

Neediness	You are beneath them, require saving in some way
Worship	You adore them and build their sense of greatness
Sales	You are a potential customer and link to other customers
Volunteer	You fill a box, are a warm body to work on a project
Social	You give them social access

Everyone in this world needs a friend. How can you be the kind of friend a friend would want to have?

DAY ONE HUNDRED & FORTY-SIX

What are your standards for intimacy with a friend?
Proverbs 27:17

Few things hurt more than finding out that someone you considered a real friend is not. People drift apart. Circumstances change. Not everyone is a friend for life. God brings people into your life for a "season" sometimes. Look for people like yourself to develop supportive friendships with - similar life situation, shared values, common interests.

Not all people are intended to be close friends. The most important thing to look for in developing close friends is does the person share your faith in Christ. If they do not, be careful that you don't deny your beliefs to conform to theirs. Jesus never rejected anyone, but he didn't form close relationships with people who rejected him or faith in God. Even Judas was a believer, but he got on the wrong path. In the end, he felt sad that he'd betrayed Jesus.

Qualities of a real friend:

- An equal in your mind and hers
- Willing and able to tell you the truth about important things
- Wants you to succeed
- Loves you despite your flaws
- Finds time to get together
- Listens to you and shares her thoughts
- Concerned about you and what's important to you
- Laughs with you and cries with you

DAY ONE HUNDRED & FORTY-SEVEN

Winning first in your head
Psalm 118

In the movie Rocky, an amateur boxer from Philadelphia gets the chance to go into the ring with the world champion. After a bitter fight, the two men agree to call the match. It's an awesome underdog story. Rocky, much like a young King David going against Goliath, won in his head before he ever went into the ring.

Every single hero in the Bible, and those in the best stories, show up for whatever the challenge having done everything they could do in their own strength. Then they leave the rest to God. Read about Abraham and Isaac, Moses, Nehemiah, Gideon, Joshua.

The trials we face require faith. You must be willing to abandon yourself to God's power and love before you see the outcome, even when it looks like there's no way the situation could end up in your favor.

DAY ONE HUNDRED & FORTY-EIGHT

Thank God for your broken heart
1 Corinthians 6:19-20

Ponder this statement from Oswald Chamber's book *My Utmost for His Highest:* "If God can accomplish his purposes in this world through a broken heart, then why not thank him for breaking yours?"

This is not an easy attitude to develop. "But what about me," you ask?

The person riding the fence on Christianity will never get to the freedom this attitude offers. It's just too hard.

Thanking God for the good and bad while believing that your literal body and life are temples of the Holy Spirit is what the Apostle Paul means when he says, "You are not your own; but were bought at a price" (1 Corinthians 6:19 – 20).

To have the intimate relationship God desires with you, and to live out the plan he has for you requires leaving behind feelings of pity for yourself or pride in your heart. This takes practice and perseverance, but it's worth it.

DAY ONE HUNDRED & FORTY-NINE

God does not discriminate between sins
Matthew 12:31

Many of the messages coming at you urge a rejection of rules and conformity either in the name of freedom or discrimination. God knew we would be confused by the enemy in many ways. He makes understanding his order simple by not placing sin into categories. Being a real jerk is just as offensive to him as murder.

He also made us to be creatures that seek order. We want to know the rules. In a culture where rules and standards based on God's sovereign design are twisted or tossed out altogether, you either give up, become reckless, or become rigid.

The public-school system's move away from moral education is an example of a form of chaos that has and continues to do great harm to individuals and society. When Americans at the behest of Massachusetts Congressman Horace Mann (1796 - 1859) determined that education at the primary and secondary levels should be paid for by the government, the foundation of that proposition was moral education which did not contradict the teachings of Catholics, Jews, or Protestants.

Mann and his contemporaries knew that with the increasing influx of immigrants from around the world, children needed to be guided in how to live in a republic with freedoms unknown anywhere else in the world.

There's no peace or joy when people do not understand the role of order and rules in managing a life well. In John 14:15, Jesus said, "If you love me, keep my commandments."

If you love him, you will want to please him and honor his rules. You will often fail, but because he does not weigh sin, forgiveness is always available. Don't let the world confuse you. There are rules and there are natural consequences. You get to choose your response.

DAY ONE HUNDRED & FIFTY

The privilege of voting for someone to protect your right to self-rule
Luke 20:25

It's easy to forget that you live in a rare historical moment. In human history, only a very few people have been blessed with the option of picking the people who would protect their right to rule themselves.

For most throughout the ages, and even now, it has been monarchs, despots, or warlords ruling over people.

Jesus of Nazareth planted the seeds for the first government to ever exist for "the people" as a whole. It would take over 1700 years to bloom.

Luke 20:25 records his simple, yet unprecedented, answer to what was a trick question about paying taxes and allegiance to Rome's dictator, Caesar. Jesus said, "Then give back to Caesar what is Caesar's, and to God what is God's."

Lord Acton, great British legislator and historian, wrote of this statement as defining the sacredness of government but also its boundaries.

Jesus simultaneously rejected governments with absolute control over people and inaugurated freedom. Political authority must have limits. The new law, spirit, and authority he proclaimed gave to liberty a meaning and a value it had not possessed in the philosophy or in the constitution of governments before this point.

The American Constitution represented the first government to draw the line Jesus proclaimed between governments and people.

Your vote is like taking part in carrying a sacred torch lit over 2000 years ago by Jesus of Nazareth. The right of American citizens to walk up to a ballot box was forged at the cost of many lives.

Vote with a sense of humility and gratitude as well as with discernment for how the people you pick will honor your right to self-rule.

DAY ONE HUNDRED & FIFTY-ONE

Commonality of Jesus' message and America
Psalm 45:4

If you study the truth about American history, your faith in God and your country will increase.

Jesus placed high value on the individual and freedom. America was founded as a reflection of that foundational principle. The early church, just like early Americans, made mistakes. They were driven by the same human nature you possess today. When you look past the imperfections at the results, you see a country that has done more for the individual and human freedom than any other throughout history.

Keep fighting for truth and your country. Demand of yourself and your country a respect for the humanity of the individual. For this is at the heart of true democracy.

A call for individual freedom is in part what Socrates, Seneca, Cicero, Jesus' disciples, and martyrs throughout history died for. They saw the evil in government that treated people like a commodity, i.e., what they could produce for the few in power.

Be leery of politicians who talk about one group of people's rights over another group's or who pit one group against another. For example, teachers, people of color, handicapped people, and so on.

If you will speak up and fight for the rights of individuals as given by God, you will help everyone regardless of profession, skin color, or any other factor.

DAY ONE HUNDRED & FIFTY-TWO

Hate being pitiful
Luke 16:19-31

The most loving thing your parents, teachers, and friends can do for you is refuse to let you feel sorry for yourself. Get comfortable saying, "It's not about me." Even when it seems to be "about you" - people talking about you, mistreating you, avoiding you.

Oswald Chambers wrote, "Self-pity is of the devil, and if I wallow in it I cannot be used by God for his purpose in the world."

The reason pity from yourself or others is so deadly is that it leads you to become over critical of yourself or insensitive to the needs of others. The person who's told they are pitiful and no one likes them is ruined. The person who's told the world owes them something is also ruined.

Power lies in knowing who you are without false pretense. You are a unique child of God, just like every other human on the planet. God has a plan for you, and it begins with learning to be humble, kind, patient, and loving. You will experience adversity and pain, but you can overcome.

God can't use you if you are pitiful, spending your time getting over on others or wallowing in your wretchedness. There are millions of people stuck at the pity party. God needs healthy people to do his work in the world. You get to choose.

DAY ONE HUNDRED & FIFTY-THREE

Getting a new dream
Proverbs 16:1

God wants us to plan and work toward dreams and goals, including big ones. He also wants us to remain ready to let go of those plans and change direction, if he directs us to do so.

Proverbs 16:1 refers to plans of the heart. Our heart is the center of our being. It's our most sensitive organ, literally and figuratively. That's why when we risk and commit and plan and work very hard and it does not work out, we can get hurt and discouraged.

The higher you fly, the farther it is to the ground.

You can't know the sensation of having a bird's eye view of the earth, without leaving the ground. Yet, there's risk of crashing to earth. You can't know the joys of love without making yourself vulnerable to another, knowing they could reject you.

You get to plan, but God knows his big picture plan for you. If he changes your plan, don't resist or get a bad attitude because that only delays the beginning of your new plan.

DAY ONE HUNDRED & FIFTY-FOUR

The devil can't read your mind, but he can hear your words
Romans 12:9-21

Only God can hear your thoughts. The Holy Spirit interprets your prayers, even your cries when you don't know what you want. He lifts them up to heaven. The enemy can only hear words.

Do your words make the enemy happy or frustrated?

Words can express faith when things look hopeless, patience when forced to wait, giving when you are poor, blessings to those who hate you, humility when you have more than others. Your words flow from attitude, which comes from your heart.

Control your words, even while your heart is still getting right. God will help you work through the disappointments and discouragement that leads to heartache. He won't make you watch what you say. That's your job.

Confound the devil by saying kind, hopeful words even when he's orchestrated situations to cause you discomfort or hurt.

DAY ONE HUNDRED & FIFTY-FIVE

Equality of women Part I
Genesis 3 and 5

It all starts in the Garden of Eden. God creates man and then he creates woman as a helpmate, partner for man. They are equally custodians of the Garden. Then comes the disobedience and eviction from the Garden.

Note these key concepts as you read Genesis:

1. God himself did the punishing of both man (Adam) and woman (Eve)
2. God did not reduce the woman to inferior status
3. God did not give man a charge or right to mistreat or disrespect women

Throughout the Old Testament you see Jewish society treating women well. Women played important and esteemed roles in their families and community. Read about women leaders from Jewish history such as Deborah, Esther, Hannah, Huldah, Jochebed, Miriam, Noadiah, Rachel, Rebekah, Rahab, Ruth and Sarah.

One of the Ten Commandments given to all people says that children must honor their father and mother (Exodus 20:12). Be clear, God did not set woman up to be mistreated or unequal to man. However, in all situations there's an ordering of people. In marriage, men and women are partners. The man is the head of the house, but this does not diminish the role of a woman.

*See http://www.christianBiblereference.org/faq_women.htm as reference

DAY ONE HUNDRED & FIFTY-SIX

Equality of women Part II
Luke 8:1-3

Jesus enters history at a very low point for women. Women were considered as inferior, little more than slaves in status. Romans ruled most of what we know as Europe and the Middle East. They were harsh rulers who believed in many gods (Pagan). Jesus came to free everyone (John 10:10). He models equality throughout his ministry.

1. Women traveled with Jesus and his disciples and even helped fund the ministry (Luke 8:1-3).
2. Jesus visited alone with a Samaritan woman; a serious taboo of the day (John 4:4-30, 39-42).
3. Jesus encouraged both Martha and Mary to sit and be taught by him. Women of that time were not allowed to participate in religious affairs (Luke 10:38-42).
4. The first person Jesus revealed himself to after his resurrection was Mary Magdalene, a former demon possessed woman (Matthew 28:1-10).
5. Women held important positions in the early churches (Acts 1:12-14, 18:24-26, 21:7-9, Romans 16:1-16). Mary, Dorcas, Julia, Lydia, Persis, Priscilla, Phoebe, Tryphena and Tryphosa

The Apostle Paul is often cited as saying women should not hold leadership roles in churches. This is a misunderstanding. Paul makes clear an equality among all Christians before God in Galatians 3:26 - 29. Paul's teachings must be read in full and considered in context of the culture and times. Christians were undergoing intense persecution.

The important thing to consider is what does God say and how did Jesus act in the Bible. Women are clearly equal in importance to men and deserve to be treated with honor. There is an order of things created by God that requires men to lead in some cases. Ideally, men lead families and churches, but this is not a "commandment" nor is it always possible. Sometimes the man dies or leaves his family. Some congregations might respond better to a woman's leadership.

The key to determining people and places you will associate with has to do with their attitude toward women. Do they see women as inferior to men or do they understand God's order?
Related more at http://www.christianBiblereference.org/faq_womensrights.htm

DAY ONE HUNDRED & FIFTY-SEVEN

Women in leadership roles
Galatians 3:26-29

Women, just like men, are often born natural leaders. You are a leader right now. It may be that you only lead your life, but eventually one or more people will look to you for leadership.

God created an order of things in marriage that places women in a ranking order as Lieutenant versus General. Both are very important, high-ranking positions. Church leadership is an area where many have struggled over what God intends. This question is answered only by individual congregations.

God does not discriminate against women.

In the home, church, government, military, or any organization, a hierarchy must exist to maintain order and achieve a mission. Unfortunately, men of all eras have at times abused and misunderstood the place of women and God's view of all people. Don't focus on the failures.

You live in a time unprecedented in history for women's rights.

There are many roles in society. There are times and places for women to lead and for men to lead. Undergirding all roles is this verse: "In Christ Jesus you are all children of God through faith, for all of you who were baptized into Christ have clothed yourselves with Christ" (Galatians 3: 26 - 27).

Don't let the mistakes of men, as well as women, be a stumbling block to your understanding of God's order and fulfillment of leadership roles he's given you. "[We] are all one in Christ Jesus" (Galatians 3:28).

DAY ONE HUNDRED & FIFTY-EIGHT

Ready for opportunity
Proverbs 21:31

Taking advantage of opportunities, achieving dreams, and success in general relates directly to what you did yesterday and the day before, etc. Feeling jealous or angry toward others who have what you want quickly becomes pride. God does not honor pride.

Think of an iceberg. What you see above water is only the tip. The great mass of ice is below water and goes deep.

When you see a person catching their dream or achieving success in a meaningful way, that's only the tip of their iceberg. The hard work coupled with the dream, often for many years, is unseen. Bill Hendrix, author of *The Person that is You*, shared research that revealed a minimum of 10,000 hours in repetitive practice prior to individuals reaching the top of their game or field.

Your mind, life's energy, and gifts are given to you by God like a blueprint. He's imagined the potential for what can be built from that blueprint, but he won't do it for you. It's up to you to investigate like a detective. The clues will be there. Find them and nurture your giftedness.

Work hard at subjects and tasks that may not come naturally but contribute to the development of a well-rounded person. For example: basic math, writing coherent papers, using a planner to schedule and keep appointments with yourself and others, telling the truth always, doing what's right when no one is looking, being the kind of friend a friend would want, etc.

You must be ready for opportunity. Don't waste your time avoiding the hard stuff or hating others for what they have. Get busy refining your gifts by using them and sowing flower and wheat seeds, not weed seeds.

DAY ONE HUNDRED & FIFTY-NINE

The high cost of being true to yourself and principles
Luke 11:33-35

You might be an Alpha personality or a more passive type, but at some point, you will face a choice that comes down to adhering to the group or being your own person. These choices are character building blocks and can be fraught with risk and pain. Some variation on the scenario below will play out in every setting of life you enter - high school, college, work, marriage, church, and so on.

There's a tight-knit group. One is a strong Alpha with a thirst for the spotlight and deference from her peers. Another in the group begins to feel unenthused about playing up to the Alpha. This leads to a "sitting out" period. The Alpha will exclude or "sit out" the gal beginning to show signs of going rogue. This is a test of the girl's fortitude. She will do one of three things: 1) rush to fawn over the Alpha and get back in, 2) become sad and isolated, perhaps depressed, 3) do her own thing while seeking new friends.

There is a healthy response to situations where a person - friend, boyfriend, teacher, boss - will seemingly out-of-the-blue grow cold. It requires great courage because the principled approach often results in a loss of belonging. The first step is to humbly confront the person. Humbly, not angry or pitiful. It goes something like this... "I sense that you are unhappy with me and that concerns me. I want to remain friends with you. Is there anything I've done to offend or hurt you?"

With this confident olive leaf, you've put the burden of proof back on them. If this person values the relationship, they will come forth with the offense or confirm there's nothing wrong. Here's the risky part, they might turn on you in a big way. You might be ostracized from the group, broken up with, fired, humiliated, blacklisted. It's a risk worth taking because unless you are willing to be the first to say you're sorry, and prepared to value yourself, you will never be free. You will spend your entire life attempting to perform by the script of others and yet often not getting it right.

Jesus died so you could be free. He said, "... I have come that they may have life, and have it to the full" (John 10:10). He warned you that it would cost you more than you ever thought possible. The thief wants to keep people bound up in a sense that they must perform for and please others to be worthy. Yet Jesus promises those who will trust him with their lives that they need not worry about the consequences of telling or living the truth. He will meet their needs.

DAY ONE HUNDRED & SIXTY

Hurt people hurt people
Matthew 18:21-35

Hurt people hurt people. It's cliche, but true. People who have been hurt in some way yet never dealt with their pain, sadness, and anger often hurt others. They don't mean to do it, but that doesn't change the facts.

You may feel sorry for a hurt person and excuse their bad behavior, manipulation, lack of commitment, etc. Alternatively, you may hate the person and want revenge.

If you start with the question of what is most loving, it is easier to care about the person as a fellow human being, sister, friend, father, etc. while refusing to go along with the behavior. Remember that the only thing in this world you ever control is yourself. You can choose your response in all cases. You may not be able to prevent someone from hurting you physically or emotionally in all cases.

If you are in a relationship, personal or professional, with a person that hurts others, find ways to distance yourself from that person by becoming less dependent on them. In some cases, you may need to remove yourself from them entirely. With family, this can be tough. You are called to honor father and mother. You are not called to be abused by anyone.

DAY ONE HUNDRED & SIXTY-ONE

Take captive every thought
2 Corinthians 10:1-6

If you watch a craftsman or physician at work, they always have an array of tools. Depending on the demands of the job, they pick their tool. Soldiers must pick the right weapon for whatever battle they must enter. You too pick tools and weapons every day of your life, whether you recognize it or not.

The methods used by the world are exactly opposite to God's. He offers us the same set of tools and weapons regardless of the situation - prayer, faith, hope, love, the Bible (God's Word), and Holy Spirt. These are the demolition tools Paul refers to for removing "strongholds" and "arguments" that distance you from God.

Paul reminded the Corinthians - "For though we live in the world, we do not wage war as the world does" (2 Corinthians 10:3).

The bulk of your daily challenges and conflicts will be carried out in your mind. How you choose to think about people and situations represents your weapon of choice. Will you respond to unkindness with same or will you wield love? When rumors are circulated about you, how will prayer fit into your plan? If fear grips you, will you call out to the Holy Spirit or give up?

DAY ONE HUNDRED & SIXTY-TWO

A bad attitude does not sway God
Jonah 4

If you feel compassion for puppies but hate for fools and the wicked, you might be in a Jonah predicament.

Jonah was the reluctant prophet to an evil, nasty, successful bunch of people. He went to Ninevah, the evil city, and pointed them toward repentance only after running away and nearly dying in the belly of a giant fish. Their changed ways were short-lived, but God kept the promise he'd made through the prophet Jeremiah (18:7,8) that any city would be saved if they repented.

After finally doing what God asked of him and seeing God's mercy on Ninevah, Jonah prayed to die. Angry and bitter, he quit on life and simply waited in a dry, desert place. God came and ministered to him by way of a lovely vine that provided shade and beauty in the dry place. Jonah was happy with the vine.

Then God allowed a worm to eat the vine and it was gone. Jonah was angry again and wanted to die.

God gives, and he takes away. He wants correction for all and a relationship with them. God is not in the revenge business toward you or others.

Check your heart. Are you running away from the difficult people and situations God has put you in because "they don't deserve" mercy and compassion? This is a tough question and one you can only get answered through prayer. God does close doors on relationships and situations. Make sure it's his hand on the door, not yours.

DAY ONE HUNDRED & SIXTY-THREE

What's luck got to do with it?
Luke 12:35-40

There's no such thing as luck for those who belong to God, at least not in the sense of some good fortune falling from the sky and onto someone randomly. Seneca (4 BC - 65 AD), Roman philosopher and martyred truth teller, once said, "Luck is what happens when preparation meets opportunity."

Every day of your life presents an opportunity for preparation. Use each day to discover your giftedness, hone your skills, be light in a dark world. Whatever good fortune you seek - health, job, husband, fame - will only arrive with lasting potential if you are prepared for it. When you go seeking "luck" on your terms and timeline, you might get what you want, for a while.

Resist the temptation to want what others have, unless you are willing to do what they did to get there. Today determines tomorrow.

Read *The Monkey's Paw* by W.W. Jacobs and *The Red Shoes* by Hans Christian Anderson.

DAY ONE HUNDRED & SIXTY-FOUR

You have the "right" to do anything
1 Corinthians 6:12, 10:31

You probably enjoy the liberty to do about anything you want.

You could run out in front of a car, hurt someone, stay up to the wee hours each night, get high with friends every weekend, yell obscenities at the police, get another tattoo, cuss out your parents, cut your hair off, or drink excessive amounts of coffee. Conversely, you could exercise regularly, help hurting people, stay in touch with those who are ill, work hard, or love those around you without condition.

Paul says in 1 Corinthians 6:12, "'I have the right to do anything,' you say—but not everything is beneficial. 'I have the right to do anything'—but I will not be mastered by anything."

He urges believers to be sensitive but to not allow their freedom to be compromised by other people's conscience. Handle yourself according to each setting and situation out of respect for other people and for your witness as a Christian. At times you will feel as if you can't get it right. Someone will always come down on you for what you did or didn't do.

Determine what you say and do in each situation with these questions in mind:

- Will this encourage the faith of those around me or could it cause them to falter?
- Is this action or my words explicitly sinful, i.e., goes against my conscience?
- Am I being selfish?
- Does this square with my personal goal and vision?
- Is it loving?

Jesus illustrated through his life that what you do is not as important as doing everything for the glory of God (1 Corinthians 10:31). Christian freedom is tied to responsibility. Keep that responsibility in mind as you go about making choices each day.

DAY ONE HUNDRED & SIXTY-FIVE

A check list for encouragers
1 Thessalonians 5:14 - 15

In everything that is of God, there's freedom and unpredictability anchored by unmoving rules and principles. This is why Christians can be neither rigid nor loose. You must call on the discernment and wisdom of the Holy Spirit in each situation. However, you know that guidance from God will never veer from the Ten Commandments.

This balance between freedom and foundational principles is at the heart of the Apostle Paul's check list for encouragers found in 1 Thessalonians 5:14 - 15 (See NIV Life Application Study Bible 1991 edition notes).

- Build people up
- Respect leaders
- Act peacefully
- Warn those prone to just sitting around
- Encourage the timid
- Help the weak
- Be patient with all
- Resist revenge
- Be joyful
- Pray continually
- Give thanks in everything
- Don't extinguish the spirit's fire in people
- Avoid all evil
- Count on God to help in all situations

DAY ONE HUNDRED & SIXTY-SIX

You can't have freedom without rules
Deuteronomy 6

The creativity to invent a useful product, confidence to be a great student, or environment that will allow you to grow into a productive person all occur within a context of rules, order, and discipline. If you never know what to expect from your parents, teachers, boss, or government, you can't create effectively.

For example, inventions that make life better take years to create. Usually an individual or group of people invested hours and hours, often unpaid, to test and develop the idea. To undertake such projects, people must first live in a society where they can earn enough money to meet basic needs. Ultimately, they must have the protection of rules and laws that enable the production, marketing, and sales across state and international borders for the product to reach the masses.

For you to succeed in school, athletics, the arts, or work, ,i.e., develop your mind and body fully, it takes living with what might look like boring and strict rules. The predictable and stable aspects of life created by families, schools, government, and employers enables the unlimited creativity God placed within each individual.

This principle is why the world has never developed, nor will it ever, an economic system able to lift more people from poverty to self-sufficiency than Capitalism. Allowing anyone the freedom to create, produce, and sell in service to their fellow humans supported by a society based on the rule of law is superior to any other idea of organization. This truth has been proven over and over throughout history.

Jesus encouraged freedom for every individual, yet he never undermined the law of God or of society.

*Go to ourworldindata.org to see facts and figures about how people and the environment are doing all over the world.

DAY ONE HUNDRED & SIXTY-SEVEN

Ultimate authority is with Jesus
Colossians 1:15-23

"All authority in heaven and on earth has been given to me," Jesus told his disciples as he sent them out to share his message with the entire world (Matthew 28:18). What a bold and serious statement; one either to be laughed off or understood.

For many, then and now, Jesus' claim to ultimate authority is infuriating.

Are you attempting to understand Jesus, yet still a bit put off by his claims of authority over every aspect of your present and future?

Human nature is to resist such submission. It's important to grapple with your feelings about Jesus. What's at stake is your entire life - now and forever. Don't ride the fence on this. Get all in or all out. Pretending to believe or doing so on and off makes for a miserable life.

In Colossians 1, Paul makes perhaps the most comprehensive statements about the authority of Jesus. He identifies him as…

- The Son
- Image of the invisible God
- Firstborn over all creation and from among the dead
- Master of all things in heaven and on earth, visible and invisible, spirit and man, leaders and common people
- Before all things, and in him all things hold together
- Reconciled all things on earth and in heaven by making peace through his blood, shed on the cross
- Reconciled you by his physical body through death so you could be presented to God the Father as holy in his sight, without blemish and free from accusation

Can you accept Jesus as all this?

DAY ONE HUNDRED & SIXTY-EIGHT

Exercising free will and maturity
Hebrews 6:1-7

Maturity implies advancing, understanding, and applying increasingly complex ideas. A mature person is "over" just being concerned about themselves. She thinks about others and seeks to be an example. This is God's purpose for every Christian, that they grow in character and ability to influence and impact others.

The Hebrews writer refers to getting certain basic tenets of the faith and says you can't go back once you have been "enlightened" by Jesus' teachings. To do so would be false and the ultimate dishonoring of Christ's crucifixion.

Imagine two sides of a divide. On one side you are a child, unaware of the truth about Jesus and his commands for life. On the other, you are an adult with full understanding of truth. As the child you didn't have much choice. You didn't know what you didn't know. Your thoughts revolved around getting what you needed and wanted. But once you become an adult and exposed to the truth through experience and teaching, there is a choice.

This choice is what we call free will. Regardless of your circumstances, you are a free agent in terms of what you believe and how you act.

DAY ONE HUNDRED & SIXTY-NINE

The gift of tears
2 Corinthians 7:1-10

Tears are a gift when they come as a result of realizing the weight of your sin in contrast to God's love. Repentance is not a personal choice. It is a gift of the Holy Spirit.

Paul's writings to the new and fragile churches throughout the Roman Empire in the years following Jesus' death and resurrection are filled with what seem like stern reprimands and warnings along with stories of great persecution and conflict.

Paul was often attempting to get people to a place where they might experience the gift of tears because he knew firsthand that the new Christians would not make it without a profound sense of God's love and power. Paul had encountered Jesus in spirit on the road to Damascus. It led to a most profound conversion within him and enabled him to persevere through horrific challenges.

You will know the difference between repentance and sorrow because the first is a realization of sin against God and desire to get right with God. Literally, repentance means to turn in another direction, to change your ways. If you are aware of offending God, it's an awful feeling.

Sorrow is often more a reaction and sense of being disgusted with yourself. You might be sorry you got caught or pushed away by someone because of your words and actions.

Understanding the nature of God and importance of a relationship with him is not something you as a human can conjure up on your own. It requires the Holy Spirit's help. An ability to see the gravity of your sin comes from the Holy Spirit. It's too much of a burden to comprehend and accept on your own.

Like the furnace that refines gold, you too only become valuable after the pain of repentance. It's necessary but counter to your innate sense of self-preservation and pain avoidance.

Paul reprimands and then reminds. "Godly sorrow brings repentance that leads to salvation and leaves no regret, but worldly sorrow brings death" (7:10).

DAY ONE HUNDRED & SEVENTY

Repetition = Who and what you are
Romans 5:4

Be thoughtful about what you repeat. The words, thoughts, and actions you repeat make up your life.

If you lift weights repetitively, muscle builds. If you study, knowledge grows. If you show kindness, you will find kindness coming to you. If you look in the mirror each day and think negative thoughts, you become negative. If you regularly tell lies, you will be a liar.

The website www.changingminds.com says, "Our brains are excellent pattern-matchers and reward us for using this very helpful skill. Repetition creates a pattern, which consequently and naturally grabs our attention at first and then creates the comfort of familiarity."

Repetition is what makes it look easy for the athlete, singer, actor, etc. No one is born a pro at anything. You become a great writer, teacher, lawyer, parent, wife, etc. Our individual personalities and gifts create a foundation for those things we have a natural tendency toward.

Think of your "God given" gifts as diamonds in the rough. You must pursue the chisel that will reveal the diamond.

What do you repeat and how is it reflected in your character and experience?

DAY ONE HUNDRED & SEVENTY-ONE

Relationships are central to life
Matthew 8

People are what make anything possible. No people means no school, family, business, town, state, country, or anything that matters. People make things difficult and they make things wonderful.

Jesus is the perfect role model for how to be in relationship with people.

Throughout the gospel you find examples of Jesus loving, enjoying, gathering, and even confronting people. He's also often shown as spending time alone. He showed us that there is a time for everything and that relationships are the foundation for life.

Jesus didn't allow everyone to be close to him, but he did have close friends. He spoke the truth about people and situations pointedly but always with respect.

Jesus' honest approach to life didn't win everyone over, especially those whose power or self-lies rested on people not speaking the truth. He was ridiculed and persecuted. It's the same today for those who live in his truth and ways.

You will be hurt, let down, and rejected by people. This is part of life.

Don't think you can go it alone or that if you just keep to a few safe people trouble can be avoided. Pray for right relationships. Don't be too critical nor fling yourself randomly into relationships.

You are valuable. God knows where he wants you.

DAY ONE HUNDRED & SEVENTY-TWO

How God works in the world
Esther 4:14

Esther became queen to the Persian king Xerxes, even though she was an orphaned Jew. She played a key role in saving the Jewish people within the vast Persian empire (modern day Middle East, mainland Europe, and over to India). Her story illustrates how God works in the world still today (See notes in NIV Life Application Study Bible 1991 edition, page 1009).

God acts through the natural order he created and set into motion, miracles, and providence. You know the natural order of things through study of the Bible and your conscience. We are born with certain attributes and abilities. In Esther's case, she was born with natural beauty.

Miracles are God's responses to people's needs or. Esther was able to speak to the king when she just as likely could have been killed for even approaching him.

Providence is God moving people, things, and situations around to enable his will to happen through people. Sometimes he overrules the natural or expected order to accomplish something. In Esther's story, her uncle overheard something that enabled him to take a step that set God's plan in motion.

You don't know God's plan for your life, but you have a map for finding out. Esther exhibits the map - plan and pray as well as trust and obey.

Make plans that fit with God's natural order and the desires of your heart. Pray about your plans and all things that concern you and the world around you. Trust that God is in control of everything and hears every prayer. Obey his commands given to everyone as revealed in the Bible. Obey the unique plans spoken to your heart personally by the Holy Spirit.

Too often people disobey God's natural order and commands, demand God do what they want, or despair when the desired answer does not come.

Have you planned, prayed, trusted, and obeyed?

DAY ONE HUNDRED & SEVENTY-THREE

Paradox of living for Christ
Matthew 11:28-30

Sometimes women say of men, and vice versa, "You can't live with them, and you can't live without them." It's an off-handed way of stating the paradox in relationship. It's hard at times but worth it. This is true of living for Christ.

Jesus tells us in Mark 8:34, "Whoever wants to be my disciple must deny themselves and take up their cross and follow me." Then in Matthew 11: 29 - 30 he says, "Take my yoke upon you and learn from me, for I am gentle and humble in heart, and you will find rest for your souls. For my yoke is easy and my burden is light."

To become truly associated with Jesus, you must accept the tension of the paradox. You will suffer at times and feel out of sync with the world. But there's nothing in the world that can give you peace like true faith in Jesus and having a real relationship with him.

Where's your relationship with Jesus?

DAY ONE HUNDRED & SEVENTY-FOUR

Right with God
Isaiah 54:4-8

Your Father in heaven is not fickle nor is his love conditional. His love is constant. Even when you are full of angst or sorrow or fear, he never stops loving you.

If you are not in a right relationship with God, you will not feel peace about your day-to-day life. However, just because you feel upset or not at peace does not mean you are on the outs with God.

God's presence, often experienced through the Holy Spirit, is delicate like a butterfly or glass ornament. You must be still and patient to enjoy them both. The Holy Spirit will withdraw when you are on a path of disobedience. Sometimes God will allow you to endure a tough time as he works out a rough spot in your character or prepares you for something down the road.

Jesus left peace behind for us so our hearts could endure and our minds would not give in to fear. As humans, we often run after what looks like peace in the world - acceptance, popularity, possessions. These things are not bad inherently but can become distractions.

In all things remember Jesus' words, "Do not let your hearts be troubled and do not be afraid" (John 14:27).

DAY ONE HUNDRED & SEVENTY-FIVE

Risking failure for God
Ephesians 1:11-22, 1 Peter 1:3-4

Living boldly based on an assurance of God's promises is risky. The world lifts up arrogant people who are often drunk on themselves. They post their face and life without reservation. They throw people away when no longer useful. The bold, self-assured follower of Christ is a different story.

Embrace your life as a "sealed" believer and heir to an inheritance that will never "spoil, perish, or fade," and the world will cringe at your audacity. (1 Peter 1: 4, Ephesians 1:13)

It will often feel like failure. Sometimes you will fail hard. God means failure to serve as a builder of your character, wisdom, humility, and knowledge. Your enemy means failure to break your faith and spirit.

Make up your mind to accept failure or success with the same kind of trust in God's care. If you develop this attitude of faith, you will avoid becoming useless to God. Some people become too confident in their success, while others become defeated by their failure.

How do you think about yourself and situations when failure comes?

DAY ONE HUNDRED & SEVENTY-SIX

Finding comfort in your own skin
Romans 8:28

The most coveted place to be as a woman is comfortable in your own skin. For the Christian, this means believing with every fiber of your being that God sovereignly controls every last detail of your circumstances.

At the heart of faith in God is accepting that he is in control of everything. We take our circumstances for granted, often assuming people are in control of what happens to us.

Because most of us only believe abstractly that God works all things together for the good of those who love him, we get stuck on one end or the other of an awful continuum (Romans 8:28). We are either arrogant and stuck on ourselves or secretly self-loathing followers. Both are destructive of your spirit and prevent enjoying meaningful relationships.

Yes, God is in control, but you get to decide whether or not to accept how he's crafted your temperament, body, life position, and everything else. Whatever it is about you and your life that is completely not of your own doing, he's done it for a reason. You may never fully understand the reasons. It does not matter.

Practice being at peace with who you are. Learn to ignore the inner voice that condemns you and judges or envies others. Become completely agnostic about what others have. Instead, place your time and energy into practicing kindness, joy, and whatever skill you find your heart desiring (art, music, building, writing, teaching, serving, etc.).

When do you feel most self-conscious? When do you feel most comfortable in your own skin?

DAY ONE HUNDRED & SEVENTY-SEVEN

Bearing up with each other and ourselves
Galatians 6:1-5

Women often want to be part of the group and unique at the same time. Just being yourself and real carries a set of risks. You may not be accepted. You could be made fun of or excluded.

Have you ever excluded someone from your group because they acted just a little too independent or maybe too needy?

Have you ever been the person pushed out and felt that horrible self-consciousness at school, work, or in some social setting of not feeling welcomed by the group?

Have you ever decided to "give them something to talk about" when people gossiped about you?

In Galatians 6, Paul says carry each other's burdens and carry your own. By saying carry the burdens of others he means be fair and honest. Give the girl who's different or messes up a break, yet don't pretend bad behavior is okay.

Extend that same rule to yourself. Be honest in judgment of yourself. Test your own actions against God's Word and your conscience. It's okay to be happy with yourself and your work. It's also important to make corrections in attitude and behavior when you realize you've been unkind, unfair, or even downright mean.

Take an honest look inside your heart right now.

DAY ONE HUNDRED & SEVENTY-EIGHT

Sooner or later you get what you expect
Psalm 27:14

What are you expecting?

Listen to your words and watch your actions. They reveal what you expect. If what you find is not in line with your deepest expectations, hopes, and dreams, change what you are saying and doing.

Your words and actions amount to your attitude. Look at your attitude and you will get a glimpse of what you can expect, sooner or later. If you are filled with doubt and negative statements about yourself, others, and what you really want, that is a reflection of what you will get.

Anything you want of value will require a wait. This is not an impatient, standing in line doing nothing wait. You will be actively preparing for what you expect and practicing skills while you wait. Your attitude should be one of hopeful expectation while waiting.

Like the nine-month gestation of a baby, all things take time to form before entering the world or becoming real. The psalm reminds you to be strong and take heart while waiting for the Lord.

DAY ONE HUNDRED & SEVENTY-NINE

How to be an interesting person
Luke 16:8-9

Think for a moment about someone you like being around. What makes them interesting? Interesting people have these traits:

1. Weave story into their conversation without slandering individuals
2. Get outside of their comfort zone to experience new people, places, food, and more
3. Question things based on reading and experience, like a scientist versus a parrot
4. Enjoy and pursue conversation about a wide breadth of topics that goes beyond the weather and famous people
5. Talk about people, situations, and the future in a positive light
6. Remain present for those they are with (turn off all those sounds on your phone and put it up for a few minutes)
7. Are authentic with people (no phony posing for the imaginary camera)

Practice being interesting. It's a great asset.

DAY ONE HUNDRED & EIGHTY

I love you and value you, no matter what
Genesis 15:1

When all the layers are peeled away, you will find that what you want most is to hear God say, "I love you and value you, no matter what." You want him to say it and prove it. Yet, he already has, and he does throughout your life.

Most of God's children have a remembering problem. You want him to show you again and again. Your memory quickly obscures that blessing of yesterday with the yearning for tomorrow's.

Abraham won a great battle in Genesis 14. The kings of the region came to him with accolades and offers to take the spoils of war. Abraham tells them he will take nothing lest they attempt to take credit for making him rich (Genesis 14: 21 - 24).

Immediately in Genesis 15:1, God comes to him saying, "Do not be afraid, Abram, I am your shield, your very great reward."

God knows what's on Abraham's mind. He's worried about the promise of a child, his descendants. We all are like Abraham. We know what God has promised, but question what if it's wrong or not really intended for me.

Don't fret. Trust God. Turn your anxiety into a prayer. God will give you everything he's promised and more.

DAY ONE HUNDRED & EIGHTY-ONE

Anxiousness is a symptom
Philippians 4:6-7

"Do not be anxious about anything," commands Paul in Philippians 4:6, but he didn't live in your world, right?

Paul lived in a time and place of difficulty and violence that you simply cannot imagine.

For his faith in Christ, he was beaten, imprisoned, and scorned. In his quest to help the fledgling churches scattered throughout the Roman world, he was shipwrecked, bitten by snakes, and often hungry and without shelter.

To be anxious about impending danger or performance in the classroom, on the field, or at work is natural. What you do with those feelings is important to your health and performance. Proper action is the secret. If in danger, get away. If there's a test, match, or big meeting, prepare, face it, and do your best.

Prolonged anxiety causes over-release of the steroid hormone Cortisol, which can lead to lots of unwanted problems. Anxiety is often a warning from the Holy Spirit that you are going the wrong way or pushing too many things onto your schedule. But the "peace of God, which transcends all understanding…" is supernatural (Philippians 4:7).

Paul's bold statement is a reminder of one of the gifts you as a believer have at your disposal.

No matter the situation or issue, you can go to God and ask for help. Precede your prayer and petition with thanks. God will give protection for the heart and mind of any believer who asks without discrimination.

DAY ONE HUNDRED & EIGHTY-TWO

Do not break faith
Malachi 2:10-16

Breaking faith means to ignore a promise, vow, or covenant. People often forget the passion and excitement felt when making a promise as time goes by and situations change.

Malachi is the last book of the Old Testament. As a prophet to the people of Israel after their return to Jerusalem and rebuilding of the temple, Malachi confronted the people about their bad behavior. They had once again begun to break the faith with God. The jubilation felt during the return to their land and rebuilding of the temple faded. They had grown bored and began to marry as well as divorce the people living around them who didn't share their faith in God.

Things began to decline for the people, and they blamed God. Malachi implored them to restore their relationship with God by asking forgiveness and returning to a true worship.

If things are not turning out well and you feel sad and let down by God, look first to your attitude and behavior. God sees everything and holds you accountable for your actions and his requirements of you. He will never break faith with you and expects the same in return.

DAY ONE HUNDRED & EIGHTY-THREE

Six things you must know about God
Malachi 4

God requires commitment and sacrifice, but it will be worth it in the end. That's a fair summary statement of what it means to follow God.

Malachi ends the Old Testament with a brief check list for the person seeking to understand God. He uses the powerful imagery found throughout the Bible to illustrate what those who love God can expect and what those who reject God will encounter.

"But for you who revere my name, the sun of righteousness will rise with healing in its rays. And you will go out and frolic like well-fed calves" (4:2).

Malachi lists six vital things you must understand about God and living for him.

1. God deserves your best because he gave you life and is sovereign over everything.
2. You must be willing to change wrong ways of living because God won't make you do it, but he will hold you accountable.
3. Family is special and should be made a lifelong priority, even if it is dysfunctional and not who you would choose.
4. Don't hate the refining process God puts his children through. It's necessary.
5. Tithing at least ten percent of your income to the church is non-negotiable.
6. Kill pride in your heart and life. There's absolutely no room for pride in the life of a Christian. God hates pride, and he will not honor it in you.

DAY ONE HUNDRED & EIGHTY-FOUR

Looking for a sign of God's goodness
Psalm 86:17

Have you ever really, really needed God to give you a sign that he cares about you?

When things are tough, everything seems to be falling apart, and you've been doing the right thing for so long with no results, you can't help but pray a King David-like prayer.

"Give me a sign of your goodness, that my enemies may see it and be put to shame, for you, Lord, have helped me and comforted me" (Psalm 86:17).

It's okay to ask God for a sign, to call his attention to your hurt, anxiety, etc. He already knows what you are going through but appreciates it when you to come to him with a humble heart. Every time you do this, an amazing thing will happen. God will show you a glimpse of the goodness he's already provided.

You will get a view of the most incredible sunrise. A friend's serious illness will remind you of your own good health. A family member will come through with the support you need.

This is not God calling you ungrateful. It's his way of saying, "I'm working on your life. Don't worry. Remember what I've already done. I'm right here all the time."

DAY ONE HUNDRED & EIGHTY-FIVE

Testing God like Gideon
Judges 6, 1 Timothy 6:6

God uses common people. They are always people who do not see themselves as great and who did what God asked, in spite of fear and weaknesses.

Gideon was a man who thought little of himself, but God used him to deliver Israel from Midian.

God directed Gideon to lead his people into a fight against an enemy much bigger than them. He doubted what he was hearing, so he asked God for a simple proof by way of laying out a wool fleece. Finding the fleece dry or wet the next morning would indicate God's answer (Judges 6:36 - 40).

This is where we get the saying, "Lay out your fleece."

God may not fulfill such a request from you, but the concept of taking tentative steps coupled with prayer is good. Give God the opportunity to affirm big decisions in your life. If you are considering a job, college, marriage, or anything that heavily impacts your life, "lay out your fleece" first.

For example, fill out an application, ask the person you are dating some hard questions, seek counsel from a Godly person with more experience than yourself. Then you often must wait. There may be more baby steps involved.

With God, timing and attitude is everything. If you respectfully "lay out your fleece" with prayer and a patient heart, God will provide.

What do you feel led to do but are not sure it is God's will?

Practice being content with not knowing and waiting until you get his directions.

DAY ONE HUNDRED & EIGHTY-SIX

God is a refiner
Proverbs 17:3

Without heat, gold and silver cannot be made into fine objects. Without pruning, a rose bush will not produce more roses.

If everything is falling apart and people have rejected you, be still and hold your tongue. God is working in your life. He's got something much better planned, but you must allow him to burn away all that is extra, the excess.

Most people never get to enjoy the best plan God has for their life and the innumerable blessings he's stored up.

They either take things into their own hands and try to control life, or they can't stand the heat during the refining process and give up. If you want to be a rare person who fulfills God's plan, trust him with every life decision. Don't judge your place in life from the world's viewpoint.

Wherever God puts you is a place of honor in his economy and worldview.

Say this prayer:

"God, I can't see beyond today. It's so hard to remain focused on you when nothing seems to be going the way I'd hoped and planned. I want to serve you. I want all of your blessings for my life. Forgive my sins. Have mercy on me. I love you. In Jesus' name, Amen."

DAY ONE HUNDRED & EIGHTY-SEVEN

The cost of breaking trust
Luke 16:9-11

Trust is the bedrock of relationship. Trust grows over time as actions and words align. A single action can tear down trust years in the making. You will pay a price much higher than expected when trust is broken.

Jordan Peterson, clinical psychologist and author of *12 Rules for Life*, notes that deception hurts you more than anything else life throws at you. People can endure cancer, natural disaster, and much more if those they trust remain trustworthy.

Your lie or indiscretion will be quickly forgiven by God if you confess what you've done to him and turn away from wrong you've done. However, it may take much longer for the lingering questions in the back of your friend, parent, or husband's mind to go away. It is often the doubt that weakens or even destroys the intimacy in a relationship.

Some people attempt to protect themselves from hurt or vulnerability by trusting no one. If you trust no one, you will never know intimate friendship. It takes a lot of courage to trust people after being betrayed, notes Peterson.

The most important trusting relationship you will ever enter is one with God. He is the creator of your life and author of your life's story. If you will not trust God, you will not be able to receive his mission and plans for your life.

DAY ONE HUNDRED & EIGHTY-EIGHT

How to succeed in God's eyes
Proverbs 19:8

The book of Proverbs is about wisdom and the results of living wisely and unwisely. Those who are wise have success and a good reputation. But there are times when even wise people experience failure and adversity.

The NIV Life Application Study Bible 1991 edition summarizes the qualities that promote success and a good reputation as described in Proverbs:

- Righteousness (acting in a morally upright or Godly manner)
- Rejecting false things and words
- Doing all work for God
- Picking words carefully, restraining the "tongue"
- Loving wisdom and understanding, seeking them
- Being humble and revering the Lord, a desire to please him

The opposite of wisdom qualities includes:

- Wickedness
- Seeking your own honor
- Hatred toward others
- Praising yourself
- Hiding sin

DAY ONE HUNDRED & EIGHTY-NINE

Be careful about what forms your opinions of people
Matthew 7:1-6

Jesus had an amazing knack for packing enormous lessons into parables. He did this in part because the crowds following him around were full of people interested in killing him. Notice too how Jesus almost always gives context and contrast when teaching.

He says, "Do not judge, or you too will be judged. For in the same way you judge others, you will be judged, and with the measure you use, it will be measured to you" (Matthew 7:1 - 2).

In the next three verses he talks about learning to look at yourself with a discerning eye before criticizing or judging someone else. Our human nature is to hate in others the very thing we hate about ourselves or to hate them because they have something we want.

Have you ever hated another female for valid reasons but deep down envied her beauty or style?

Jesus is warning us against judging the way people look or who they are based on bias or a sense of being better.

He also provides the flip side, which is judgment. You should use good judgment and discernment when picking boyfriends, friends, jobs, churches, etc. Don't avoid the truth. Always seek the truth but be careful about how you speak it and use it.

This is what Jesus means when he says, "Do not give dogs what is sacred; do not throw your pearls to pigs. If you do, they may trample them under their feet, and turn and tear you to pieces" (Matthew 7:6).

You are a pearl. Pigs represent the things and people that can't or won't appreciate what you know or who you are. It's not your job to "judge" them. Only God can do that. It is your job to use judgment in deciding if or how you associate with those people and things.

DAY ONE HUNDRED & NINETY

Ask, seek, knock
Matthew 7:7-12

Many deep-down yearnings and dreams may seem so crazy or personal that you don't want to talk about it.

Jesus tells you to ask, seek, knock because everyone who does so will get an answer. You've got to take steps. Not one step but multiple. There's action in asking, seeking, and knocking.

Many times, you will wish and hope but never take the action or you will take some action, not get the results desired, and give up.

In the giving up stage, you will often say something like this, "I guess God does not want to bless me," or "I'm not smart (pretty, good, rich, lucky) enough to get that."

This is why Jesus says, "Which of you, if your son asks for bread, will give him a stone? Or if he asks for a fish, will give him a snake" (9-10)?

God is all powerful and loves you. He will not withhold any good thing from you, especially if you ask.

In closing, Jesus places the notion of asking and receiving in a human context. "So in everything, do to others what you would have them do to you, for this sums up the Law and the Prophets" (7:12).

If you give freely of yourself and what you have to those asking, seeking, and knocking at your door, you are acting as an agent of God. Everyone will have what they need as each gives what they themselves want.

Think about this idea. Have you ever wanted kindness, love, a job, a coat, a meal? Are you giving those things you have wanted?

DAY ONE HUNDRED & NINETY-ONE

The narrow and wide gates
Matthew 7:13-14

There are stories of people dying briefly and getting to glimpse heaven. Revelation 4 provides imagery using words like crystal, jasper and rubies, a rainbow that shone like emeralds, and angels who sing without ceasing. It is a perfect place without any of the pain and limitations of being human on earth.

Once you get to heaven it's forever, but entrance is through what Jesus calls a narrow gate.

If you come to understand that Jesus is the only "gate" to heaven and that what he demands of you is to walk a road that will require a lot from you, it will often feel as if you are missing something on the parallel road filled with many, many people. They will look to be having a grand time. Many will be experiencing all the excitement this life has to offer.

The narrow path created by Jesus also offers excitement at times, but most of all it provides peace, which will never be found on the wide road.

Pick which road you will take with eyes wide open.

DAY ONE HUNDRED & NINETY-TWO

True and false people
Matthew 7:15-23

Have you ever seen an apple tree in the spring? Without the apples, you may not have known how to identify it. Unless you are a student of apple varieties, you may not know if apples found on a tree are any good or not until you pick one and take a bite.

Jesus often compared people to fruit trees. He said, "By their fruit you will recognize them. Do people pick grapes from thorn bushes, or figs from thistles" (7:16)?

Your fruit is your actions. An apple tree is expected to produce apples. If it does not, it is not a good apple tree. The owner of an apple tree that is not producing good apples on a regular basis can be expected to cut that tree down and replace it with another.

If you are a Christian, God expects you to produce a certain kind of fruit. See Galatians 5:22 - 23 for a list. This list includes kindness, goodness, patience, etc.

The plan God has for your life cannot be fulfilled if you insist on producing bad fruit. For example: jealousy, bitterness, hatefulness, gossip, distrust, cussing, getting drunk, sleeping around, disrespecting people, taking without giving, laziness, and so on.

Jesus says that those people who claim to be Christians but are false will come to him one day and want to be recognized and included in him. But it will be too late.

DAY ONE HUNDRED & NINETY-THREE

What is wisdom?
Proverbs 8

The ways God designed people to live is the essence of wisdom. The Bible is full of references to wisdom (219, according to Bible Gateway) as well as contrasts between the wise and foolish person.

In Proverbs 8, wisdom is said to dwell with prudence and possess knowledge and discretion (8:12). She hates pride and arrogance, evil behavior and perverse speech (8:13). She has insight and power (8:14). Anyone who seeks her finds her, and they find riches, honor, and enduring wealth and prosperity (8:17 - 18).

Wisdom is timeless and was created by God before there was an earth, people, or anything. She accompanied God as he created everything. "I was there when he set the heavens in place, when he marked out the horizon on the face of the deep" (8:22 - 31).

God promises wisdom to anyone who seeks it as stated in James 1:5, "If any of you lacks wisdom, you should ask God, who gives generously to all without finding fault, and it will be given to you."

You don't need to be smart or particularly gifted to be wise. It starts with an attitude of humility and willingness to be taught and grows through perseverance. Don't stop seeking and doing the right thing day in and day out. One day you will realize that you are a wise person.

It's interesting that the Bible gives wisdom a female personification. Just a note for those who think God discriminates against women.

Who do you consider wise? Are you wise?

DAY ONE HUNDRED & NINETY-FOUR

Building capacity in kids
Deuteronomy 11:19, Proverbs 22:6

Capacity is built by exposure, training, and practice. Children and adults must be exposed to opportunities that build skill and confidence. Scouting is designed to do these things. Work in a family business, whether it be retail, farming, insurance, or manufacturing gives kids a challenge that leads to confidence in their abilities.

The human brain is like a computer. It can and will be programmed. Children are like blank slates seeking to be filled. Someone or something will do the programming. The Proverb encourages you to start children off on the way they should go. Deuteronomy 11 speaks of weaving conversations about the truth, principles, and how to live into every aspect of life from an early age.

Successful young adults are not the product of wealth or of special favors but of attitudes given to them from birth in the home and to some extent their community. Dependent, defeated people will raise the same kind of person. Hopeful, confident, interdependent people raise children with those attitudes.

It's never too late to start raising yourself or your children with hope and skills building. Read a Proverb a day. Believe that you have a gift and role to play.

DAY ONE HUNDRED & NINETY-FIVE

Christians are united as one people by God
Genesis 11, Acts 2

Following the flood, Noah's sons Shem, Ham, and Japheth reproduced and repopulated the earth. "Now the whole world had one language and a common speech. As people moved eastward, they found a plain in Shinar and settled there. They said to each other, "Come, let's make bricks and bake them thoroughly."

They used brick instead of stone, and tar for mortar. Then they said, "Come, let us build ourselves a city, with a tower that reaches to the heavens, so that we may make a name for ourselves; otherwise we will be scattered over the face of the whole earth" (Genesis 11: 1-4).

The bricks and tar along with building a "tower to the heavens" represent pride among humankind, the same pride that led to rebellion and the fall of Lucifer.

"The Lord said, "If as one people speaking the same language they have begun to do this, then nothing they plan to do will be impossible for them. Come, let us go down and confuse their language so they will not understand each other." So the Lord scattered them from there over all the earth, and they stopped building the city" (Genesis 11: 5 – 8).

All of the world's people groups develop from this scattering of Noah's children's children. Only on God's terms could humanity be one, a united people. The prophet Joel prophesied that God would pour out his Spirit on all people (Joel 2:28). Then somewhere between 500 and 900 years later, Immanuel - Jesus Christ, the Son of God arrives. Immanuel means "God with us." Jesus demonstrates to mankind the meaning of God's desire for fellowship.

Jesus dealt with the problem of sin via the cross. His sacrifice made fellowship with God possible again. Jesus' death expands the "borders" of God's people. God chose the Jews, or sons of Shem, to bring forth Immanuel, the Messiah. After Jesus entered the world, shared God's message, and died on that cross for all sins, there was no longer a need to limit membership into God's family.

The Day of Pentecost was a dramatic revelation of God's desire to end the division created by the Tower of Babel (Acts 2:17-21).

DAY ONE HUNDRED & NINETY-SIX

Wise, foolish, and evil people
Proverbs 2:11-15

In his book, *Necessary Endings*, Dr. Henry Cloud says there are three kinds of people: wise, foolish, and evil. Each must be handled differently.

Wise people are those you want to hang around. They are people open to feedback who care when you tell them something has hurt you. They say, "I'm sorry. I don't want to hurt you." They want to learn how to do things right and do not reject instruction. Read Proverbs 8 for more on wise people. Talk directly to wise people about issues and concerns.

According to the NIV Life Application Study Bible 1991 edition, the foolish are not stupid. They do not know the difference between good and bad or right from wrong. They are often sincere, but sincerely wrong. Be patient with foolish people and be a friend. Avoid going into business with or marrying foolish people.

Foolish people are child-like, only caring about themselves when you boil it all down. They may be very nice, smart, beautiful and even seemingly concerned about doing the right thing. But they usually have an excuse for not changing behavior or following through in the end. They say things like, "It's not my fault. You're the one who…" They talk about what they will do later or tomorrow. They take silly risks, hold poor attitudes, and don't think God's principles apply to them.

Evil people want to do you and others harm. The reasons are not relevant. Most evil people did in fact endure some past abuse, but that should not be a reason for you to allow them to hurt you or others. At the first sign you are involved with an evil person, take action to get away from them. Delete them from your contacts. Move away if necessary. Break up with them. Get them out of your business. If things escalate and they don't lose interest and move on from making your life difficult, get a lawyer or call the police. Seriously, don't risk your life or even waste any time attempting to reason with or be friends with people who have tried to harm you either physically or by way of reputation and harassment.

DAY ONE HUNDRED & NINETY-SEVEN

A time for everything
Ecclesiastes 3

Even by today's measures, Solomon is considered the richest, wisest man to ever live. He was King of Israel from roughly 971 BC to 931 BC. His father was King David, born around 1040 BC. David was King of Israel for 40 years. Ecclesiastes is Solomon's summary of his search for meaning in life.

He spared no cost in the quest for wisdom, pleasure, accomplishment, and relationship. He realized that all people, regardless of intelligence or wealth, die. He found that pursuit of the "good things" in life become meaningless in light of death.

Solomon acknowledged that there is a time for everything. His famous list is found in chapter 3 of Ecclesiastes - a time for life, death, planting, uprooting, peace, war, weeping, laughing, and so on.

Underlying this understanding of life's natural yin and yang, he saw God's sovereignty. He realized that only when humans submit to God's timing and seek God for all meaning will they find what is ultimately the sweetest gift in anyone's life, and that is peace that comes from knowing, trusting, and obeying God.

How do you feel about endings? Some people cringe at the thought of a relationship, job, or phase in life ending. Endings are necessary for beginnings. Even if something ends in failure, this too is part of life. Every successful person will tell you that they have failed many times. The only thing that makes failure permanent is if you don't get back up and try something new or the task again.

Accept that there is a time for everything in some form or measure. Acknowledge that the human experience and inherent nature of people is not evolving or changing. Culture and conditions may change but not people. Scientific research, study of history, and human observation allows you to see God's design and work.

Don't be afraid of endings or beginnings. Work on assessing situations to determine when something needs to end or continue. The Holy Spirit will lead you in every detail of life, if you will ask.

DAY ONE HUNDRED & NINETY-EIGHT

Obedience and blessing
Deuteronomy 8

Does God have a right to tell you what to do?

This is a fundamental question to determine whether or not you will live the Christian life. If no one, not even God, is going to tell you what to do then you are wasting your time with Christianity. The book of Deuteronomy is full of inspiring and difficult words from God.

Deuteronomy is documentation of God's Word given through Moses to the children of the Israelites. Their parents were the ones that God brought out of Egypt. However, disbelief and disobedience led to God making them wander around in the desert for 40 years to be tested and humbled.

Moses speaks to these now adult children of the Exodus as they stand at the River Jordan looking toward the Promised Land, a whole generation that has never known a homeland or a stationary home. They are sojourners, homeless drifters, but they are about to move into the equivalent of the best neighborhood and the fanciest house.

Think of this context as you read chapter eight fully.

In 8:3 Moses says, "He humbled you, causing you to hunger and then feeding you with manna, which neither you nor your ancestors had known, to teach you that man does not live on bread alone but on every word that comes from the mouth of the Lord." Jesus quoted this verse to Satan in Matthew 4:4.

It is a reminder that God's blessings are not intended simply to satisfy your desires.

He goes on to remind them that their clothes did not wear out nor did their feet swell during the forty years (8:4). God disciplines you like a good father (8:5). You must obey and revere God (8:6). He's about to give you everything you've ever wished for and so much more. Don't mess this up (8:6-7).

Those same words are for you. Whatever long wait or discipline you've endured will have an end, if you get yourself right with God. He can't give you the big stuff until you are ready, or it will just ruin you.

The NIV Life Application Study Bible 1991 edition lays out the anatomy of obedience to God:

Heart	Loving God more than any relationship, activity, achievement, or possession
Will	Commit completely to him
Body	Strengths, talent, and sexuality are God-given to be used for pleasure and fulfillment according to his rules, not yours
Finances	All resources come from God, you manage them for him
Future	Make service to God and people the main purpose of your life

DAY ONE HUNDRED & NINETY-NINE

Prayer, meditation, study
Mark 1:35, Luke 5:16, Luke 18:1-3

To live your life to the fullest extent you must develop a relationship with God and understanding of his ways. This is a definitive. Everything else in the world defies an absolute, unwavering formula. But with God, prayer, meditation, and study of the Bible are key.

Prayer (talking to God), meditation (listening for God), and study (reading the Bible for context and understanding) are three vital steps to having everything God promises his people.

If you will daily pray, meditate, and study, God will lead you and intervene in your life. He has a plan for you devised before you were born. Your choices can delay or alter that plan. Even if you get off track, misunderstand, or disobey he will still work all things together for your good (Romans 8:28).

Unless you are praying, meditating, and studying, you will get scared and confused or arrogant and forgetful at times. Stick with the formula, and you won't get too far off track.

Ultimately, you must trust God's direction, which he will reveal. It may not be what you planned on the timeline you devised. Pray.

When and where can you daily pray, meditate, and study? Start with a non-negotiable 15 minutes every single morning.

DAY TWO HUNDRED

God will not withhold anything you need to live for him
Romans 8:31-34

God will not withhold anything I need to live for him. Make this your mantra. When things get tough, say it out loud.

Paul writes, "If God is for us, who can be against us? He who did not spare his own Son, but gave him up for us all—how will he not also, along with him, graciously give us all things" (Romans 8:31 - 32)?

This is very hard to believe every day, no matter what.

Our wants often exceed our needs. You wanted that and God provided this. Disappointment sets in and can turn to despair, if you do not have God's promises memorized. Go to his word daily, to him in prayer.

Say this out loud: My Lord will not withhold anything I need to live for him.

DAY TWO HUNDRED & ONE

Your "flesh" will never be satisfied
Ephesians 5:8-21

You cannot overcome desires that get you off-track or in trouble. It may be a desire for a man's attention, to buy things, to get high, to relax, to be popular, to be successful. There are so many facets of the human heart that can turn into a troublesome area.

Remember that all sin is something good gone wrong or in excess. God created everything for good, but the enemy wants to disfigure and destroy it.

Jesus came as your solution to overcome whatever you face. He steps in for you, but you must ask. It's not a onetime thing for most. You've got to go to him day after day like a drink of water. This is what he meant when he said, "Let anyone who is thirsty come to me and drink" (John 7:37). You can't live, i.e., thrive, without water. We are all thirsty because deep down we know it's just not possible to thrive on our own.

Paul says, "For you were once darkness, but now you are light in the Lord. Live as children of light" (5:9).

Children of the light are careful about how they live. They make the most of every opportunity. They are wise not foolish. And you know how the foolish live. They are those getting drunk and high, experimenting with sex, wasting time, gossiping, disrespecting parents and teachers, demanding others worship them, etc.

Imagine how you would like your life to look five years from now. What you are doing with your life now is a predictor of what you will be doing in five years.

DAY TWO HUNDRED & TWO

Surprises
Revelation 1:7-8

A "black swan" is a person, movement, event that is unexpected, has a major impact, and is usually rationalized or downplayed with hindsight.

After all, who believes in black swans. Most people would say that swans are white, but black swans, while rare, exist. The first documented black swan sighting was in Western Australia by a Dutch researcher in 1650. John Stuart Mill, a British philosopher and economist living in the 1800s, coined what has become known as "black swan theory" or "black swan events" within his writings on logical fallacy.

Our expectations are often for much less than is possible. Many sell themselves short because to believe in the miraculous is just too risky.

Jesus Christ is the embodiment of a black swan event. He is so much more than anyone every expected. Jesus defied expectations throughout his life and continues to do so today in the hearts and lives of children and adults worldwide.

When he traveled for that short three years about Judea, people expected healing. He forgave sins. Fishermen expected to catch fish, but they encountered the Messiah (Luke 5: 1 - 11). A widow expected to bury her son. Jesus restored his life (Luke 7: 11 - 17). The disciples expected to send the crowds home to eat. Jesus fed 5,000 with a few fish and loaves (John 6: 1 - 15).

The people wanted a political leader to overthrow Rome. Jesus offered an eternal kingdom and ability to overcome the control of sin and death. Leaders and other educated, important people felt threatened by Jesus. They crucified him because he didn't look or talk like a messiah.

He rose again three days later and lives still today (John 20: 1 - 29).

DAY TWO HUNDRED & THREE

Bringing God a broken spirit
Psalm 51:10 - 12,17

Broken or "broke" has a bad connotation. People are broken by addictions. An empty bank account represents a "broke" person or family. At some time in life you will be broken. It will represent the beginning of a new phase of growth or descent into sadness. You get to choose.

God accepts the broken spirit as a sacrifice. Offering it to him with request for renewal is the first step toward the healing and ultimate growth.

Read the words of King David in Psalm 51 as a model for how to cope with the brokenness life brings. Remember he spent many years in hiding and running from someone who hated him for no reason other than he was loved by people and chosen by God. David knew something about a broken spirit and heart as well as loneliness.

Don't keep your brokenness to yourself or turn it into hate toward others. Share it with the Lord. He will take it away and in return give you a new hope.

DAY TWO HUNDRED & FOUR

The command to love
John 15:17

Jesus told his disciples to love each other. His command is for us as well.

He didn't mean you should send your mother a Valentine card or text a friend periodically or feel romantically toward your husband. He meant love as in an action that requires something.

Love is a verb.

This command from Jesus is in the context of him telling the disciples that he's going to leave them, and life is going to get very harsh. He knows that unless they remain tight knit and in relationship, they'll never make it through the coming persecution.

Life is about relationship and relating. Love is the currency that makes it work.

When Jesus commands you to love, he means to listen, help, encourage, and give to those you've chosen to have in your life and those he chose for you.

You will not give love in the same way to all people. The resources (time, money, relationship) you give to your child or a parent are very different than those you give to the hurting stranger you meet on the subway or the "loner" kid at school.

Yet the command remains - Love one another.

Jesus expects you to give and then give even more because the world will never have enough love to go around to meet all the needs. Many people will look to receive but never give love.

How can you love by listening, encouraging, helping, or giving today?

DAY TWO HUNDRED & FIVE

God's view of life
Genesis 9:1-7

Prior to the flood, God handled everything for his creation. He filled the roles of Sheriff, judge, CEO, and pretty much all other executive leadership roles.

When the flood waters receded, God had a meeting with Noah and his family. He blessed them and initiated a new covenant with mankind. Noah and his family marked the beginning of a major job promotion for humans.

God said something like this, "You all need to go forth and repopulate the earth. I'm going to make you above every other living creature - beasts, birds, lizards, fish, everything. All orders of life beneath you, ,i.e., non-human is now yours to steward. Develop and care for them well or you won't survive."

But as in Eden, God made blood off limits for consuming. He emphasized blood because it represents life. He instituted the practice of removing the blood of an animal before eating it.

God also placed a very high value on human life, making it clear that murder is wrong. "I will demand an accounting for the life of another human being. Whoever sheds human blood, by humans shall their blood be shed; for in the image of God has God made mankind" (Genesis 9: 5 - 6).

God values all human life born, unborn, strong or weak, rich or poor, any color or nationality.

DAY TWO HUNDRED & SIX

If it's worthwhile, it will be hard
Nehemiah 1:1-11

Nehemiah was charged with rebuilding the wall in Jerusalem. In 445 B.C., it took Nehemiah and his men 52 days to complete the entire construction project. If you get serious about fulfilling whatever plan God has given you, learning to resist detractors is vital to success.

Just like Nehemiah, you will encounter people that do not want you to finish your project or stay focused on school, children, husband, job, etc. They often offer very reasonable and appealing reasons for why you should stop.

When the lure of fun or belonging does not work on you, some will resort to threats such as "It seems you don't really care about our group," or "People are saying you...," or "If you don't..."

Nehemiah told those who wanted to intimidate him to stop the wall project, "Nothing like what you are saying is happening; you are just making it up out of your head"(Nehemiah 6:8).

The courage to speak that kind of truth to people that can ruin you socially or professionally comes only when you are walking close to God and know that you know what he's asked of you.

Everything that really matters to God and to the fulfillment of his plan for your life will require very hard work. It will demand that you keep going in the face of disappointment, set-backs, people who are jealous or don't understand, and more.

You will have to make choices in the now that impact the distant future. Many of those choices seem insignificant, but in total they will add up to your character and the outcomes of your life. Will you study or go out, be with your children or accept one more volunteer position, spend money on that thing now or save for the bigger thing.

Nehemiah had to get the wall built. That was God's call for him. He filtered everything through that goal. What wall has God called you to stay on until it is finished?

*Consider reading Nehemiah chapters 1 - 6.

DAY TWO HUNDRED & SEVEN

You were born this way, but staying this way is a choice
Ephesians 2:1-10

Have you ever said someone was "just born that way," or "a natural born (fill in the blank)?"

You were born with a desire to have whatever you want without concern for others. It is natural for you to never be satisfied, to overindulge, to hurt others in a quest to satisfy whatever catches your eye.

If you are not trained to deny yourself and to consider others, you won't change much over time. Your character - how you treat yourself and others - is the result of how you deal with your natural self.

When you encounter someone who was never denied their whims as a child and over indulged, they will hurt you eventually. They might seem very fun and whimsical but sooner or later you won't do or be what they want in the moment. This is when things get tricky.

If you are someone "made alive with Christ," as Paul says in Ephesians 2:1, God will allow you to feel the hurt of those who are selfish. He will then urge you to reflect on that feeling. You will not want to do this to someone else. Also, you will see that it is wrong to allow yourself to be mistreated.

This natural born selfishness is why we need a Savior. Christ was the only perfect human and God. He traded his physical life in the great exchange so you might have access to his perfection. Over time he helps you overcome childish, sinful ways, if you will allow him to help you.

Changing from being a selfish, all-about-me person is a choice. It's very, very hard. You must be committed. Welcome those times when through the mistreatment of others, you see the truth about yourself.

DAY TWO HUNDRED & EIGHT

Learn to use God's weapons
Psalm 37

Everyone has problems, disappointments, failure, and enemies. When you focus on any of them you will become anxious and angry. Psalm 37 is designed to encourage you to use God's weapons to combat all the evil that will come at you in life.

These are God's weapons for you:

- Do not fret over those who are evil
- Do not envy those who do wrong
- Trust in God
- Do good
- Take delight in God
- Commit your ways to God
- Be still before God
- Turn from evil
- Hope in God
- Claim the authority of Jesus
- Speak His words to yourself and others

In return, God will give you the desires of your heart that are best for you, a future, including forever with him.

He will vindicate and reward you, give you a place to live, make your steps firm, and not leave you under the power of wicked.

What if you laid down the emotions and behaviors of human nature and the world that lead to frustration - worry, revenge, anger, etc. - and simply trusted in the power God offers freely and then trusted he would reward as promised?

DAY TWO HUNDRED & NINE

True love
1 Corinthians 13:1-7

If you think about it, there's nothing you want more than love.

Jesus is the embodiment of love. The Gospels chronicle God walking among people, fully human and fully God. He modeled to us what it means to love a friend, a parent, husband/boyfriend, fellowman.

A list of those who you feel love you would include people you feel accept you. In spite of all your faults and imperfections, they stick around and engage with you.

Therefore, love is action first and foremost. It requires something of you. The Apostle Paul says that it requires everything of you. He says that even if he had every spiritual gift and gave all his possessions without love, "I am nothing" (13:2).

Here's his love checklist:

- Love is patient and kind
- Love does not envy, brag or indulge in arrogance
- Love honors others instead of seeking honor
- Love is slow to anger and keeps no record of offenses
- Love hates evil and always looks for the truth
- Love protects, trusts, hopes, and does not give up when things look bad

Who do you love? Who loves you?

DAY TWO HUNDRED & TEN

Faith, hope, and love
1 Corinthians 13:8-13

Love conquers all, so the saying goes. Love does overcome much when understood through God's eyes. Love strips away anything selfish by becoming a verb. Love costs. It sees past bad attitudes, habits, and even hate, yet it never condones or encourages those things. Love places every outcome in God's hands.

In 1 Corinthians 13:8, the Apostle Paul says, "Love never fails." He does not mean that acting in love nothing will ever go wrong or that relationships won't end.

If you love in the active sense described in verses 1 - 7 and offer God unselfish service, love never fails. Love is not part of an equation that has a right or wrong answer. Love is a sum total in and of itself.

When acting in love you are the closest to experiencing God that is possible on earth. This is why giving gifts or giving of yourself in service to others feels so very good. Love and that special feeling it brings is why we give gifts at Christmas and other holidays.

In 13:12, Paul says, "For now we see only a reflection as in a mirror; then we shall see face to face. Now I know in part; then I shall know fully, even as I am fully known."

Love enables us to know God, yet only as a reflection.

Paul sums up in 13:13 with "And now these three remain: faith, hope and love. But the greatest of these is love."

Your faith, based on God's Word and help from the Holy Spirit, enables you to search for God's reflection. Your hope is the attitude required to believe. With faith and hope you can love. It is a choice manifested by thoughts, words, and actions.

List three love actions you can take today.

DAY TWO HUNDRED & ELEVEN

From thoughts to destiny
Genesis 37 & 45

You can't underestimate the power of your thoughts. What you are thinking right now correlates to your destiny. You may already be living out a destiny that you can trace back to thoughts, for better or worse.

Many verses from both the Old and New Testament tell us this: Thoughts lead to action. Actions lead to habits. Habits result in character. Your character sets your destiny.

You can control what you think. You can choose how you interpret life's situations.

A guy breaks up with you. Thought: Thank you, God for ending that sooner than later. I know you have a better relationship for me.

You get fired. Thought: God, help me to see where I need to improve. Thank you for closing that door and please help me prepare for the next one you will open.

The test results are not so good. Thought: God, help me to do better next time or work this out for my best.

Notice the difference in attitude toward outcomes. The thoughts that lead to growth and a better destiny are rooted in giving thanks to God for all things, owning up to the facts, and believing things will get better.

God has given you this amazing superpower. It is an ability to choose your thoughts no matter what the circumstances. When you think hopeful, positive, loving thoughts it's like opening a secret door. You get results that often seem impossible from a distance.

He's always nudging you toward the secret door because on the other side of that door you become the person of character he intended. He won't force you there. The power only works when freely taken. No one can take it for you. Sometimes it is only in pain, at the end of your "rope" that you see an alternative way of thinking.

Have you experimented with your superpowers – ability to choose your thoughts?

DAY TWO HUNDRED & TWELVE

Guard your heart, you will follow it anywhere
Proverbs 4:23

As a blessed people, we've come to expect upward spiraling lives. You will get a degree, great job, perfect husband, two lovely kids, a bigger house every few years as well as car. There will be promotions and accolades for service. You will take trips abroad, do weekenders with insanely fun friends.

This may not be your personal map of success but many of us have an idea or goal for some level of greatness. All of those things are good, and God does want to give you the desires of your heart.

Proverb 4:23 says, "Above all else, guard your heart, for everything you do flows from it."

"Heart" connotes what you love and desire. You follow your heart. You make time to pursue what you love. God wants you to love him and his word. If you seek after him, he will give you the desires of your heart (Psalm 37:4).

You can get fixated on wanting something good, like a husband or a personal achievement. The desire and pursuit come to define you, making you unhappy during the wait. You chase after every possible angle in hopes of getting it. You pray. You cry. You mope. You get heart sick, which can lead to physical sickness.

Beware of this path. God is unmoved by a desperately yearning heart for anything other than him. You should have dreams and goals, but pray for them like this:

"Dear God, I want your will for my life and to use my abilities and gifts for you. I want _____. If it's in your plan, show me how to get it."

What do you yearn for the most?

DAY TWO HUNDRED & THIRTEEN

Is your prayer for forgiveness of sin or forgiveness from consequences?
Job 4 - 5

Our most heartfelt prayer often comes when the consequences of bad choices catch up with us. It is not wrong to pray that God will lighten or even lift consequences. In his mercy, he often enables us to live with or through hard situations that may or may not have been our fault.

Do not go to God in prayer with fake repentance of sin. To repent means to turn around or away from the sin. Consequences may remain and usually involve broken trust, owing money, extra responsibility, overcoming guilt, loneliness, ridicule, etc.

If you pray for forgiveness, God will forgive, and he will make a way for you to live with the consequences. In his mercy, he often will turn the consequences into a blessing for you and others. The key to restoration of closeness with God, others, and even within your own heart is the commitment to turning away from the tendency to repeat the wrong again, and again, and again.

DAY TWO HUNDRED & FOURTEEN

Dealing with difficult people in touchy situations
2 Corinthians 13:7-10

"Be careful not to win the battle but lose the war," is a common saying. With trying situations, it's easy to focus on winning in the moment but at the cost of relationship with the people, i.e., losing the war.

Even in the best relationships, tough situations will arise. The Apostle Paul is our worldly role model for dealing with people and situations with love. He teaches us that the loving action is to confront the issues with the right people and in the proper manner. The three most common approaches are the wrong way to handle people and situations.

- A legalistic, condemning approach pointing to laws and consequences
- Gossiping about the person(s) and isolating them from the group
- Writing them off all together

The best approach, which takes time and courage, is to speak to the individual(s) about the problem or issue. It's also important to take actions that limit damage the person can do to themselves and others. Ultimately, the key is going to God for wisdom and direction. Ask him to do the fighting and to give you the courage to take the steps he gives you.

American President Ronald Reagan illustrated how to properly deal with problems on a big scale when he ended the Cold War without ever firing a shot at the Russians. He didn't fear or coddle them. He stated the evils of communism. He called out, "Mr. Gorbachev, tear down this wall."

All the while he was employing enormous diplomatic resources, building up the U.S. military, and keeping economic pressure on the Russians. During this time, he was also building a personal relationship with Mr. Gorbachev.

It's much harder, riskier, and time consuming to deal with people in a Christlike way. Yet to simply meet aggression with aggression or ignore bad behavior, only prolongs the problem and the pain.

Where do you need to take the time to call out wrong in a loving way?

DAY TWO HUNDRED & FIFTEEN

Living a salt life
Matthew 5:13, Leviticus 2:13

Salt is almost magical. We can't live without it, but too much will harm us. "Salt Life" is a term seen pasted on the vehicles of those who enjoy the ocean. Salt is referenced in many ways throughout the Bible in both literal and figurative terms.

Most notably when Jesus said in Matthew 5:13, "You are the salt of the earth. But if the salt loses its saltiness, how can it be made salty again? It is no longer good for anything, except to be thrown out and trampled underfoot."

In the Old Testament, God makes a "salt covenant" with the people and requires salt be added to all their offerings.

Seasoning the offerings with salt and becoming like salt in the way Jesus references were both symbolic of God in a person's life. Like salt, God permeates, preserves, and aids in healing.

God wants to be like salt in your life, and he wants you to be like salt in the lives of others.

Remember, too much salt ruins the dish. It takes just the right amount of seasoning, based on the type of food and method of cooking to flavor something properly.

Whose life can you salt?

DAY TWO HUNDRED & SIXTEEN

A light in the world
Proverbs 20:27, Matthew 5:13

Imagine a world, a life without light. In darkness, you could not see those you love, read, work, plant, drive, or go about in any way. Light versus darkness is used throughout the Bible to illustrate the presence or absence of God.

Proverbs 20:27 explains how God placed his Spirit in all humans. We are distinguished from other forms of life by having this element of God. It gives us the ability to reason and have a conscience. His Spirit in us is like a lamp illuminating our soul or inner being.

This analogy is carried by Jesus into the Sermon on the Mount. "You are the light of the world," he says (Matthew 5:13). For now, the world needs the sun and the moon as well as you to contrast the darkness with light. One day history will end, and God promises a new earth where "the glory of God gives it light, and the Lamb is its lamp" (Revelation 21:23).

Keep your light burning always.

DAY TWO HUNDRED & SEVENTEEN

You must own your faith
John 3:1-21

Statistics show that most people who identify as Christians say they joined the church, got baptized, or were "saved" before the age of 13. These actions do not necessarily equate to responding to the urging of God – Father, Son, and Holy Spirit – to enter your heart and life.

Salvation (becoming one of God's children for eternity) happens only when you are invited by God's Spirit and you accept that invitation.

Young people often sense that God is real and believe that what is taught from the Bible is true. They also often simply follow what others are doing or want to do what they are told. Unless they received and accepted God's invitation, they won't continue on a path of owning their faith because it will be too hard to wrestle with the questions and resist the temptations that come with growing up.

Questioning is important and often lifesaving. God is not offended or threatened by questioning and even doubts about who he is. Ask the people you encounter that claim to be Christians questions. Don't be afraid to admit your fears, doubts, and even disbelief.

One of the ways you can evaluate a religion or philosophy is by whether it stands up to honest intellectual scrutiny or not.

Christ and his message are not a religion, and your honest inquiry will reveal this truth.

Don't take anyone's word for it. Delve in yourself. Kick the tires, look under the hood, so to speak. You won't believe it until you've done the research. You must own your faith. No one else can believe for you.

Ask God your toughest question, right now.

DAY TWO HUNDRED & EIGHTEEN

Fruit, branches, and vines in Christ
John 15:1-5

Vineyards make excellent analogies for explaining the relationship between the Christian and Christ. Only branches that are grafted firmly into the main vine and pruned early in the season and often throughout will bear real fruit.

Jesus makes clear his role, our role, and God's.

Jesus is our vine. Apart from him we can do nothing (15:5). God is the gardener who knows just how much to prune and how much to cut away in order to produce the greatest amount of fruit. Your character and willingness to be useful to God is the fruit.

It's useless for you to dread or hate the cutting and pruning process. You, like the fruit of a vineyard, can't see the harvest to come. Trust the painful pruning and cutting process. Let God shape you to become all he's planned for you.

With reliance on your place in the vine (Christ), there's nothing to fear. You get the strength to hang-on with him.

Let the pruning begin!

DAY TWO HUNDRED & NINETEEN

Sin crouching at your door
Genesis 4:1-16

Cain was the first child born to man. He killed his brother Abel out of jealousy.

God told Cain, "If you do not do what is right, sin is crouching at your door; it desires to have you, but you must rule over it" (4:7).

God corrected Cain when he chose not to bring his best offering, but gave him encouragement saying, "If you do what is right, will you not be accepted" (4:7)?

Cain chose not to listen. He took out his feelings of inadequacy on his brother. How was it easier for him to kill his brother than to take corrective instruction from God?

A hard heart will lash out when corrected; will deny correction. The only way to overcome sin crouching at your door is to keep an attitude of willingness to hear correction from friends, parents, teachers, bosses, and most of all God.

If you will come to the Lord with a humble attitude, he offers the Holy Spirit. He will help you through the lifelong battle of overcoming sin until you see Christ face-to-face.

DAY TWO HUNDRED & TWENTY

Beware of doubt, discouragement, diversion, defeat, and delay
Job 4:4-6

You have an enemy that wants to keep you from receiving everything God has planned for your life. If you can be kept bound up with the five "D's," your life will have little impact for God.

- Doubt makes you question God's Word and his love for you
- Discouragement results when you focus on your problems instead of God
- Diversions get you to think the wrong thing is better than the right things
- Defeat keeps you from trying because you feel like such a failure
- Delay prevents you from getting around to doing the important things

Which one has you right now?

*See NIV Life Application Study Bible 1991 edition page 15, "Satan's Plan."

DAY TWO HUNDRED & TWENTY-ONE

One main point to make
1 John 5:1-11

In your travels through life you will encounter hundreds of beliefs, philosophies, and superstitions. If you live as a Christian openly, you will meet others who hold many varying beliefs about the faith. You will also meet many who reject, don't believe, or don't understand Christian faith.

Some don't believe evil exists. Others are not sure if the Bible is fact or just stories. It is easy to get into theological disagreements that place a wedge between people. At root of these problems lies discomfort with being challenged, called wrong or ignorant.

When you have opportunity to probe beliefs and understanding, start with questions. There's no need to ever argue with someone about faith in Christ. Unless they ask, don't attempt to teach them theology or history.

Christ is not a religion. He offers a relationship that leads to eternal life as well as life lived to the fullest on earth.

There's only one point you need to make when the opportunity arises - Jesus lived, died, and came back to life, all to pay the way for you to live eternally with God.

Leave the rest to God. Your willingness to take a step of faith in sharing the information opens the door to all manner of encounters and understanding that God will provide.

DAY TWO HUNDRED & TWENTY-TWO

On laws
Psalm 19:6-8

Laws governing a free society are tricky. Everyone has an opinion about the veracity of each law. Often those opinions are based on personal preference.

The absence of law is anarchy. People cannot form a society without laws because even the best people will eventually do something that infringes on the property and freedom of another. Most societies throughout history, and even today, operate under a form of dictatorship or absolutes imposed by force on a people through a military.

When you hear people promote or disparage a law, enter the conversation from the standpoint of why a free society has laws, i.e., to protect people's property, rights, and freedom.

Next, it is important to understand that any law not grounded in God's basic laws given in the Ten Commandments and elevated by the teaching of Jesus will ultimately serve to diminish freedom of individuals and societies.

Jesus said, "Do not think that I have come to abolish the Law or the Prophets; I have not come to abolish them but to fulfill them" (Matthew 5:17).

Moses says to the Israelites, "See, I have taught you decrees and laws as the Lord my God commanded me, so that you may follow them in the land you are entering to take possession of it" (Deuteronomy 4:5).

Laws governing a free people must be built from a foundational understanding of justice and liberty as defined by God. With this basis, men and women elected by and accountable to the people who will live under the laws will be able to make rules and laws that help hold society together within any given historical context.

Think about laws being made today. Are they just and wise?

DAY TWO HUNDRED & TWENTY-THREE

Only you are accountable to your conscience
John 3:27

You are not responsible for the conscience of anyone else. Isn't that freeing?

"If you are led by the Sprit, you are not under law" (Galatians 5:18).

Paul refers to the qualities of character and behaviors that a person led by the Holy Spirit pursues. It is not a law to love, express joy or self-control, to avoid hatred or sexual immorality. People from different faith traditions within Christianity or altogether different religions may believe various things about what to eat and wear or interpretations of the Bible.

If you are led by the Spirit and have studied Christ's teachings, your conscience will guide you away from vices and toward virtues. The Spirit may give you an awareness that certain things are not acceptable for you to do or say. As you get closer to Christ and the Spirit, you will understand more about God and his plan for your life.

Don't expect others, even your friends and family, to have the same awareness as you. He may not touch the conscience of someone else in the same way.

Unnecessary barriers or judgment between people often arise because of differences in what they each feel led to think or do (or not think or do). This is tricky because you often either conform to them or try to get them to conform to you.

If you feel led to avoid certain situations or things, God expects you to obey. Your friends may or may not understand.

DAY TWO HUNDRED & TWENTY-FOUR

Great difficulty is the door to greatness
Proverb 16:18

You will have difficulties to bear. In fact, the bigger your personal difficulty, the greater God's plan for shaping your character.

Anyone who has achieved any form of success or greatness spent years working hard and overcoming something. Endurance is part of every path to getting better.

James Madison, the fourth American President and "Father of the Constitution," suffered from some form of epilepsy. He was a small and very sensitive man. As a Christian in the 1700s, he would have read the stories of Jesus healing children described as lunatics and possessed due to the same symptoms he likely suffered. That, coupled with teachings of the time that interpreted such afflictions as incurable and the result perhaps of some wrong or weakness of spirit, even a punishment, made him doubt his future opportunity.

Madison came out of college at Princeton so weak and sickly that he believed there was little future for himself. In spite of his frailties, a lack of real treatment, and even misunderstood teachings, Madison prevailed, and his life is a testament to what happens when people who won't give up intersect with a sovereign God.

He married the buoyant Dolly Payne Todd from North Carolina. She was outgoing and loved by Americans for opening the White House to a wide cross section of people through her many events. She complemented him and together they made a mark on society as he served two terms as President (1809 - 1817). He studied and practiced the arts of good manners, listening, and diplomatic exchange that enabled him to accomplish so much in one of the most pivotal times in history.

Those who cannot accept that God is in control and that Christianity is a way of life not a religion, scoff at Christians as unintelligent and superstitious.

How could people like James Madison and even wise people today believe that Jesus miraculously healed a boy with epilepsy or that people were in various ways possessed by demonic forces?

They accept that to live in this world and under the authority of a sovereign God involves tension. They cannot and will not understand everything. They do not reason away obstacles and hardship. On a deep level they understand that the brilliant person with power who does not also suffer in some way would become rotten with pride.

Pride is the source of every fall. It is a false belief that you have the looks, money, popularity, and intelligence to do anything you want without God. Thank God for your "thorn" or stumbling blocks. Without them you would be useless and intolerable.

DAY TWO HUNDRED & TWENTY-FIVE

Working like it's all up to you while trusting like it's all up to God
Proverbs 16:3

Proverbs 16:3 says, "Commit to the Lord whatever you do, and your plans will succeed."

A simple statement, but hard to live by. There is a balance to living for God and committing all you do to him. This balance looks much like a person walking a tight wire while holding a long pole. It requires focus, knowing when to slow down and when to speed up, and keeping the weight of the pole evenly distributed at all times.

Committing your plans to God requires turning complete control over to him. Your human tendency is to either give him only superficial or temporary control. Succeeding in a plan will require work on your part, but it is not all up to you. Trusting God's subtle cues and following his known commands are critical.

You can't break God's law and expect to succeed. You can't refuse to do your part or give up and expect to succeed.

Many plans take years and years to come to fruition. You will get tired, confused, and distracted along the way. Write your goals for the plan down and go back to them often. Pray for God's daily intervention and guidance in your life. Be careful about taking steps that deviate from the path leading to your goal. Don't give up the path, unless you are sure God has redirected you.

Any plan God has led you to undertake will succeed in his time and on his terms. Trust him, even when you are unsure – especially when you are unsure.

DAY TWO HUNDRED & TWENTY-SIX

People have not changed nor has God
Leviticus 26:40-46, Jeremiah 29:10-14

Have you ever done something in spite of warnings about the harm and consequences?

Much of the Old Testament is one repeating story of God giving people a lot with a few requirements, the people forgetting the requirements and becoming prideful, God humbling them and then restoring them. This cycle reaches a crescendo with God coming to earth in the form of a Savior - Jesus Christ. God sent Jesus and his Holy Spirit to make the requirements for his gift of eternal life even easier.

People have not changed. We still become prideful and God still humbles us, but we live under the new covenant. God and forgiveness are accessible through our hearts. We never need a human intermediary or a live sacrifice. "It is finished," as Christ said on the cross (John 19:30).

The stories of men and women's lives, the failure followed by redemption, and the many signs pointing toward the arrival of Christ make the Old Testament critical to a full, contextual understanding of God.

Thousands of years ago and still today, God's purpose is not to destroy you. His desire is to help you use time on earth to grow in character and understanding of his purposes. He has a plan for you that is unique; a purpose carved out for you alone. There will be hardships and loss. You will experience correction from God when you go astray. He may even allow severe consequences to occur as the result of your decisions or as the result of evil in the world.

As Winston Churchill said, ""Never give in--never, never, never, never, in nothing great or small, large or petty, never give in except to convictions of honor and good sense. Never yield to force; never yield to the apparently overwhelming might of the enemy."

DAY TWO HUNDRED & TWENTY-SEVEN

Answer me when I call to you
Psalm 4:3

God sets apart the godly for himself and hears when they call (Psalm 4:3). You are "godly" if Christ is your acknowledged savior. When you need God's answers to prayer most, it is often when you feel the least godly.

Don't ever doubt God's love for you and that he can hear your prayer. Patience and perseverance are often required to see the answer fulfilled completely.

King David prayed fervently to God because he was often in great danger and facing enormous personal problems. His prayers always praise God and acknowledge his love for and trust in God.

"Look at your problems in the light of God's power instead of looking at God in the shadow of your problems" (NIV Life Application Study Bible 1991 edition notes page 1086).

DAY TWO HUNDRED & TWENTY-EIGHT

Acting like you believe
John 4:46-54

Saying you believe in Christ is a simple first step. Acting like you believe leads to the kind of faith that becomes a witness to others. Faith is like a muscle. The more you use it, the bigger it gets.

A royal official walked 20 miles to find Jesus because his son was near death. He said, "Sir, come down before my child dies" (John 4:49). This man was desperate.

Jesus told him to go home and find his son well. The Scripture says, "The man took Jesus at his word and departed" (John 4:50). His servants met him on the road to report that the boy was alive and well. When the official inquired about the time of his recovery, he found it to be the same time he spoke to Jesus the day before.

This man, who held a societal position far above Jesus, first sought the person called the Messiah out of a "nothing left to lose" place.

The next step was a much bigger leap of faith. He left Jesus to go home based on his word versus his initial mission of getting Jesus to come with him and perform a miracle. He acted like Jesus could change things with a word.

His faith proved right and it grew, and he surely told many others about what had occurred.

You can't have what Jesus offers until you begin acting like you believe.

Until you experience his power and presence in your life, you can't tell others a personal story. This is a vital concept to understand. You will only parrot what others say or half-heartedly believe before you have a first-person experience with Christ and a unique story of your own to tell.

Will you seek Christ and then act like he's capable of taking care of your need long before you see the result?

DAY TWO HUNDRED & TWENTY-NINE

Waiting for God's "plans to give you hope and a future"
Jeremiah 29:9-14

Many hope for a happy and prosperous future, regardless of present situation. This hope is an element of God that resides in every human. He has a good plan for every believer during their life on earth. It prepares them for eternal life with him in heaven.

The plan will not come together without a time of waiting and doing in preparation. Sometimes things happen to derail or delay the plan. You make mistakes, natural disasters occur, wars break out, people harm you, etc.

Jeremiah 29:11 is one of the most comforting verses in the Old Testament - "'For I know the plans I have for you," declares the Lord, "plans to prosper you and not to harm you, plans to give you hope and a future.'"

The verses just before and after are rarely quoted because they are tough.

The full context of this section finds the people in captivity. They rejected God's covenant by breaking about every condition he'd given them and becoming prideful. Jeremiah is the prophet bringing them the bad news and the good news.

The bad news - they are going to be under the rule of the crazy Babylonian pagans for seventy years. A whole generation will not enjoy the land God gave them and the blessings he'd promised, if only they would honor him.

The good news - God is going to remember the covenant with their ancestors. Those were the people he brought out of Egypt and made into a nation that caused the world to revere and fear them. He's going to bring them back to prosperity one day.

God also relays that something important is going to happen in the hearts of the people in that long stretch between trouble and prosperity. "Then you will call on me and come and pray to me, and I will listen to you. You will seek me and find me when you seek me with all your heart" (29:12 - 13).

Don't despair if the future you hope for seems lost. God is always working out your plan. Your job is to seek him with your whole heart while waiting.

DAY TWO HUNDRED & THIRTY

Finding your tribe
Revelation 5

You may feel out of place or out of sync in your current family or community. Many people don't "find their tribe" until later in life. Tribes share customs, language, and beliefs. Don't despair if you have an unfulfilled yearning for others like yourself.

Those you seek are seeking you too.

The key is to keep looking without impatience. You may be tempted to disdain those in your life because they "don't get it" or try to change yourself in order to fit in with where you are right now.

God made each of us to be unique and to fulfill certain purposes. His larger purpose is to bring all of those who belong to the Lamb (Jesus) into one kingdom forever. With his blood, people "from every tribe and language and people and nation" were purchased (Revelation 5: 9 - 10).

Keep seeking your tribe and while you look enjoy those around you and pursue the interests God has placed in your heart.

DAY TWO HUNDRED & THIRTY-ONE

Loving Jesus more than myself
John 4:15

Being a Christ-follower in the world is hard and confusing. In the story of the Samaritan woman at the well, she says,"...'Sir, give me this water so that I won't get thirsty and have to keep coming here to draw water'"(John 4: 15).

She wanted Jesus to make life easier. He did not do that for her. He does not make life easier for you either. He makes life harder because he calls you to an abandonment of yourself, your desires, and even your inborn compulsions. Jesus often does not take away your challenges or the "thorn in your side."

He does empower you to deal with everything from societal issues to your personal issues through God's perspective.

You must be willing to acknowledge that without the pain of struggling and self-denial you will never gain strength and overcome the enemy's most powerful weapon.

His weapon is a twisting of the freedom for every individual that Christ brought to this world. He convinces you that it's about what feels good to you now. When this selfishness is wrapped in the cloak of "I was born this way" and planted in a morally permissive culture, you get people rationalizing all sorts of new laws and behaviors.

What "born this way" trait is your conscience and knowledge of Christ's ways urging you to overcome?

DAY TWO HUNDRED & THIRTY-TWO

Sinners and the church
1 Corinthians 5, Romans 3:21-26

The world claims there is no moral right and wrong. But as a Christian you know this is not true, yet you are called by Christ to live your life in love and truth among fellow believers as well as the world at large. The result is a temptation to skip or misinterpret parts of God's Word in order to avoid offending anyone. Romans 3: 23 - 24 says, "For all have sinned and fall short of the glory of God, and all are justified freely by his grace through the redemption that came by Christ Jesus."

Be clear on this: no one is without sin. Christ's message was simple. He came not to undo the laws of God but to strip away all the manmade complexity and burdens of animal, grain, and drink sacrifice before priests and in a temple. Through Christ you are forgiven once and for all but called to live your entire life as a living sacrifice. He is your king and priest. He gives everything and in return demands one hundred percent of your heart and mind.

So is the liar, the adulteress, the homosexual, or the murderer to be treated differently in the church? No, all are the same before God.

What is different for members of the Church is attitude toward sin and God. Anyone living in open defiance against God's Word and commands is not seeking a place in Christ's Church. Anyone actively seeking forgiveness, healing, growth can be part of Christ's Church in good standing (1 Corinthians 5).

The teaching in 1 Corinthians 5 is tough to understand from a modern perspective. Yet it is sound for a Christ-follower at any point in history. He's speaking to the Church about members of the Church openly practicing sexual immorality. "What business is it of mine to judge those outside the church? Are you not to judge those inside? God will judge those outside. Expel the wicked person from among you" (1 Corinthians 5: 12 - 13).

He's not calling for witch hunts, public humiliation, or hypocritical thinking. He's being emphatic about the need to acknowledge defiant sin among your church membership. This is an important responsibility. Look carefully at how your church leadership addresses lifestyles and behaviors among its members.

DAY TWO HUNDRED & THIRTY-THREE

Holy Spirt and self-discipline = successful people
Romans 2:6-8

You may wonder what formula successful or popular people apply to life.

Every life is unique. No two people will ever walk the same exact path. Personality, past life experience, and how a person self-evaluates determine many outcomes.

There are traits, practices, and habits to emulate for success. For example, Rules of Civility by George Washington is a book outlining practices useful even today.

Often you see only one dimension of a person, and it looks good. But there's another side that may reveal a person running on empty, tempting fate to get what they have in the moment, or miserable with the trade-offs and sacrifices made to get that public facing success.

Everything of God is simple, including the formula for success.

He doesn't promise anything will be easy, but he does not give a lot of complexity when it comes to the rules for fulfilling his unique plan for you or for just being human.

1. Take time to study God's Word and learn how the trinity of Father, Son, and Holy Spirit work
2. Commit to living a life of self-discipline. Figure out what you need to live in a disciplined way. For example, you may need a coach or accountability partner. Everyone needs a daily schedule. To be self- disciplined means that at the most basic level you can be counted on to generally do the right thing in life whether at home, school, work, church, civic, or other. Don't be a "problem child." Be a trusted contributor everywhere you go.
3. Know and trust the Holy Spirit on a moment-by-moment basis. Many of the situations you face will not be covered in the Bible or any other book. Only with an ear toward the Holy Spirit can you succeed in situations that will often make no sense.

DAY TWO HUNDRED & THIRTY-FOUR

Personal sin versus personal indulgencies
1 Corinthians 8

It is impossible to be human and not have personal indulgencies. But when do indulgencies become sin?

Paul says, "We all possess knowledge. But knowledge puffs up while love builds up. Those who think they know something do not yet know as they ought to know" (1 Corinthians 8:1-2).

In the Corinthian context, Paul is speaking of differences in individual conscience regarding food. He's clarifying that sin to one person's conscience is not so to another. There are only a few things God directly commands you to avoid.

How do you know if something is sin?

Sin is anything that rules you and makes you turn away from God. Sin is lawlessness, an absence of God. Sin literally means to miss the mark for what is God's best.

You sin daily in some form. You withhold complete obedience and love from God when you cherish some sin. Don't feel condemned or proud of this condition. As Paul urges, use your knowledge to pursue love of God and others. Don't exercise your freedom of conscience in an area that makes your friend stumble or feel uncomfortable.

DAY TWO HUNDRED & THIRTY-FIVE

Secrets and intimacy
Proverbs 17:17, Proverbs 18:24

Secrets can be the glue that makes for intimacy with a friend, husband, or parent. They can also be your downfall. God knows all your secrets. Sharing them with him builds intimacy, just like with people.

Inherent in a secret is a sense that knowing this thing about you creates vulnerability. You can reveal secrets only with those you trust. Not everyone can be trusted with your most private thoughts, heart, physical being, indulgencies, and weaknesses.

The best friend is someone who can bear up with your secrets, even when they are a reflection of something less than lovely about or in you. They can remind you to be careful or watch bad habits. They can look at your failures and weaknesses and still love and like you.

Our yearning for this intimacy and safety is a reflection of the need for a savior.

No one is without a secret. No one is without sin. Many people abandon a faith in Christ and live isolated, lonely lives because they can't accept the darkness in themselves. The result is they can't tolerate the light in others.

Don't hide behind the darkness in others or compare yourself to their darkness in order to prove that you are not so bad.

If you do this, you will become vulnerable to condemnation from within, others, or the enemy. You will end up either a hateful hypocrite or an undisciplined burden on others.

If it's hard for you to love people in spite of their failings, it could be that you are carrying around shame for things you've done and don't feel forgiven for. Don't run away from what feels like a dark place within yourself. Keep putting it in Christ's hands to help you. Allow him to forgive you, and then go on with the life he's given you.

DAY TWO HUNDRED & THIRTY-SIX

Allowing imperfection in those we love
Galatians 6:2-10

Love goes far beyond feelings. Love bears up with the hypocrisy, failure, and ugliness in me and in you. Yet love welcomes God to reshape and transform behaviors and attitudes that limit a person.

Paul tells us to "carry each other's burdens" and our own (6:2,5).

You must allow yourself to be less than perfect yet still okay, still lovable. Then you can allow this in others. Refusing to allow yourself or others to be "okay" while still needing improvement eliminates the chance for intimate friendship and mutual submission.

If you can't look at your own darkness and failure, when others make themselves vulnerable to you, all you will be able to see is weakness. You will take advantage of them or run away from them.

Intimate relationships are a symbolic reflection of what the Lord wants to have with you. You must come as you are, as just human, with both darkness and light in your heart. You need acceptance and forgiveness every day.

Jesus renews you each day, forgives you every time you ask. He loves you even though you are imperfect. Extend that same gift to those in your life.

"Let us not become weary in doing good, for at the proper time we will reap a harvest if we do not give up. Therefore, as we have opportunity, let us do good to all people, especially to those who belong to the family of believers" (6: 9 - 10).

DAY TWO HUNDRED & THIRTY-SEVEN

The Lord is close to the brokenhearted
Psalm 34

When you truly seek God in times of hurt, confusion, and pain he will come near you. When you are struggling with your humanity and inability to overcome your many faults and sins, he is present.

"The Lord is close to the brokenhearted and saves those who are crushed in spirit" (Psalm 34:18).

When someone says God spoke to them or they experienced God, this likely means the Holy Spirit showed up in their life. You will know when the Holy Spirit is near.

You might be overcome by a shudder and spontaneous tears. You will feel the comfort and warmth that comes when hugged by a special person but multiplied times a hundred. It's his way of letting you know the Father loves you and that you should not give up.

He comes subtly because we can't tolerate the whole presence of God. Like the experiences of Daniel and Moses, as mere mortals his power is too awesome for people to experience him face-to-face. Even the Holy Spirit's dove-like approach is almost too much at times. But if you seek his presence through quiet time alone and in whispered prayer throughout each day, you will come to sense him without being overwhelmed. You will know a quiet comfort. If you've felt nothing for long periods, you have stopped seeking him.

Stop what you are doing and call to him. Ask the Spirit to be near you and then wait. He will return.

DAY TWO HUNDRED & THIRTY-EIGHT

Faith in God's plan when your plan has fallen apart
Lamentations 3:18-33

Sometimes your plan does not work out. Sometimes you don't have a plan, but a dream burns in your heart. The dream light goes on burning, but you see no sign of it coming to pass.

In Lamentations 3: 18, Jeremiah says, "My splendor is gone and all that I had hoped from the Lord."

He remembers affliction, wandering, and bitterness. His soul is downcast. At some point you will feel this way. But do not stay in that place. Like Jeremiah, call to mind hope. "Because of the Lord's great love we are not consumed, for his compassions never fail. They are new every morning; great is your faithfulness" (3: 22 - 23).

When all your plans have failed and you want to give up, that is when God shows up with the unexpected. He will not cast you off forever. The grief he allows will always be followed by compassion for those who love him because his love is unfailing.

Even as you may feel it is too late for you, God is working out some new plan and working to prepare you to receive it. It is never too late for God. Open your hands to let go of the old plan and open your heart to receive the new one.

DAY TWO HUNDRED & THIRTY-NINE

A woman of God flees, pursues, fights, and perseveres
1 Timothy 6:11-12

Paul instructed Timothy in preparation for his role as a church leader. His instruction remains solid for you today.

The woman of God flees from anything that will distract her from God's best and his plan. This can be wrong friends, a lust for money or beauty, relationships with men that are harmful. You will know in your gut the things you should flee from, if you pray for Holy Spirit guidance.

The woman of God pursues "righteousness, godliness, faith, love, endurance, and gentleness" (6:11).

Fleeing and pursuing require a fight. You must become intentional about what you flee from and run to. "Fight the good fight of faith," Paul urges Timothy (6:12). It is never a onetime battle. Whatever makes you weak, will always be with you.

Know that you must persevere in this diligence to live well. Do not fear or despair. God remains close to the woman who makes effort to flee, pursue, fight, and persevere. Trust him each day with your life and your will.

DAY TWO HUNDRED & FORTY

No middle ground with Jesus
John 6

As Jesus made his way to Jerusalem for the last time, he became emphatic and bold in his interactions with everyone. The time to explain and teach was short. He was an all or nothing choice for people then and remains so today.

Be clear. If he knocks at your door, you either accept him or reject him.

Jesus said, "I am the bread of life. He who comes to me will never go hungry, and he who believes in me will never be thirsty" (6:35). His teaching revealed throughout John 6 is hard to grasp. He is comparing the choice to accept and follow him to life itself. He speaks of his flesh in analogy to bread and that he is giving that bread in exchange for "the life of the world" (6:51).

Many followers left Jesus at this point. Many today turn away when they realize that Jesus demands loyalty and obedience in exchange for the life he gives on earth and eternally in heaven. It is easier for them to reject the messenger than to accept the message.

Jesus requires that you believe who he was and is, love God and others as yourself, depend on his teachings for guidance, and trust the Holy Spirit for power to do it all (See NIV Life Application Study Bible 1991 edition notes). That's what it means to "take of" his flesh as living bread.

Make your choice to follow or reject. Don't be lukewarm.

DAY TWO HUNDRED & FORTY-ONE

Understanding sin
1 John 3:4-10

"Everyone who sins breaks the law; in fact, sin is lawlessness" (3:4).

The message of 1 John is designed to reassure you and clarify how to walk through life as a Christ-follower. You will sin, likely each day. The Christian life is a process of becoming more like Christ. It will not be done until you meet him. It takes effort in this life to stay in the process.

You must be honest with yourself about the difference between committing sin and continuing in sin. You have areas where temptation is strong. Perhaps the enemy has a foothold in some area because you are vulnerable. The Holy Spirit will work in you and through others to reveal continuing sin and to overcome it. The believer repents, confesses, and finds forgiveness.

Never practice sin and look for ways to justify it. True Christians will not be indifferent to God's moral law, they will not willfully sin.

Follow these steps in your life:

1. Seek power from the Holy Spirt and God's Word
2. Stay away from tempting situations
3. Seek other Christians to trust and hold you accountable

DAY TWO HUNDRED & FORTY-TWO

Repent every foolish, sinful thing
2 Samuel 24:10

King David led a major expansion of the Israelite territory and ushered in a peace they had not known under any former judge or King Saul. He placed God first in his governance of the people and his own life. He also committed sins that led to great pain for himself, his family, and the entire country.

King David was a sinner, but he also found favor in God's eyes. In Samuel 24 the secret to King David's success is revealed.

He initiated a census of the people out of pride and excessive ambition, even though he knew God would not approve. The land was at peace. He didn't need to reinstate the army at that moment. In Samuel 24:10 it says, "David was conscience-stricken after he had counted the fighting men, and he said to the Lord, "I have sinned greatly in what I have done. Now, Lord, I beg you, take away the guilt of your servant. I have done a very foolish thing."

God gave him a choice between three punishments. David chose a punishment directly from God's own hand because he knew that even in anger, God's mercy far exceeds that of man.

What foolish, sinful thing do you need to ask God's forgiveness for in order to rest?

"Great are all his results, small are all his beginnings."

-George MacDonald

DAY TWO HUNDRED & FORTY-THREE

Confession and relationship
Psalms 4:4, 19:3, 67

"In your anger do not sin; when you are on your beds, search your hearts and be silent" (Psalm 4:4). Confession before God is about attitude and relationship, not remembering every sin.

Think about your closest relationships. Are they not marked by an ability to trust, to say I'm hurt, I'm sorry, I love you? Real relationship does not exist without mutual willingness to communicate, and the ability to say you are hurt, angry, irritated, happy, sad, etc.

Honest expression of your full range of emotions is like a spring that continually renews and restores relationships. God offers this and he expects it in return, like a best friend. He's not touchy or jealous or intent on hurting you, but he needs your honesty and respect.

A refusal to repent, to express sorrow over wrong creates a wall between you and God, just like it does with people. Whether with a parent, teacher, friend, or God, relationship must rest on love and respect.

DAY TWO HUNDRED & FORTY-FOUR

The sovereign God of the universe wants to be in relationship with you
Psalm 66

You have been set apart by God because he loves you. Is this hard for you to hear?

He hears every prayer of those who belong to him, and he does answer every prayer. The answers are often longer in coming than expected or different from what you desired. You may delay an answer or prolong a difficult season by holding onto worry or sin.

Sin separates you from God, but only for as long as you refuse to give it up to him. Pride is at the root of all your sin and separation from people and God.

Sin in the form of unkindness, lying, jealousy, stealing or any other form should cause feelings of sadness and guilt. It is a reminder of a need to seek forgiveness and restoration, but guilt is not to become a burden. When you come to God requesting forgiveness sincerely, it is given. Don't sin willfully or in defiance.

Your responsibility is to ask for forgiveness from people and God. Do so with a heart set on not repeating the offense. You cannot make people forgive. Do not carry their burden of unforgiveness.

DAY TWO HUNDRED & FORTY-FIVE

Each person pays for her own sin
Deuteronomy 24:16

You will be held accountable for your sin. You are not responsible for the wrongs of your parents, children, or anyone else.

However, you will often suffer for the sin of others, and others will suffer for your sin. Sin splatters, as they say.

Sin came into the world with the first couple in the form of pride, which is the pathway to disobedience. Your enemy whispers pride into your ear so you will become fallen and separated from God, like him.

Pride is the urge to do things your way, take what you want, do what feels good no matter what. God can't tolerate sin - disorder, disobedience. Putting limits on disorder, which leads to chaos, and constraints on pride is the purpose of rules. Every loving home and civil society reflects this need for limits and order.

Take responsibility for curbing your own pride with God's help. Don't fall for the lie that if it feels good do it or that everybody is doing it. What feels best will come after you have submitted yourself to the hard work, to resisting some of your urges for something bigger, more important.

Ask God to forgive your sin and ask him for your heart's desires too. He cares about both.

DAY TWO HUNDRED & FORTY-SIX

Waiting prayerfully
Daniel 10:10-12

Answers to prayers can seem long in coming. Never give up on receiving an answer to a prayer, if you have "set your mind to gain understanding and to humble yourself before your God" (10:10).

Daniel is most remembered for his time in the lion's den. His life story also involved being taken by force from his home and put into the service of the very leader who destroyed his country. Yet Daniel remained faithful to God and calm in the face of life-threatening trials. His steadfast prayer life and faith led to an extraordinary relationship with God.

God relates directly to the person who loves and seeks him. He sends all manner of favor and assistance to the faithful person who remains confident while waiting for answers to prayer.

In Daniel 10, you see that many unseen forces can impact the timing of your answer. Some practical, some spiritual, and many times unseen. An angel told Daniel that from the moment he began asking, his words were heard.

Seek God in prayer for the answers to everything. Wait patiently while you go about the tasks before you.

DAY TWO HUNDRED & FORTY-SEVEN

Acknowledging the truth is loving
John 7:45-52

Truth is often seen as confrontation. Lies are often the price of "getting along."

Many people do not want truth. They want to tell a story or "narrative." They want you to say things like "it's all good" or "there are no wrong decisions."

But some things are not good, they are bad. Everything you need to know about what is good and what is bad can be found in God's Word. The Bible is timeless because it explains and illustrates life's principles and what God expects of people.

Human nature is to pick and choose parts and pieces of the truth to suit our desires. When someone says or does something that conflicts with your behavior and choices, do you call them a hater, judgmental, not loving?

Sometimes the most loving thing a person can do is speak truth even when they know it will upset others. Silence and pretending wrong is right can have dire consequences.

What if your parents never told you no? What kind of friend pretends "it's all good" when someone is doing something that could ruin or even end their life or the lives of others?

DAY TWO HUNDRED & FORTY-EIGHT

Not because you are righteous but because God is merciful
Daniel 9:17-19

Confessing wickedness and rebellion, acknowledging that you are covered in shame, is very hard. You probably don't see yourself that way because you can look around and see so many truly wicked and awful people.

Yet you are not called to compare yourself to others. You are to compare yourself to Christ and God's commands. By those standards, we all fall short. This is by design, and the place God wants you to start - acknowledge your need for him, for salvation.

Until you get to that place, you can't go to the next higher step, which is to accept that you deserve to be disciplined by God and are not above whatever hardship has come your way.

Daniel prayed, "Just as it is written in the Law of Moses, all this disaster has come on us, yet we have not sought the favor of the Lord our God by turning from our sins and giving attention to your truth. The Lord did not hesitate to bring the disaster on us, for the Lord our God is righteous in everything he does; yet we have not obeyed him" (9:13 - 14).

Get okay with the fact that you are rebellious by nature and sinful. Accept that a sovereign God controls everything, must demand order, will discipline you, and loves you infinitely.

Then you can sincerely pray as Daniel did saying, "We do not make requests of you because we are righteous, but because of your great mercy" (9:18).

God in his mercy cares for you and will answer all of your prayers, many he will answer by giving you the desires of your heart, but only if you are ready, and it aligns with his ultimate best for your individual life. Never doubt this and you will live in peace with God and yourself.

DAY TWO HUNDRED & FORTY-NINE

Killing prophets and embracing demons
Psalm 31

In the story of Jesus' life, all the people who should have recognized him and heralded his coming wanted to kill him. The rulers, law keepers, and even one of his own disciples rejected Jesus and embraced a demon in one form or another.

Our innate drift is toward pride. It is often quite subtle and disguised by busyness, false humility, hurt emotions, and so much more. Pride is a sense that the rules don't apply to you or that you are better than others in some form or fashion. It leads you to take things into your own hands, often on behalf of God. It whispers that risky behavior will work out for you.

God will send many prophets, in varied forms, into your life to instruct, warn, and even to help you live day-to-day. They often appear in human form but can just as likely come as an illness, some innate handicap or fetish, a billboard or song, a challenging experience, and all manner of other encounters.

Demons come from your enemy and they appear in many forms, just like the prophets, except the demons have one singular purpose. They turn your heart and mind away from God. They feed and grow pride.

Learn to recognize your prophets and demons. Don't kill the prophets and embrace the demons.

Pray like King David, "Into your hands I commit my spirit; deliver me, Lord, my faithful God. But I trust in you, Lord; I say, 'You are my God'" (31:5).

DAY TWO HUNDRED & FIFTY

Only a true friend makes a good husband or wife
John 15:12-14

Don't you envy those girls who can mold their wishes and likes to whomever they are with at any given time? Everyone loves them. They are the first chosen by "cute guys" and always invited to the party. Is that you?

As girls, we often live with the conundrum of wanting to fit in and be like everyone else and wanting to be unique and special. But the person who's always shape shifting, focused on pleasing the crowd, and doing things to be seen may not make the best friend.

A best friend is our favorite person to spend time with. You look out for each other. There's exclusivity between the two of you on some levels. You are committed to being there through thick and thin. Developing and maintaining a best friend is good practice for successful marriage.

If you toss away friends at the first sign of trouble, you will likely have a hard time making the kind of commitment required for marriage.

It takes practice to be the kind of friend a friend would want to have. You must be willing to be a friend even when no one notices, when there seems to be no payoff. The person capable of being a real friend at times will sometimes feel unnoticed and alone.

The enemy will tell you to "show them" and be like all the rest, or he'll say you don't have what it takes and can never be loved. It's a lie. Trust God. Be calm. Wait. Pray.

You have the power to choose your reaction and action. Be yourself and be a good friend. What you want is so much bigger, so much more satisfying long term. You want to be a woman of character, blessed with an important role to play, and peace and confidence as you go about getting it done.

DAY TWO HUNDRED & FIFTY-ONE

Truth and light
John 3:19 - 21

An important part of growing up is learning to overcome your innate selfishness. Naturally, you want to make people characters in a play about you. Loving people up close and loving them like yourself is hard.

Jesus said, "This is the verdict: Light has come into the world, but people loved darkness instead of light because their deeds were evil" (3:19).

He is the light you can trust to shine into the dark corners of your life. You can't do it on your own. But you must allow light or else you will hurt others without concern. You won't say, "I'm sorry" before the sun goes down or ask forgiveness. You will think being good is all up to you, and you will fail.

Many people don't want to be exposed by the light but living by the truth means the light is on you, all the time for God and people to see (3:20 - 21).

Don't be like everyone else and fear the light. You don't need to force light on others but stand in it yourself. Let the light shine in and through you. Darkness causes confusion and fear. Light chases all that away.

DAY TWO HUNDRED & FIFTY-TWO

Pride and faith both start small
Matthew 17:20; Genesis 3:6-7

Throughout your life a spiritual battle for your heart, mind, and soul will never cease. The agents of heaven will fight for you to choose faithfulness in the smallest acts to the biggest decisions. The mercenaries of hell will tempt you with pridefulness.

Both start small, like the tiny mustard seed Jesus referred to when he said, "Truly I tell you, if you have faith as small as a mustard seed, you can say to this mountain, 'Move from here to there,' and it will move. Nothing will be impossible for you" (Matthew 17:20).

Willing yourself to choose the right response, to choose God's urging versus what feels good or reasonable to yourself is the seed of faith that can grow into mountain-moving proportions.

Pride too begins very small with promptings just like Eve in the garden. The devil said, "Did God really say, 'You must not eat from any tree in the garden?'" (Genesis 3:1). That's all it took for Eve.

A few verses later we find that "When she saw that the fruit of the tree was good for food and pleasing to the eye, and also desirable for gaining wisdom, she took some and ate it. She also gave some to her husband, who was with her, and he ate it. Then the eyes of both of them were opened, and they realized they were naked; so they sewed fig leaves together and made coverings for themselves" (Genesis 3: 6 - 7).

Doing the right thing or wrong thing starts small with a thought, and that leads to an attitude which becomes a word or action. Take your thoughts to God in prayer. Ask the Holy Spirit to guide and show you how to think about what you see, hear, and experience.

DAY TWO HUNDRED & FIFTY-THREE

Setting expectations
Matthew 9:18-34

Most people set low expectations for themselves and others when it comes to relationships. They create narrow boxes for each individual they know and for categories of people.

Throughout his ministry, Jesus exceeds expectations with his actions and illustrates God's high expectations for people. Yet with Jesus, he does not disqualify people from a relationship with him if they do not meet expectations.

Creating small boxes for people with low expectations is convenient and safe. It demands very little of you. If you keep people at a safe distance or within a box, they can't ask too much of you or confront you about dishonesty or weaknesses.

With people, as with God, you are free to keep a safe distance and to rationalize why it's not a good idea to get too close, but you miss out on the sweetness that lies past the uncomfortableness of being known or trying new things, and the time commitment involved with being present.

Look closely at the boxes you've put people into. Could some of those boxes afford some expansion?

DAY TWO HUNDRED & FIFTY-FOUR

I don't condemn you, but stop sinning
John 8:1-11

When they brought to Jesus a woman caught in the act of adultery and demanded she be stoned to death because that was the law of Moses, he said, "Let any one of you who is without sin be the first to throw a stone at her"(8:7).

It was a powerful moment. One-by-one they dropped their stones and quietly slipped away. Left alone with the woman, Jesus - God in the flesh - turned and asked her, "Has no one condemned you? Then neither do I condemn you," Jesus declared. "Go now and leave your life of sin" (8:10 - 11).

In our present-day churches and society, we've dropped a lot of stones. Hallelujah!

But we've also stopped saying, "Leave your life of sin."

It feels good to put down the stone because it takes the pressure off dealing with your own nasty little sins. The unspoken words go something like this - "If you will let me go on telling "white lies," withholding my tithe, gossiping, hating, disrespecting my husband, getting drunk on Saturday night...Well, I'll gladly let you have any sin you'd like; no questions asked."

Urging each other to "leave your life of sin" is the yin of the stone dropping yang. Smiling and patting heads while saying, "You were just born that way" is shallow and a cop out on Jesus. He meets you in your sin without condemnation, but he can't leave you that way. There's always a calling up to a higher place. If you are going to be his follower, his hands and feet, you've got to drop your stone and say, "Leave your life of sin."

Begin with being intentional about living morally upright and with integrity. When you get it wrong, confess it to God and those you influence, if necessary. Love those heading in the wrong direction or who don't understand that Christianity costs an honest look at sin by speaking truth about leaving sin behind in the right contexts.

When the church and society put down their stones as well as stopped acknowledging right and wrong and setting boundaries around what is good and not good for children and adults, we did not end up with a freer, happier society. We ended up with a lot of emotionally confused people and a decaying civil society.

DAY TWO HUNDRED & FIFTY-FIVE

Can you really trust God?
Romans 15:13, Deuteronomy 31

If you seek God and the Christian faith, there will be critical times when you must confront the hardest question of all: Can I really trust God?

Life at times will look to be falling apart. Your dreams will seem shattered. Everyone around you will be getting what they want. You will think that God might not get around to really working all things together for your good (Romans 8:28). You've leaned on him, but the path does not feel straight (Proverbs 3:6).

The tendency is to conclude that you have not been diligent enough, have sinned, or that God's promises don't apply to you. Your enemy is happy to have you in any one of these spots.

You overcome by not concluding anything other than this: God is alive and hears every prayer and answers in due time. The answer may be no or wait, but he will never forsake the one who continues to seek, ask, and pray.

Don't allow disappointment to turn into a bad attitude because that is the lead up to taking things into your hands. When you've done your part, followed direction available, and results are still not coming, stop and listen. God is the author and finisher of all your circumstances. Never give up believing that his plan is far better than yours.

The direction you take at the crossroads when the pain is greatest is the most important decision you will ever make. Before you decide, look for any blessing in your life and search your memory for any signs that God loves you and has answered your past prayers. You will find blessings and answered prayers.

Recommit to trusting God in that moment. Confess your confusion, anger, and, disappointment.

DAY TWO HUNDRED & FIFTY-SIX

Your crazy dreams
2 Timothy 2:20-22

Your crazy dream may not be realistic, but God will take your passion and hard work to reach that dream and shape it into something that serves his higher plans and your greatest good.

However, you must ask yourself a very hard question for this to happen: Am I preparing myself daily for the arrival of the dream?

Preparation takes place in the mind, body, and soul. It takes shape through thoughts, attitudes, actions, and words. The girl who wants to marry a loving, handsome man of God is practicing being loving, taking care of herself, pursuing a relationship with God. The girl who wants to be a successful attorney or doctor or teacher or whatever profession is daily studying up on the topic, working at some internship or job that exposes her to others in this profession, etc.

You must live in the present while pursuing dreams. Make time for rest and play and remain committed to active pursuit of your crazy dream.

DAY TWO HUNDRED & FIFTY-SEVEN

Hypocrites and liars
Luke 12:56

Do you know anyone who is not a hypocrite or a liar? How about yourself, what are you?

Hypocrites apply a different set of standards to themselves than others. They say one thing and do another. They judge without compassion or willingness to walk in another's shoes.

Liars tell the truth when convenient, their version of the truth, or not at all. They often speak without thinking of the impact their words might have.

Jesus said, "Why do you look at the speck of sawdust in your brother's eye and pay no attention to the plank in your own eye? How can you say to your brother, 'Let me take the speck out of your eye,' when all the time there is a plank in your own eye? You hypocrite first take the plank out of your own eye, and then you will see clearly to remove the speck from your brother's eye" (Matthew 7: 3 - 5).

Remember, he does not offer the teaching as a reminder to mind your own business. He's urging you to take an honest look at yourself so you can "see clearly" what's in someone else's hurt, problem, or untruth.

It's easy to become one extreme or the other; either the hypocrite who only sees other's failings or the "it's all good" person who believes there's never a time to speak loving truth. There is bad behavior. There is right and wrong. You are called to recognize them all, and in some cases call it out.

This is why walking the life of a Christ-follower is so very hard. You must renew daily your commitment to truth and seeking Holy Spirit guidance. Don't be a hypocrite and liar or allow hypocrites and liars to run your world.

DAY TWO HUNDRED & FIFTY-EIGHT

What was Jesus like as a person?
John 1

The Gospels reveal everything you need to know about who Jesus was as a person and as a divine member of the Trinity. His ways as a human are a map to follow. Your sin, wounds, and human nature make it hard to be like him all the time. He doesn't ask you to be perfectly like him but to strive to follow his example and God's will.

Following God's will entails studying his Word and listening very closely for his voice every single day and obeying whatever he says. Jesus' humanity helps you know what to aspire to in day-to-day life on earth. His divinity gives comfort and encouragement when you get tired, confused, angry, sad, or feel like giving up.

Jesus...
- Told the truth always, sometimes softly and sometimes bluntly
- Loved and respected everyone but didn't condone bad behavior and attitudes
- Felt angry and expressed it when people disrespected God
- Humbled himself
- Got up early to pray and seek God
- Took care of himself by working, resting, and enjoying fellowship
- Honored his family and made effort to ensure their well-being but didn't take responsibility for their actions and attitudes
- Didn't pretend anything
- Never discriminated
- Never played the victim
- Discerned between honest people and liars, good and evil
- Kept an inner circle of friends
- Did a lot for others but never allowed himself to be taken advantage of
- Put God's will ahead of his own will and the will of his friends
- Hung out with lepers, widows, prostitutes, single women, tax collectors, Romans, Greeks, Jews, divorcees, sick, poor, powerful, weak, rich, insane, adulterers, leaders, beggars, blind, blue collar and white-collar workers
- Influenced people from all walks of life and in every sort of condition by accepting them as individuals while speaking truth about their wrong behaviors and attitudes
- Limited no one based on their past, present, or future but called all to their highest and best in the here and now

DAY TWO HUNDRED & FIFTY-NINE

Don't despise small steps
Zechariah 4:10

"Oh, that's nothing," you say of so many things. The small way you helped someone. The good grade on a test or paper. The smile he gave you today. The short run you took. The sketching for your dream home.

Zechariah was a young prophet destined to encourage the Jewish exiles in Babylon. It had been seventy years since God, in his anger, allowed the Babylonians to conquer his people. Finally, word from God came - you will go home, prosperity will return to Jerusalem, you are still a chosen, and loved people.

The beautiful temple built by Solomon had been destroyed. Now, the measuring line would be brought out to begin planning for a new, albeit smaller, temple. It was a very small step, and many of the people knew they'd not live to see it completed.

God told Zechariah to say to the people, "Who dares despise the day of small things, since the seven eyes of the Lord that range throughout the earth will rejoice when they see the chosen capstone [measuring line] in the hand of Zerubbabel" (4:10)?

God's "seven eyes" see everything. The seven eyes are his seven Spirits of God (Revelation 5:6). He has a plan and is in control of everything. You often know only what's happening right now. The building or the rebuilding of your "temple," ,i.e., life, may begin with a very small choice that you make.

Many small actions combine to make for something big. Don't "despise" or take lightly the small beginnings. You have no way of knowing which ones will lead to the big dream in your heart.

DAY TWO HUNDRED & SIXTY

Asking (or not asking) the "dumb" questions of God
Job 38:2-4

"There are no dumb questions," says a loving teacher. It's meant to encourage critical thinking and a confidence in searching for answers. Many questions really have no definitive answer. It all just depends. However, sometimes we ask "dumb" questions of God because we already know and don't like the answer.

Being honest about your own questions that already have answers is hard. Doing the right thing day in and day out is not easy. Sometimes you just need a break, to have some fun and relax. True, but be careful because giving yourself "a break" can lead to developing bad habits and attitudes.

Here are some common "dumb" questions girls ask of God and themselves:

- He feels so right. Shouldn't I "be with him" to know for sure
- It's on sale. I can charge this and pay it off next month, right
- Some people don't deserve respect
- Getting high is okay, because everyone does it
- I don't have to always do the right thing. Sometimes we need to just have fun
- Exercise and eating healthy food is not mandatory
- God is everywhere, I don't need a church

DAY TWO HUNDRED & SIXTY-ONE

God is the CEO, and you are an employee
Psalm 139

God is the CEO of a corporation called Kingdom on Earth. You can be his employee, if desired.

Traits that make for a good employee include treating the business like it's your own, showing up ready to work, respecting management, representing the brand well everywhere you go, doing your best work, and having a positive attitude.

Everyone who works for God has a few of the same things in their job description: produce fruit of the spirit like kindness (see Galatians 5:22), love everyone, support those who hurt, share your faith through stories about personal experiences working for God, and seek peace with others.

In Kingdom on Earth there are many, many positions requiring a lot of different skills and talents. You will be given opportunities by management to take on jobs that fit your level of maturity, skill, and talent. It's up to you to take those opportunities as they come and approach them with the traits of a good employee coupled with your unique talents.

At Kingdom on Earth, sometimes promotion looks like a step down, but the CEO is in total control and never makes a wrong decision. He always handles missteps in management. The benefits and salary are designed to fit the needs of every individual employee. A bad economy never affects the company. This company will never go out of business, and in fact will be the last company standing when everything comes to an end.

The best news of all is that there's a place for everyone who wants to get on at Kingdom on Earth. You just apply directly to the CEO, anytime day or night. You will be hired on the spot. Take whatever job you are given, and do your best. Promotions come when you least expect them, not when your sole focus is on promotion.

DAY TWO HUNDRED & SIXTY-TWO

You can never do enough
Psalm 119:29-30, Matthew 11:11-19

Do you ever feel exhausted by trying to do the right thing, get everything done?

A powerful tactic of the enemy is to work in your mind to "damn you if you do and damn you if you don't." Jesus said, "For John came neither eating nor drinking, and they say, 'He has a demon.' The Son of Man came eating and drinking, and they say, 'Here is a glutton and a drunkard, a friend of tax collectors and sinners.' But wisdom is proved right by her deeds" (Matthew 11: 18 - 19).

The problem is twofold. You can't do it alone. It's just not feasible to do it all right, to serve, and love, and work, and keep up your home, health, etc. in your own strength. Simultaneously, action on your part is required. Passivity leads to sin.

Dr. Charles Stanley speaks of opportunity as the doorways to God's will for your life. He also says that how far you are along in life is a reflection of your response to opportunity.

You have the opportunity each day before your feet hit the floor to choose an attitude. Each person you encounter is an opportunity to lift-up or tear down, simply with a smile or frown, a kind word or none at all.

The bigger picture opportunities that set the course for a life come in many forms - an invitation, acceptance letter, job offer, volunteer spot, date, try out, etc.

Most of the fateful opportunities only come around once. You must be awake, ready, in-touch with the Holy Spirit to take those opportunities. Alternatively, you must be in a position to know when to decline an opportunity. Some opportunities rejected based on a "gut feeling" can mean the difference between life and death.

If you think too much about future opportunities, it can become overwhelming. Pray as King David did in Psalm 119: 29 - 30. "Keep me from deceitful ways; be gracious to me and teach me your law. I have chosen the way of faithfulness; I have set my heart on your laws."

DAY TWO HUNDRED & SIXTY-THREE

Steps toward restoring relationships beyond forgiveness
2 Corinthians 13:11-14

When someone hurts you, forgiveness is not an optional choice. It is an absolute necessity for you, not them. You are called in no uncertain terms to forgive even those who may not be sorry one bit or simply sorry they got caught or called out.

Often the difficult part is restoration of the relationship. The forgiven person may be allowed back into your life and soon repeat the offense. Forgiven yet unrepentant people mistake the passage of time and your willingness to forgive as signs that there's no need to change anything.

Repent means to turn away from the actions or attitudes that caused the hurt.

Time is often part of restoring relationships and certainly actions, but there's another key element - a heartfelt acknowledgement and apology, where appropriate.

You know in your own heart the difference between sincere and obligatory repentance. The person who is ready for a restored relationship names what they have done and acknowledges the hurt it caused.

Relationships patched only with time enough to "get back to normal" or tepid "sorry you were mad" faux apologies are destined to backslide. It may not make sense at first, but love involves protecting yourself and others from patterns of negativity. Forgiveness is the first step. Restoration takes time and sincere repentance.

Don't withhold forgiveness awaiting an apology or change in behavior. It may never come. Forgive quickly, even when your forgiveness is not sought. When you remember the offense, forgive it again. Pray for the strength to do this as many times as it takes.

DAY TWO HUNDRED & SIXTY-FOUR

Choosing life
Deuteronomy 30:15-20

When reading the words of Moses to the Israelites about choosing life and prosperity over death and doom, it seems so cut and dry (30:15). The problem is that the choice is made day in and day out. It's not a one-time event.

Moses hints at the nature of choice saying in 30:16, "If, however, you turn away your hearts and will not listen, but are led astray and adore and serve other gods, I tell you now that you will certainly perish; you will not have a long life on the land that you are crossing the Jordan to enter and occupy."

These "other gods" represent a minefield of distractions and pitfalls from social media to money, unhealthy relationships, food, drugs, and so much more. No one is without some sin, a temptation they must face down or give into on a regular basis. However, you must strive to reject morally wrong attitudes and acts within your heart.

If you will not willingly limit your own desires and attempt to curb your own sin, your private condoning will influence your children, family, friends, and co-workers. When people refuse to limit themselves privately it becomes difficult to uphold public limits.

Communities that refuse to set limits on behavior and to state the difference between right and wrong eventually lead to societies with public policy condoning all manner of things harmful to many people.

The millions of daily choices still make up the big-picture life as described by Moses. Your life direction impacts those coming behind you as well. "I have set before you life and death, blessings and curses. Now choose life, so that you and your children may live and that you may love the Lord your God …" (30:19 - 20).

Choosing life is more than simply a free will matter of accepting God's law. Many of the plans he has for you are not spelled out anywhere in the Bible. People support all manner of sin by pointing out that Jesus didn't address a particular area. Your path that leads to life and prosperity versus death and destruction unfolds by heeding his voice and holding fast to him. Love the Lord, your God, and seek him every day. It takes a daily choice. You will have good days and bad days, but never give up on choosing life.

DAY TWO HUNDRED & SIXTY-FIVE

The nature of hate
Luke 23:33-35

Have you ever stood by and watched as someone was mistreated? Have you ever been mean to someone you love?

A great deal has been written about how whole populations of people either participate or stand by and watch atrocities take place against their neighbors. The Germans during the Nazi reign is likely the most egregious.

There's an uncomfortable phenomena we humans experience when we betray someone, especially someone we love or a person that's done us no harm. We come to hate the one we've hurt. If they remain humble and don't fight back, we hate them all the more. Then something even stranger happens, our disdain for them boomerangs back on us.

Jesus modeled love as action, not feeling. The more you act in love, even when you don't feel like it, the more you stave off the self-hatred that comes from mistreating others. When you betray or harm someone, it's critical that at some point you sincerely apologize, ask for forgiveness, and repent (turn away from the behavior or attitude).

When you don't own up to a betrayal, mistreatment, or disrespect of someone a form of rationalization takes root in your mind – it's okay to diminish them. If you are not willing to apologize and ask for forgiveness, you believe they deserved what you did to them. Perhaps you think they had it coming, are stupid, don't understand (respect, appreciate) you.

Over time your attitude grows like a cancer as hate toward the person. You can't respect them because in some sense they allowed you to betray them. Even seeing them can come to give you a sick feeling. Maybe you even stoop to talking about them in a condescending manner. The longer you go, especially if this is a parent or husband or anyone you must encounter regularly, the worse it gets.

You hate them because deep down you hate yourself. You know what you did is wrong and that your continued disdain for them is adding coal to the fire inside your heart.

You may begin making fake attempts at doing nice things for them or even calling them under the pretense of "checking in." But invariably you will go away feeling aggravated because either they continue on as if everything is just great between you, further convicting your barely alive conscience or they act a bit sensitive, cautious, and distant letting on that they are hurt, yet not flat out confronting you. That's even worse because you feel guilty and put out at the same time.

Can you think of someone you were once very close to but now have at best a superficial relationship with? Did you betray them or vice versa? If you secretly hate them, take this to the Lord and work it out.

DAY TWO HUNDRED & SIXTY-SIX

Don't sweat the small stuff
Amos 5:13-15

Eliminate the word worry from your vocabulary. Worrying entails spending time in the present fretting over what might happen in the future. This is not the same as planning or concern. You should be concerned about some future events and plan for your life.

Worry can prevent you from facing the challenges or the joys of the moment. Concern activates your wisdom and common sense to work in tandem with God.

Amos says, "Seek good, not evil, that you may live" (5:14). Life is complex, but on a basic level your job is simply to seek out what is good and to avoid what you know in your gut and heart is evil.

You can't know today what opportunity or conflict is coming or the outcomes of those brewing around you presently. You can prepare and ask God for what you want.

Jesus said, "Do not worry about your life, what you will eat or drink; or about your body, what you will wear..." (6:25). Any real need you have will be taken care of by God. Resist reasoning based on what happened in your own family. Don't expect God to let you down or over-indulge you.

If you felt hungry or without necessities as a child, don't assume you must worry about preventing those situations today. Ask God and thank him in advance for providing everything you need to live for him.

If as a child you had plenty and even too much at times, don't worry about how to keep getting more and more today. Ask God and thank him in advance for providing everything you need to live for him.

Letting go of worry may feel hard. Just start practicing. Begin each day asking God to take care of you and to help you lay down worry. Become like the horse training, preparing, and waiting patiently for opportunity.

DAY TWO HUNDRED & SIXTY-SEVEN

The temptation to avoid pain
Matthew 16:21-28

Jesus told the disciples that he would suffer, be killed, and on the third day come back to life (16:21). Peter, who would become the original leader of the church, even after denying Jesus three times and abandoning him during his hour of need, said, "Never, Lord! This shall never happen to you" (16:22)!

Jesus spoke firmly to Peter saying, you are a "stumbling block" and "do not have in mind the things of God, but the things of men" (16:23).

Peter, like your friend or parent that loves you, loved Jesus and didn't want him to suffer. Peter also thought Jesus was going to be a national leader. He anticipated holding a pretty high-ranking position in Jesus' regime. Imagine telling people that instead of pursuing a lucrative career you are going on the mission field. What if you are a natural born athlete but feel led to pursue social work? Maybe you are married to a real jerk and everyone keeps telling you to leave, except God.

After the blistering one-on-one with Peter, Jesus goes to the whole gang of disciples and says this:
"Whoever wants to be my disciple must deny themselves and take up their cross and follow me. For whoever wants to save their life will lose it, but whoever loses their life for me will find it. What good will it be for someone to gain the whole world, yet forfeit their soul? Or what can anyone give in exchange for their soul? For the Son of Man is going to come in his Father's glory with his angels, and then he will reward each person according to what they have done" (16: 24 - 27).

Carry a cross? They knew exactly what this meant. Crucifixion was common. Minutes before Jesus made this statement, they were all reveling in a belief that God was finally showing up to put the Romans in their place.

Jesus is still delivering this message to you. Put the well-meaning people who don't want you to suffer behind you, including yourself. Following Christ at times is going to mean pain, suffering, and humiliation. You will be reminded over and over that it is not about your happiness and comfort.

The proposition of "carrying your own cross" is daunting. At first glance, it seems ridiculous, not worth the cost. Why would Jesus ask you to do something so hard, so awful? It was exactly what God asked Jesus to do on your behalf. Mercifully, your cross is not a literal one. Your cross may be a handicap, a parent, a lust for something, a task, or something else.

Running away from the pain instead of dealing with it or even enduring it for a season, of whatever Jesus has put before you will result in spiritual and emotional death. You will lose your reward. And that is exactly what your enemy wants. If he can get you to listen to the voices saying, "How could a good God expect you to suffer," you will be of no threat to him or of use to God.

DAY TWO HUNDRED & SIXTY-EIGHT

Opportunities, decisions, and your life
Psalm 32:8-10

Opportunities, information, and decisions come at you daily. There will be crossroad moments that literally determine your entire future. The weight of reasoning and sorting out options to make decisions when you have limited information can be debilitating. Yet you careen through life often making thousands of decisions in a day.

God makes one of his most practical and powerful promises in Psalm 32:8. "I will instruct you and teach you in the way you should go; I will counsel you with my loving eye on you."

He means you. Yes, out of the billions of people, he has an eye on your life. He knows every fear, pain point, sin, talent, and future opportunity. He devised a plan for your life before you grew in your mother's womb.

In the next verse, God states a warning. "Do not be like the horse or the mule, which have no understanding but must be controlled by bit and bridle or they will not come to you" (32:9).

God is telling you that he will guide and teach you like a free individual, if you will let him. However, if you are obstinate, unruly, hard-headed, and insist on going your own way based on worldly reasoning, you will be taught like animals that have no ability to choose.

The one who trusts God is surrounded by his unfailing love while those who go their own way experience many woes (32:10). God always gives you the choice: trust him or trust yourself and the world. Throughout his Word the outcomes for each choice are made clear.

DAY TWO HUNDRED & SIXTY-NINE

The faithful few
Malachi 3:16-4:6

When things are not going well, do you begin wondering if God is testing or disciplining you or if the enemy is trying to break your faith?

The answer could be "all of the above." In some ways it does not matter. What's important is that God promises over and over throughout the Old and New Testament to redeem the faithful. Those who:

- Love God with all their heart, soul, and mind
- Love their neighbor as themselves
- Obey God's Word
- Trust God with every aspect of their lives
- Follow the promptings of the Holy Spirit
- Forgive others and ask for forgiveness quickly

The Old Testament illustrates a pattern of people straying from God followed by his allowing or causing things to happen that call them back. He always follows an admonition with a reminder that he will not forget the faithful. He also speaks through the prophets of the coming Messiah who will once and for all cover all sins.

Malachi, a prophet, warned of coming destruction for those who have broken faith and his commands, but he says they will "see the distinction between the righteous and the wicked, between those who serve God and those who do not. Surely the day is coming; it will burn like a furnace. All the arrogant and every evildoer will be stubble, and the day that is coming will set them on fire," says the Lord Almighty. "Not a root or a branch will be left to them. But for you who revere my name, the sun of righteousness will rise with healing in its rays. And you will go out and frolic like well-fed calves" (4:1-3).

God's fulfilled promises for the faithful few are always something wonderful. However, they come at the cost of remaining faithful through thick and thin and always after what seems like a very long wait.

DAY TWO HUNDRED & SEVENTY

Standing at the edge   Part I
Psalm 57

Today, you or someone you know feels they have reached the edge. The relationship is over or the money is all gone. Someone is dying or dead. You no longer remember what really happened, only that the dream is shattered. The edge represents the end of yourself and your sense of control.

These are the most important times in life. They are the places God's Holy Spirit hovers and waits, ministers and directs. Many of King David's Psalms were written for times such as these. The enemy does not want you to know or share them because they are like a drink of water in hell. They revive and give hope.

Study the verses in Psalm 57 and write those that touch you most on your hand, wall, a card. Pray and remember them during your time on the edge.

"Have mercy on me, my God, have mercy on me, for in you I take refuge. I will take refuge in the shadow of your wings until the disaster has passed" (57:1).

DAY TWO HUNDRED & SEVENTY-ONE

Kneeling on the edge   Part II
Psalm 55

In Part I, you found yourself standing on the edge. The edge is the place where you feel options are none or limited. Maybe it's your fault or someone else's fault. It no longer matters. All seems lost or failed.

Many go from standing at the edge to jumping. It's an alluring option when you first stand looking down at all that nothingness. If you are seeking Christ, and he lives in you, the next move you make will not involve jumping but kneeling.

Yes, this is very humbling.

Study the verses in Psalm 55 and write those that touch you most on your hand, wall, a card. Pray and remember them during your time on your knees at the edge.

"But you, God, will bring down the wicked into the pit of decay; the bloodthirsty and deceitful will not live out half their days. But as for me, I trust in you" (55:23).

DAY TWO HUNDRED & SEVENTY-TWO

Hanging off the edge   Part III
Psalm 25:16-21

Perhaps you jumped instead of kneeling while at the edge.

Even if you jumped, it's not too late to call on Jesus. This is part of the amazing mystery of Jesus, he will never reject your call no matter what you've done. Unfortunately, when you jump there's often an even bigger mess to clean up. It will take time.

If you are kneeling and do not yet have an answer, stay on your knees at the edge. Wait and pray actively. This means go about your daily business with a smile. You may cry and be sad in your private time with the Lord, but do not let yourself be overcome by grief for too long. Circumstances may get worse, and you might find yourself hanging from the edge. Don't let go.

Study the verses in Psalm 25 and write those that touch you most on your hand, wall, a card. Pray and remember them during your time hanging from the edge.

"May integrity and uprightness protect me, because my hope, Lord, is in you" (25:21).

DAY TWO HUNDRED & SEVENTY-THREE

God will rescue you   Part IV
Psalm 37:3-7

If you find yourself standing, kneeling, hanging on, or even having gone over the edge in your life, God will rescue you. He may come in a manner you do not expect.

Psalm 37 calls you to four habits of the heart and mind:

- Trust in the Lord and do good (37:3)
- Take delight in the Lord, and he will give you the desires of your heart (37:4)
- Commit your ways to him, and he will reward your righteousness and vindicate you (37:5-6)
- Be still before him and wait patiently for him (37:7)

This is a crossroads in your faith. Will you really believe in God's ability to rescue you or not? Don't try to ride the fence. Make a choice and stick with it.

DAY TWO HUNDRED & SEVENTY-FOUR

When a sparrow falls to the ground
Matthew 10:29-31

Jesus says you are worth more than a sparrow (10:31). He claims that the very hairs on your head are numbered (10:29). These are words to treasure up in your heart. But they do not mean that trouble will not come into your life. Sparrows do fall to the ground.

No one wants to fall or fail. When God allows you to fall, it is always for some reason designed to carry you farther along in the sanctification process. It is natural to grab on to something to break a fall. Anything you grab for other than Jesus himself will surely break off in your hand.

Trust and obey. Wait. Trust and obey. If you feel a falling sensation, reach for him. The falling is scary, and it may even hurt. Yet, he will be there. "So don't be afraid" (10:31).

DAY TWO HUNDRED & SEVENTY-FIVE

Living by the T.K.N. Code
Philippians 4:4-8

The T.K.N code involves asking yourself three questions before speaking:

1. Is it the **Truth**?
2. Is it **Kind**?
3. Is it **Necessary**?

Living out the T.K.N. code is not easy, but it is an important discipline for every Christian woman. Many things are true but not necessary. Some things may seem kind but not true. The code demands that you listen more than you speak, that you treat words like dollar bills and spend them with frugality.

If you intentionally filter your words, thoughts, and actions through the code, you will live much like the way Paul urged the Philippians and other early Christians to get along in a hostile world. After writing to them about many things, he left them with his version of the T.K.N. code:

"Whatever is true, whatever is noble, whatever is right, whatever is pure, whatever is lovely, whatever is admirable—if anything is excellent or praiseworthy—think about such things"(4: 8).

The context in which Paul spoke to these men and women is not entirely unlike the one you live in today. The society around them did not share their values or beliefs. They had to do jobs with and live next door to people who didn't respect them. They were countercultural.

Paul urged them to not worry about everything and everyone around them. He told them to focus on being excellent and those things that are worthy of praise and admiration.

You too can do this.

DAY TWO HUNDRED & SEVENTY-SIX

Will you be god, or will God be God – The problem with being your own god
Genesis 3

In the book, The Cost of Discipleship, Dietrich Bonhoeffer (a German pastor and anti-Nazi dissident who was executed by the Nazis on April 9, 1945), wrote that when Adam and Eve ate of the tree of wisdom and knowledge, they became like gods unto themselves, in a sense. Therefore, they no longer had the true God.

This is what is meant by the fall of man. They had everything and were in perfect union with God before their disobedience.

God was not surprised by what they did nor is he shocked by the horrible things you do. He made us in his image. That means we are not robots. We have free will and a mind that can reason. God wired us with incredible power. We get to decide whether we use our power for good or evil.

Even in the Garden of Eden, God had a plan to send his Son to make things right. We return to God and the fellowship afforded Adam and Eve through the very image of Christ. He lived once to set us an example, to usher in the Holy Spirit as our counselor and guide, to conquer death by dying and rising again. He is coming again to judge the living and the dead (Revelation 20).

When Christ comes back, he will usher in return to that perfect state Adam and Eve originally had with God. This experience is possible for those who, during their short time alive on the earth, chose to believe in and follow Christ.

DAY TWO HUNDRED & SEVENTY-SEVEN

Guaranteed success
Joshua 1

After Moses died at the age of 120, God comes directly to Joshua, Moses' aide, and tells him it is finally time to cross the Jordan and enter "the Promised Land." God says to Joshua, "No one will be able to stand against you all the days of your life. As I was with Moses, so I will be with you; I will never leave you nor forsake you. Be strong and courageous, because you will lead these people to inherit the land I swore to their ancestors to give them" (1: 5 - 6).

You may not be anything like Joshua, but you do have a job to do that will require strength and courage. It will be challenging and risky. God also promises to never leave nor forsake you. If you ask and obey, he will help you take whatever hill or mountain stands before you.

The trap is that you might think prosperity and success come only to those who have talent, power, drive, and connections. God does not always measure success the same way people do.

He will ensure your unique success, if you believe in his power and remain close to him through prayer and his Word.

Success always requires strength and courage, obedience to God, and close study of his Word.

He commands you, just as he did Joshua, to be strong and courageous and to not be afraid and discouraged. "God will be with you wherever you go" (1:9).

DAY TWO HUNDRED & SEVENTY-EIGHT

Loving the world
1 John 2:15 - 17

"Do not love the world or anything in the world. If anyone loves the world, love for the Father is not in them" (2:15).

John, one of Jesus' closest friends, has a way of being blunt when relaying Jesus' teaching. You live in the world. God created it, and it's full of amazing beauty. The world is also the realm of your enemy, and he's placed lots of lures to trap people into believing this world is all there is.

"The world and its desires pass away, but whoever does the will of God lives forever," says John in 2:17.

Worldliness is not just behavior. It begins inside of your heart and mind with attitudes. John identifies the three primary areas that cause humans to fall. They are the same three areas Satan used to tempt Eve in the Garden (Genesis 3:6) and attempted to tempt Jesus in the desert (Matthew 4: 1 - 11).

- Lust of the flesh: gratifying physical desires
- Lust of the eyes: materialism, craving things
- Pride of life: boasting, obsession with status or importance

You fall into those three areas of worldliness when you doubt that God will provide for your needs. God values self-control, generosity, humble service, and a good attitude.

DAY TWO HUNDRED & SEVENTY-NINE

A call to build your house for the Lord
Haggai 1:5 - 2:9

Haggai was one of the prophets God spoke through to get the attention of his people. Eighteen years after their return to Jerusalem following the long exile in Babylon (538 BC), God tells the people, "Give careful thought to your ways. You have planted much but harvested little. You eat, but never have enough. You drink, but never have your fill. You put on clothes but are not warm. You earn wages, only to put them in a purse with holes in it" (1: 5 -6).

The people had put a great deal of effort into building their own homes, but the temple remained a mess. God tells them to build his house so that he can be honored and take pleasure in their worship (1: 7 - 9).

Sometimes the harder you work for yourself, the easier it is to ignore your relationship with God. The work seems reasonable and responsible. You have so many responsibilities and priorities. It's easy to get confused.

What is most important to you? Make a list. Where is God on that list?

If anything takes God out of first place, it won't be satisfying or enough. He's promised to provide for all your needs.

As Haggai's story goes on, the people listen to God and get busy putting his house in order and focusing on their commitment to him. As soon as they put words into action, God moved. He sent word back saying, "I am with you" (1:13).

He tells them not to worry about how at first their efforts seemed like nothing. "Be strong, all you people of the land and work, for I am with you," he says (2:4).

Then, like he always does, God provides way more than they could have ever imagined just for being obedient and doing their best. He promises to bless them (2: 6 - 9).

For every small step of obedience, God takes three. He is eager to bless you, but he can't if you are out of sync with him. Get your priorities straight. You are chosen. Quit worrying and rebuild "the temple,", i.e., your commitment to worship and honor God.

DAY TWO HUNDRED & EIGHTY

Why can't we just co-exist?
John 17:13-19

The "Coexist" bumper sticker began showing up not long after 911. Each letter in the word is formed from some religious or philosophical symbolism. Those who "wear" this statement on their car, t-shirt, or in conversation are saying that every belief system is equal, there's no absolute right or wrong, so why all the hate and prejudice.

As a Christian you too wonder why all the hate and prejudice, but you know that all beliefs are not equal and there is in fact right and wrong.

If you've ever been friends with a "Coexist" person, you may have found that it's hard for them to walk their talk. They coexist as long as you don't walk your faith's talk. Jesus warned you about how this would go as he prayed aloud to God in front of his disciples just before the end of his human life on earth.

"I have given them your word and the world has hated them, for they are not of the world any more than I am of the world" (17:14).

Why does the world hate you?

You are a living accusation against the world's immorality. You need not judge in words. Your actions that run counter to theirs incite discomfort. When we are confronted by our conscience, one of two things will happen. We look at it and consider a change, or we reject it.

When friends, family, and co-workers seemingly reject you for no reason, this might be why. Remain in God's Word daily. It will change and strengthen you, if you will let it.

DAY TWO HUNDRED & EIGHTY-ONE

Rejoice, pray, give thanks, and hold on
1 Thessalonians 5:16-24

After you have lived for a while, you will see a pattern to life. It ebbs and flows. It's full of peaks and valleys. God uses every aspect of your life to shape you, bring you closer to his ultimate plan for your life, or to play a role in another's life.

Paul's life was an example of how living for God is never boring and often unpredictable. Remember to practice the actions Paul gave the Thessalonians or else you will easily become complacent or despaired.

- Rejoice always (5: 16)
- Pray continually (5:17)
- Give thanks in all circumstances; for this is God's will for you in Christ Jesus (5:18)
- Do not quench the Spirit (5:19)
- Do not treat prophecies with contempt, but test them all (5: 20 -21)
- Hold on to what is good (5:21)
- Reject every kind of evil (5:22)

It takes practice. Try not to give up. Be gentle on yourself and others when the time comes to be reminded of these things.

DAY TWO HUNDRED & EIGHTY-TWO

When the answer to your prayer is within reach
Joshua 5:12

The book of Joshua is about the moment they'd all been waiting for since the exodus from Egypt forty years prior. Many of the Israelites had died out in the desert, including Moses. These were the sons and daughters of slaves. Yet they'd seen or been taught firsthand that a mighty God had a plan of greatness for them.

They had received their daily bread, i.e., manna, every single day in the desert without lifting a finger except to pick it up and eat it. Then as suddenly as it had started, it stopped.

God stopped producing food for them because it was time to produce food for themselves using their minds to think and bodies to labor. During their days as children, so to speak, unable to do for themselves, God miraculously provided. Now, he'd given them a fertile, solid place in the world. They graduated.

It may be time for you to graduate to the next level in some area of life.

Notes for Joshua 5:12 in the NIV Life Application Study Bible 1991 edition say this:

"Prayer is not an alternative to preparation and faith is not a substitute for hard work. If prayers are unanswered perhaps what is needed is within reach. Pray instead for the wisdom to see it and energy and motivation to do it."

DAY TWO HUNDRED & EIGHTY-THREE

When your righteous plan blows up
Joshua 7:1-9

Under Joshua's leadership, the Israelites watched the walls of Jericho miraculously crumble and then they won a resounding victory over Jericho's army. They were on a high that comes only to those who get to be a part of a God-sized win. Joshua sent a small force in to take the next city, called Ai. They were nothing compared to Jericho. Defeating Ai looked like a piece of cake for a people fighting on God's side.
But that's not what happened.

"So, about three thousand went up; but they were routed by the men of Ai, who killed about thirty-six of them. They chased the Israelites from the city gate as far as the stone quarries and struck them down on the slopes. At this the hearts of the people melted in fear and became like water" (7: 4 - 5).

Joshua was devastated. He "freaked out" and went to God with a prayer that you may be able to relate to. It contained these sentiments (7: 6 - 9):

- Why have you let this awful thing happen to me/us
- I should have never thought anything good would ever really happen to me/us
- This whole thing was a big mistake on my part
- Forgive me. I'm a loser; this is so embarrassing for you and everyone else
- They are going to do us in, and God, your good name is at stake
- What in the world will you do now without me/us to make you look good

Have you ever been confused by defeat in a small battle after winning a big battle?

Sometimes God enables us to take a big leap. We think, "This is it. God's going to really open doors for me now." Then something unexpected and often horrible happens.

Joshua's prayer was not a formal rehearsed prayer. It was a prayer of someone confused and afraid. He just poured it out not thinking about how silly some of it sounded. That's how you need to pray when your righteous plans go awry. Be honest with the all-powerful, loving God of the universe. He already knows what you need, and he saw what you did or said or thought. Give it up to him. But then shut your mouth and listen.

DAY TWO HUNDRED & EIGHTY-FOUR

When God calls you out on sin
Joshua 7:10-26

After Joshua freaked out and prayed his blubbering angst-filled prayer to God about losing the battle with Ai, God responded.

"The Lord said to Joshua, "Stand up! What are you doing down on your face? Israel has sinned; they have violated my covenant, which I commanded them to keep. They have taken some of the devoted things; they have stolen, they have lied, they have put them with their own possessions. That is why the Israelites cannot stand against their enemies; they turn their backs and run because they have been made liable to destruction. I will not be with you anymore unless you destroy whatever among you is devoted to destruction" (7: 10 - 12).

Smack down for Joshua, and the people.

Keep in mind that Joshua had just become the God-ordained leader over the two-million strong Israelite nation. God had told him to never be afraid, to be strong and courageous because God himself would be with Joshua. They were taking the Promised Land, finally, after forty long years of wandering around like a bunch of nomads without a home.

Just because God speaks a promise to you does not mean you get a pass on sin or that you will not be delayed in getting the promise. In some cases, you will suffer for the sin of others around you. That's why my grandmother said, "If you are in the room when !*#* hits the fan, it's going to get on you."

Disobeying God's explicit commands is dangerous for you, entire families, and even entire nations. There are no "victimless" sins or crimes.

DAY TWO HUNDRED & EIGHTY-FIVE

Dealing with sin, repenting of sin, and how Jesus saves
Joshua 7:13-26

Joshua's men lost an easy battle and some lives. Joshua went to God confused and angry. God called him and the people out because someone in their midst had sinned in a big way. One of Joshua's own family members, Achan, had done something God explicitly forbade the Israelites to do during the battles to take the Promised Land.

Achan had taken some of the "booty" from Jericho and hidden it in his own tent. It was a "victimless" sin, right. No one was left in Jericho to care. It was just a pretty robe and some gold. Rationalizing sin is a temptation you will face. Sometimes what God commands doesn't make "common sense."

God does not tell Joshua who committed the sin or exactly what happened. He just tells him to deal with it. Ultimately, Joshua confronts Achan saying, "My son, give glory to the Lord, the God of Israel, and honor him. Tell me what you have done; do not hide it from me. Achan replied, "It is true! I have sinned against the Lord, the God of Israel. This is what I have done..." (7: 19 -20).

Joshua has the stolen items unearthed. Achan, his entire family, all his possessions, and the stolen stuff are brought together and everyone and everything is destroyed. This is a very hard thing for us as modern people living in the "civilized world" to grasp.

Here are the key points for you as a "modern" Christian:

1. God will not settle for doing what is right some of the time or when it feels good or comfortable. The NIV Life Application Study Bible 1991 edition says, "We are under his orders to eliminate any thoughts, practices, or possessions that hinder our devotion to him."
2. Don't fool yourself into thinking that your sin, regardless of how small or personal, won't hurt anyone. Learn to recognize rationalizing and talk back to it. Some things God commands for us all, e.g., Ten Commandments. Some things God will command to you personally. If you are not listening and willing to obey, you will miss it and pay the price.
3. God does not revel in punishing you. Just like you, hopefully, do not enjoy speaking truth to or disciplining those in your life. When you remove sin, God will

immediately encourage you, be with you in whatever battle you face, guide you, bless you with everything you need and more.
4. There are still times today in society when capital punishment or incarceration are necessary. Serious punishment for crimes (sin) that threaten the innocent or the stability of the whole society must be an option. Those punishments must be seriously applied through the use of laws and court systems based on justice blind to race, religion, or any other discriminating factor.
5. Jesus changed everything for the individual. His literal blood covered every sin you will ever commit. It does not mean that there will not be consequences. It means that your family will not be called to stone you to death for a sin that hurts you and them. You can ask for forgiveness from Jesus. You can make reparations and be restored.

DAY TWO HUNDRED & EIGHTY-SIX

The day after sin catches up with you
Joshua 8:1-4, 30-35

Joshua and the Israelites faced some major setbacks in their campaign to take the Promised Land, as the result of one man's sin. People died, including the man who broke God's command and his entire family as well as some of the soldiers. Their progress toward a huge promise God had made to them was delayed unnecessarily, again.

These people had already languished in the desert for forty years due disobedience. Now, with the prize in sight, they faced the same problems, and delay, once again, was the result.

Human nature does not change, and God does not change.

Whatever promise from God you are pursuing is bigger than you are right now. He can't magically take you from A to Z because it would destroy you. Three things must happen before you can reach the promise:

1. You must do your part to train and fight for the promise
2. You must follow orders explicitly, even when they seem unfair or harsh
3. You must check yourself when sin creeps in - confess it, repent, and get back to 1 and 2

After the Israelite's defeat, confrontation with God over the sin, and acting to completely eradicate the sin and repent, God did for them what he'll do for you: forgive you, give you a new set of orders, and bless you by providing what's needed.

DAY TWO HUNDRED & EIGHTY-SEVEN

Killing anything that holds you back from God's best
Joshua 10:40 - 43

The book of Joshua, like much of the Old Testament, is rich with metaphors for your life. In order to truly "take" the Promised Land, Joshua had to subdue the whole region. "He left no survivors. He totally destroyed all who breathed, just as the Lord, the God of Israel, had commanded" (10:40).

What area of your life must be subdued in order to receive the best? Are there relationships that must be totally removed so you might move to the next level of growth?

God's command that Joshua wipe out everything that existed in the Promised Land before moving in symbolizes the importance of removing anything that distracts you. If God reveals to you that something or someone is hindering your walk with him, don't debate or wait. Remove it, avoid it all costs.

Any relationship or activity that leads you into sin must go. Sin can involve wasting time, a bad attitude, partial obedience - anything that you sense is not what God wants you doing or involved in becomes sin.

What is sin for you right now may not be sin for your friend. Seek God for guidance and then don't delay in addressing the area he shows you.

DAY TWO HUNDRED & EIGHTY-EIGHT

Unwavering faith
Joshua 14:6-15

Caleb and Joshua were young men when Moses sent them to scout out the promised land. They found abundant natural resources and giants. Their faith in God's ability to make anything happen enabled them to come back with a positive report while the others melted in fear. Forty years later, Caleb remained ready to fight the giants and claim God's personal promise to his family.

Caleb came to Joshua when the land was finally being divided up among the tribes of Israel and reminded him of God's promise that he would inherit the land he'd seen. "Now then, just as the Lord promised, he has kept me alive for forty-five years since the time he said this to Moses, while Israel moved about in the wilderness. So here I am today, eighty-five years old! I am still as strong today as the day Moses sent me out; I'm just as vigorous to go out to battle now as I was then. Now give me this hill country that the Lord promised me that day. You yourself heard then that the Anakites were there and their cities were large and fortified, but, the Lord helping me, I will drive them out just as he said" (14:10 - 12).

He never stopped believing God's promise. He was still alive and strong. He was still prepared to fight the giants living in the land he'd been promised. Just because God leads you to pursue something does not mean it will be quick or easy.

There will always be giants in your promised land. Remain faithful. Do not assume reputation or past efforts will get you there.

DAY TWO HUNDRED & EIGHTY-NINE

Putting off the hard part of a goal
Joshua 18:2-6

Years after Joshua had led the people into the Promised Land, seven tribes still had not gone in and done the work to fully clear and claim their tribe's inheritance. "So Joshua said to the Israelites: 'How long will you wait before you begin to take possession of the land that the Lord, the God of your ancestors, has given you?'" (18:2 - 3).

It sounds crazy. After forty years of waiting, how could they possibly delay? The heavy work had been done by Joshua and the army.

The path of least resistance is always the most traveled. To fully take the land, those tribes would have to do some very difficult and unpopular things. It was easier to mingle and trade with others living in the land.

When you leave the hard part of a job undone it reveals a lack of discipline and poor time use. Procrastination is a bad habit. If you have yet to take some steps that will help you cross a finish line, look for ways to focus attention on the detail, build a team, and get encouragement and accountability from others.

God will open doors, but you must walk through them.

DAY TWO HUNDRED & NINETY

Leaders go last
Joshua 19:49

Joshua had been a faithful servant to Moses. He never doubted God's promises. After forty years of desert wanderings, God charged him with leading the people through the toughest battles they'd ever known.
Yet, Joshua and his family were the last to receive their inheritance of land.

This fact is not coincidence. True leaders always go last. They are the last ones off the boat, the field, the job, etc. Leadership is hard and costly. Leaders are servants.

Some are born with innate leadership tendencies, but we all must learn to lead on some level, even if only in our own homes.

Where do you need to lead?

DAY TWO HUNDRED & NINETY-ONE

In the belly of the beast
Jonah 2:1-10

Jonah was a prophet by God's appointment. He was called to take a message of repentance to Nineva. Sin ran rampant in Nineva, and God was about to bring serious repercussions. Jonah didn't want to help save them. He hated Ninevites. So, he attempted to run away from God's call.

Running away from anything God has asked you to do will not turn out well.

Jonah ended up in the belly of an enormous fish for three days. Being in "the belly of the beast" is symbolic of a dark, confusing, and scary time. You are completely helpless with only three options during such times: call out for God's mercy, struggle in your own strength, or give up.

Jonah said, "In my distress I called to the Lord, and he answered me. From deep in the realm of the dead I called for help, and you listened to my cry" (2:1).

Giving up is not really an option. Whatever dark place you might find yourself in right now or one day in the future, call out for God's help. When he pulls you up, set about doing whatever he's called you to do.

DAY TWO HUNDRED & NINETY-TWO

How to know sin
Romans 14:23

Paul simplifies the sin question by stating that anything and everything that is not done in good faith is sin. In other words, outside the matters God speaks directly to as sin, if you don't feel convicted about something, it may not be sin for you. God extends a great deal of mercy to those young in years and in maturity of faith.

This is why things you may have done years ago without a second thought now pierce your conscience.

The Holy Spirit is used by God to reveal truth to you when the time is right. Once you've been given truth, you can't unknow it. You can choose to ignore it, but you will no longer be exempt from respecting that truth.

Listen carefully for leading from the Holy Spirit. Once you know what sin is for your life, respect it.

DAY TWO HUNDRED & NINETY-THREE

Valuable and vulnerable simultaneously
Luke 12:24

Allowing yourself to be vulnerable with people can be risky. When you trust and make yourself vulnerable, sometimes others take advantage, reject you, or simply turn away. Do you still feel valuable when someone does not honor your vulnerability?

Your sense of self-value will determine how you cope with the fear, shame, and disappointment.

When your vulnerability is not honored or reciprocated, the tendency is to try harder to get the respect or attention desired from others or to crawl in a personal hole hoping no one will see you. Neither response is necessary. Hold your head up and remember that you are valuable in God's eyes. Every single person is equally valuable to God, no matter what they've done or who they are.

Jesus used the birds as examples of how vulnerable we are yet valuable to God. Like a bird, many things can harm you, but nothing can get to you without God's permission. Rest in the knowledge that you have value.

Vulnerability is key to truly loving a husband as well as your family, friends, and fellow man. Allow yourself to be vulnerable and know that you are valuable.

DAY TWO HUNDRED & NINETY-FOUR

The prudent versus the simple
Proverbs 27:12

The prudent or wise person turns away from unhealthy, unproductive, or dangerous situations and people. The word prudent has been contorted into the derogatory term prude, which is often used by foolish people to unnerve prudent people. The simple or foolish person keeps going right past warning signs. There's a price or penalty for those who keep going.

Prudent people are those whose lives may not be full of glitter and glamour, but they are peaceful and have enough. Simple people are those that appear to be having a blast on the highway of life, but you often see them in a ditch down the road.

But how do you know? Sometimes there's a need to run into danger. The way you know how to avoid danger and the associated penalties is through discernment, which is a gift of the Holy Spirit.

Discernment is available to every Christian. It is what you just know, if paying attention, about people, situations, and choices. It is a sense you have, usually accompanied by warning signs along the way.

Make your choices based on being honest with yourself about the costs of having what you want, taking a particular road or path. On big decisions that could have high penalties such as where you go to school, who you marry, or hanging out with people who do drugs, consult God in prayer, the writings of notable people, and people older than you with a stable life.

There are three habits to practice that will keep you prudent:

1. Be honest with yourself. If it's too good to be true or too complicated or too confusing, it's probably not a good idea.
2. Keep at least one person in your life that is wise and willing to tell you the truth.
3. Pray and wait about everything. Yes, everything, even if it is years. God's silence means he's not finished working things out.

DAY TWO HUNDRED & NINETY-FIVE

A few good friends
Proverbs 27:17

"As iron sharpens iron, so one [woman] sharpens another," states Proverbs 27:17.

Do you have a real friend? Friends that you can trust with your successes and failures are few and far between. Everyone's connected 24/7 through social media, but it's mostly a mile wide and an inch deep.

The Proverb analogy of iron and sharpening may sound harsh, yet as the NIV Life Application Study Bible 1991 edition note says, "There is a mental sharpness that comes from being around good people."

"Good people" are those willing to discuss ideas, share insights, tell the truth, rejoice when you succeed, and mourn with you when you fail. You may not know anyone quite like that. Start acting that way yourself. Like attracts like. Don't falter in being a friend and treating others the way you want to be treated, just because others don't reciprocate.

No one succeeds unless someone else wants them to. Be generous with your ability to connect people, your skills and talents, and most of all with your encouragement.

DAY TWO HUNDRED & NINETY-SIX

How to know your own individual sin
James 4:17

James puts to rest the question about personal sin. "If anyone ... knows the good they ought to do and doesn't do it, it is sin for them" (4:17).

The Ten Commandments cover a lot of ground, but your life will be filled with times when you are unsure of right and wrong in a specific situation, in a moment. Whatever has been revealed to you becomes your responsibility. If God has opened your eyes to something that he does not approve of for you, avoid it.

This verse explains why you often see people "getting by" with things you feel convicted to not do. Children are given a lot more leeway than adults in society and by God. This is why many want to remain immature. Growing up comes with responsibility and accountability.

Do you want to remain child-like and have only the benefits and freedom of a child, or do you want to grow up and go to increasingly higher levels of God's unique plan for your life? It won't be easy. You will have to make many tough choices, often in a split second. However, the blessings for those who do what is hard are extraordinary.

DAY TWO HUNDRED & NINETY-SEVEN

Turn knowledge into wisdom and live well
Proverbs 1:7

"The fear of the Lord is the beginning of knowledge, but fools despise wisdom and instruction" (Proverbs 1:7).

Knowledge is about facts. Wisdom is about applying knowledge to your life. The world's accumulated knowledge is as vast as the stars. The Proverbs speak to the knowledge of how to be a successful human in business, relationships, parenting, and much more.

God set the world and laws of nature in motion. He wired principles into the human experience that are applicable to all regardless of belief. He didn't do this so you would fear him. He wants you to respect and revere his principles and sovereignty. The "fool" is the one who refuses to accept God's order and his place of authority.

The fool suffers mostly at her own hand while the wise builds a good life based on God's unique plan for her, one decision at a time.

Are you turning knowledge into wise living?

DAY TWO HUNDRED & NINETY-EIGHT

Living with treasure in a fragile vessel
2 Corinthians 4 and 5

In this life, you will experience death in many ways. Dreams and relationships will die. People around you will die. Ultimately, you too will face a physical death. However, Christ has made death of the body temporary for his followers. Paul writes, "We have this treasure in jars of clay to show that this all-surpassing power is from God and not from us" (2 Corinthians 4:7).

The treasure is your knowledge of Jesus and his power brought to you through the Holy Spirit. Our physical bodies are jars of clay. They are fragile and have an expiration date. Having such power within such a breakable vessel is the downfall of many.

"We are hard pressed on every side, but not crushed; perplexed, but not in despair; persecuted, but not abandoned; struck down, but not destroyed. We always carry around in our body the death of Jesus, so that the life of Jesus may also be revealed in our body" (4: 8 - 10).

The Corinthians are reminded to not lose heart, renounce secret and shameful ways, avoid deception of all kinds (5:1 - 2). The external troubles and natural aging that humans face is contrasted to the spiritual renewal and building taking place in the soul (5:16). It is important that you not get caught up in worry over troubles nor think that you are invincible because this Christ-power lives inside of you.

"So we fix our eyes not on what is seen, but on what is unseen, since what is seen is temporary, but what is unseen is eternal" (5:18).

DAY TWO HUNDRED & NINETY-NINE

When you're too scared and weak to talk
Ephesians 6:18, 2 Corinthians 12:9

You know the feelings associated with news or a revelation that something has gone terribly wrong. It may be an accident, your perfect plan derailed, a test of your faith, or some other twist in your individual path.

Fear and the overwhelming sense of weakness are crushing. Does your mind rush to solutions, or do you shut down?

Your weakness is designed to be replaced by Christ's strength. Any resistance to this fact will be your downfall or delay.

Paul shared with the Corinthians that he struggled with a "thorn in my flesh" (12:7). He pleaded with God to take it away. "But he said to me, 'My grace is sufficient for you, for my power is made perfect in weakness.' Therefore I will boast all the more gladly about my weaknesses, so that Christ's power may rest on me. That is why, for Christ's sake, I delight in weaknesses, in insults, in hardships, in persecutions, in difficulties. For when I am weak, then I am strong" (12: 8 - 10).

You too may be tormented by a thorn. Pray "in the Spirit" for the will to either fight the thorn or live with it (Ephesians 6:18). Don't give up, no matter what. God uses every person who seeks him, and he knows what you need to become exactly who and what he needs in the world.

DAY THREE HUNDRED

Thoughts, attitudes, and responses to opportunity
Psalm 139:23-24

Your enemy cashes in every day on ignorance about the mind. Your mind and its programming are your responsibility. You can't always control what is being put into your mind, but you can control what stays inside your mind.

Think of your mind like a computer. Each time a computer is exposed to the internet, fragments are left behind, "cookies." You must periodically clean out all those fragments or the computer will slow down and eventually stop working.

Your mind requires daily "cleaning." As Paul puts it, "Do not conform to the pattern of this world, but be transformed by the renewing of your mind. Then you will be able to test and approve what God's will is—his good, pleasing and perfect will" (Romans 12:2).

To renew your mind no special software is needed nor do you even need electricity. All you need is a commitment to start and finish each day with God. A Bible is good to have on hand for reading what God has to say about every possible situation you will ever face. If you go to him asking for renewal, he will show up.

He tells you to not be anxious but to give thanks for everything and ask him for anything (Philippians 4: 6). That means come to him with gratitude for what you have and be honest about what you want. He may not instantly grant your wish, but he will give you peace beyond what anyone can understand, and he'll guard your heart and mind with the power of Christ (Philippians 4:7).

DAY THREE HUNDRED & ONE

Grounded for life
Jeremiah 10:23-24

Loving parents don't like to ground their children. They do it to get their attention, to make a point about bad and disrespectful behavior. A parent who let's anything go and places no limits on the words and actions of a child is not being loving.

Being grounded usually means not going where you want to go, losing privileges and access to things you find entertaining. When grounded you still have food, clothing, and shelter. You often still get to partake in family activities.

God is an unwavering, unerring, and loving parent to his children. He will ground you for life, if necessary.

He will keep you tucked away until you learn the lesson that builds your character. God never gives up on disciplining you. He won't tire of keeping you at home on the weekends. He's unemotional about your disobedience. It does not offend him. Your tears and claims of unfairness don't annoy him or change his mind.

God knows that how you behave now has implications for where you are in life ten, twenty years down the road. He knows that the plan he's laid out for you will not work if you are not mature enough to handle it. How cruel would it be for God to put you in a position of responsibility without the ability to handle it.

Use your grounded time to learn patience and discipline. Pray for God's help in becoming responsible and ready for his plan. Anticipate a renewed life on the other side of being grounded, but don't take it into your own hands to decide when it's time to get back out there.

DAY THREE HUNDRED & TWO

The reliability of scripture
1 Peter 1:16-21

People often say things like, "The Bible is made up of fables and myths written by men long ago. It's not practical or relevant to modern times." You might also hear them say, "How can you believe that the Bible is literal, science has disproven most of it."

The Bible is God's ideas, commands, and promises written by people for people throughout the ages. Every story and verse have meaning and truth. Science has not disproven the Bible. In fact, science has increasingly verified the Bible.

The same people who make these statements about the Bible, generally say similar things about the U.S. Constitution. "The Constitution is out-of-date. It was written by white men. It's a living document that must be interpreted for the current times."

Peter writes, "For prophecy never had its origin in the human will, but prophets, though human, spoke from God as they were carried along by the Holy Spirit" (1:21).

He's pointing out that from beginning to end, the Bible was brought to people by God's Holy Spirit. God also speaks to men and women post-biblical times, including the American founders, regarding the way they should go and how to apply his unchanging principles.

Without the Bible, you cannot adequately understand how God wants you to live and the principles he designed to make the world work.

If you want to learn more about how science supports the Bible, go to www.answersingensis.com: "Answers in Genesis is an apologetics ministry, dedicated to helping Christians defend their faith and proclaim the gospel of Jesus Christ effectively. We focus on providing answers to questions about the Bible—particularly the book of Genesis—regarding key issues such as creation, evolution, science, and the age of the earth."

DAY THREE HUNDRED & THREE

Faith in the face of your nothingness
Hebrews 11:1, Revelation 13:10, 2:10, Ephesians 2:8-9

Living a life of faith is simultaneously the easiest and the hardest way to live. Faith is trust and confidence that the Trinity - Christ, God, and the Holy Spirit - is real and working directly in your life, no matter how lost, meaningless, or afraid you feel today.

Hebrews 11: 1 describes faith as "confidence in what we hope for and assurance about what we do not see."

The simplicity of faith is that you receive Christ's salvation and invitation to live eternally in heaven through no effort of your own outside of acceptance in your heart. The difficulty lies in retaining that confidence and assurance while facing the trials and temptations of life.

Amazing promises are made to "the faithful" throughout the Bible from Genesis to Revelation. Yet the Christian finds those promises do not work like magic. They come often slowly and through trials, loss, and years of waiting. Jesus warns followers of all eras that "patient endurance and faithfulness" will be required (Revelation 13:10).

In Revelation 2:10 he says, "Do not be afraid of what you are about to suffer… Be faithful, even to the point of death, and I will give you life as your victor's crown."

Your God knows how difficult it is to endure. You will never become self-sufficient in maintaining faith. He gives you grace and assistance as a gift through the Holy Spirit (Ephesians 2: 8 -9).

Don't be afraid or give up when you are overcome by what feels like God's silence, your own nothingness and doubt. This is normal. Speak to yourself and God about your concern, pray God's Words back to him, and list your blessings.

God will not leave or give up on you. Don't give up on him. Seek him out.

DAY THREE HUNDRED & FOUR

The cost and promise of faith
Hebrews 11:6

You have hopes and dreams for a steadily improving life for yourself, those you love, and your country. Right now, your dreams and prayers are about a better situation for yourself or someone. If you live in a box, you want a house. If you live in a house, you want a bigger or nicer one in a better location. If your children are in school, you hope they get out of school one day. Think about your list of prayers and notice that none of them contain elements of life getting harder in any way.

Faith allows you to continue hoping for life to get better. You can't see it now, but you believe because some time in the past you hoped, and things got better, even if just a little. Combined with hope there was action on your part in some form. Even prisoners can scratch out the passing of each day on a wall.

Sometimes life seems to get harder instead of turning out the way you had hoped. Don't stop taking actions based in faith and hope. God will honor your continued efforts.

God's promises and his blessings are activated by those who act on his word or his urging through the Holy Spirit. Hebrews 11 is a reminder list of people featured in the Bible for their faith in action. "And without faith it is impossible to please God, because anyone who comes to him must believe that he exists and that he rewards those who earnestly seek him" (11:6).

DAY THREE HUNDRED & FIVE

Faith like Joan of Arc
James 1:12

Joan of Arc, the 14th Century French army commander and martyr, is the patron saint of all who remain faithful to God's call on their life and to the truth, even to death. She, like so many truth-tellers, throughout history was killed for unwavering devotion to that which God placed on her heart to accomplish.

God often takes an unlikely servant to carry out his will and when they succeed the powerful hate them.

Joan was only seventeen, illiterate and without any prestige. She was a mere shepherdess. Because of her simple faith, when God called her to lead French armies against the occupying English, she didn't know to be fearful or doubt.

Church leaders, the king she saved, and the civil authorities all conspired to have her ultimately burned at the stake although innocent of any crime. She loved God and her country and died for both.

God has ordained a plan for your life. It may be grand from an earthly standpoint, or it may be quiet and solitary, but you can be assured it is important. Your enemy, the devil, will work to dissuade and distract you from remaining obedient and faithful. It may cost you life on earth, but never falter in standing up for what you know is truth and to fulfill whatever you know God has asked you to do.

Your reward from him will always be far greater than any punishment people can deliver.

DAY THREE HUNDRED & SIX

Generosity makes you richer
Proverbs 11:24-25

God has created a paradox that shows itself in nature as well as the lives of humans - with proper use things multiply. Think about how your muscles grow with use, cutting grass leads to it becoming thicker, or trees harvested make way for even more to regenerate. It is the same with love. The more you give, the more you have. The more you have, the more you want to give.

Jesus taught us that love is a verb. We express God's love when we give of our time, energy, and possessions. God blesses those who give their time, possessions, and energy by increasing what they have.

Sometimes we develop a scarcity mindset because of things that have happened in life or things we fear might happen. This thinking leads to selfishness. Poverty comes to those who are selfish with the gifts and resources God has given - financial, emotional or spiritual. "One person gives freely, yet gains even more; another withholds unduly, but comes to poverty" (11:24).

Get a hold of this fact - everything you have from breath in your lungs and food to talents and a home are not yours. They all belong to God.

He gives freely to you so you can serve others. It makes God smile when you do this. As his image-bearers you too get true joy when giving.

You should hoard nothing. Living by percentages to give, live, and save is wise, but do not attempt to "store up" too much, or it will become a burden to you.

DAY THREE HUNDRED & SEVEN

Recognizing a bully, and how to handle them
Psalm 141

Society has gone somewhat overboard to stop bullies. It's hard sometimes for children and adults alike to know how to joke around and even show appropriate affection to classmates and coworkers.

When the term bully is used, we think of the big kid at school taking lunch money from the weak kid or someone making fun of another for being different in some form or fashion.

A bully is anyone who manipulates you emotionally or becomes physically aggressive in order to get you to do what they want.

Do you know anyone that becomes sad, aggressive, combative, or silent when you disagree with them or don't do what they expected you to do?

In a healthy relationship, when someone you are close to acts "different" suddenly, you ask them what's wrong or apologize for the action that upset them. A conversation occurs where you both talk about the situation and then "move on."

However, if your sincere outreach results in more of the same or an escalation in behavior and you walk away feeling confused or abused that is unhealthy.

We have the Holy Spirit to give wisdom and discernment in order to know when to speak or not. In a moment of conflict, it's often best to hold your tongue. Let things cool down, pray about the person and situation, but always come back to them with what you feel is the appropriate words. Don't compromise to appease the bully. Always "tell the truth or at least don't lie," as Jordan Peterson, author of *12 Rules for Life* writes. A bully will always want more and will keep pushing you until you initiate a stop. Children and adults are both looking for boundaries. They may not be aware of it but that's human nature.

You are responsible for setting boundaries around your heart and self. It is the most loving thing toward yourself and others to have lines that you draw and enforce for behaviors, words, spending, and so on.

DAY THREE HUNDRED & EIGHT

Make up your mind to press past the hard part
1 Peter 4

If you've ever walked into a rough ocean, you know that swimming is easy once you get out past the breakers. Life gets easier too once you make up your mind to live for God, no matter what.

Before you "suffer in the body," as Peter says in 1 Peter 4:1, you fear the consequences of going against the grain or taking a leap of faith. But once you have faced it, you are done with it. Not that you will never be tempted again in various areas. The person who has committed in their heart to take the high road or the road less traveled passes through a form of temporary darkness. Once on the other side, whatever it was that felt so hard no longer seems so daunting.

Maybe you feared not having any friends if you didn't go along or that a boyfriend might break up with you or a teacher would fail you. The list goes on and on. Your enemy wants you to become a prisoner to those fears and addicted to whatever substance or behavior that he's convinced you goes along with the deal.

If you feel condemned or convicted by something, don't let it keep you trapped. Nothing is beyond the reach of Jesus' forgiveness. Once you confess it, it is finished. Yes, we all "will have to give account to him who is ready to judge the living and the dead" (4:5). However, God has the power to redeem all things. Focus not on the consequences of your past but on the opportunity your future holds.

DAY THREE HUNDRED & NINE

Never be fooled, God is real
Romans 1:18-25, Hebrews 4:13, 13:5, Psalm 103:19

You will be confronted with doubts about God's existence or his goodness. Challenging circumstances may cause you to doubt. Hurt or evil people will attempt to fool you into forsaking what you know. Be prepared so you won't falter.

Paul wrote, "For since the creation of the world God's invisible qualities—his eternal power and divine nature—have been clearly seen, being understood from what has been made, so that people are without excuse" (Romans 1:20).

God is omnipotent, omniscient, and omnipresent. Therefore, for those willing to see and hear, he is impossible to miss. We have historical and biblical documentation of Jesus' life, death, and resurrection. The Holy Spirit works in and through us so we know the truth of it all.

Why would some go to such lengths to kill your knowledge of and love for Jesus Christ and to tear down your belief in God?

Our enemy, Satan, rules this world and while he knows that the story ends with his ultimate defeat, his mission is to destroy as many lives as possible along the way. His weapon is deceit, and the human mind is his arena. It all starts there.

He can do nothing, but humans have free will. The enemy works with your human tendency toward pride, discouragement, and desire for power. He attempts to convince you that God is not enough, does not have your best interest in mind, and that you deserve more.

Pray that God will protect your mind, body, and spirit. Hang onto your faith and knowledge no matter what happens in this life.

DAY THREE HUNDRED & TEN

Be alert and self-controlled
1 Peter 5:1-10

Danger always has and will exist. The world is not a friendly place. It is only safe in small pockets because individuals decided to sacrifice in order to make it safe by agreeing to social norms, pooling resources to hire police, educating their young, and so on. Don't let fear of random violence or anything else keep you from living life fully. You have the first tangible tools of defense against harm already in your hands: be alert and self- controlled.

Safety trainers tell men and women alike to always be aware of their surroundings. Always be alert whether in a classroom or on a city street or wooded path.

Self-control means deciding to not be controlled by anxiety, addictions, habits, people, or anything else. Being a person with self-control does not just happen. It is hard work and takes commitment to discipline from within.

The woman prepared to take on any assignment God hands her and who lives her life to the fullest heeds all of Peter's direction:

- Be alert and self-controlled (5:8)
- Humble yourself under God's mighty hand (5:6)
- Cast your anxiety on him because he cares for you (5:7)
- Resist your enemy, the devil, by standing firm in your faith (5:9)

Take one step today toward making yourself more alert and self-controlled.

DAY THREE HUNDRED & ELEVEN

Like mother, like daughter
Genesis 1:27

God created us in his own image, both male and female. We carry many of God's attributes as humans. Yet, each person is unique. No one has the same fingerprint. Personality and life experience mingle to shape a person. Of greatest influence on the "shape" you become is your parent's genetic material, attitudes, and culture.

You are very much like your mother and your father.

There are things you like and don't like about each parent. Take an honest look at yourself, and you will find many of those same things within you. Embrace the good and commit to changing the attitudes and behaviors you do not like.

Change is very hard. Pray for God's help. Intentionally put yourself around people who model the kind of character you desire. Don't give up and don't believe for one moment that you can dishonor your parents and get by with it. No matter how much you dislike your parents, how embarrassing they are to you, and so on, you are required to honor them.

Do the best you can to love them as they are and yourself as their continuation of life.

DAY THREE HUNDRED & TWELVE

What if God really does answer every prayer?
1 John 5:14-15

To those who believe in Christ and have accepted him as their Savior, God makes amazing promises. The most powerful promise is that if you ask anything according to his will, he hears you (1 John 5:14). He meets all your needs as if heaven were on earth (Philippians 4:19).

Why do you not embrace his promises and claim them every day?

You've prayed and not received what you asked for quickly, or the door closed on what you wanted.

If you live for a God that can create and manage the whole world and every single soul in it, you can trust that he's going to answer your prayers in the manner that is best for all concerned. What if you began to pray bold, righteous prayers every day and then go out and do your best no matter what the situation?

Pray something like this: "God, today use my life. I want your will not mine. You know that I need _____. You've heard me ask for _____. I come to you again not in my righteousness but seeking your mercy on me, my family, community, and country. God, I love you more than myself. Help me to be the servant you've created me to be. Amen."

Jesus said, "And I will do whatever you ask in my name, so that the Father may be glorified in the Son" (John 14:13).

DAY THREE HUNDRED & THIRTEEN

Expectation is the root of unhappiness and the fuel for our faith
1 Peter 1:3-7

Shakespeare is often quoted as saying that expectation is the root of unhappiness. In reality, he penned a few lines in *All's Well That Ends Well* that say miracles happen most when least expected. It's when you're sure that something is yours because you deserve it that disappointment often visits. Expectations you place on others can lead to turmoil.

"When miracles have by the greatest been denied. Oft expectation fails and most oft there Where most it promises, and oft it hits Where hope is coldest and despair most fits" — William Shakespeare, All's Well That Ends Well.

It may feel like a paradox that expectation is both the root of unhappiness and necessary to a vibrant faith. Much of life as a Christ-follower does require holding tension between what feels like two opposing emotions or ideas. The very essence of Christianity is knowing the journey's end but having no idea what the journey itself holds.

Peter wrote, "In his great mercy he has given us new birth into a living hope through the resurrection of Jesus Christ from the dead, and into an inheritance that can never perish, spoil or fade. This inheritance is kept in heaven for you…" (1 Peter 1: 3 -4).

You have a "living hope" because a promise of eternity with God is being kept safe for you. The problem is you must run the gauntlet of this life first, which is fraught with many pitfalls. Peter warns and encourages. "For a little while you may have had to suffer grief in all kinds of trials. These have come so that the proven genuineness of your faith—of greater worth than gold, which perishes even though refined by fire—may result in praise, glory and honor when Jesus Christ is revealed" (1 Peter 1: 5 - 7).

DAY THREE HUNDRED & FOURTEEN

Standing with Christians and Jews
Romans 11

Judeo-Christian (Jewish and Christian) principles, ideologies, and culture are rooted in God's Word. The culture you enjoy, known as Western Civilization, comes from Judeo-Christian ideology. The cornerstone of that ideology is individual freedom, value, and responsibility. Wherever this belief prevails, societies prosper. There are two common lies that weaken the civil society and individual freedoms you enjoy in America.

Lie # 1 = God is unfair.

Deep down many are angry at God for things that have happened to them and offended by his claim of authority over every life and the entire earth.

Lie #2 = Christians and Jews are all hypocrites and liars.

Many people of your own faith will do despicable things. People you know and trust will lie and act in hypocritical ways. If your brother or sister commits a crime, you must turn them over to the proper legal system for justice. However, you should not abandon your faith because hypocrites and liars exist. Human nature is the same across all people groups and creeds.

Don't place your political identity above your cultural or spiritual identity in hopes of being accepted or seen as intelligent.

DAY THREE HUNDRED & FIFTEEN

Know the Ten Commandments
Exodus 20

God gave people ten simple rules to live by. They are intended to prevent you from hurting yourself or others. Living by these commandments allows you maximum freedom.

When Moses presented the Ten Commandments, he said, "Do not be afraid. God has come to test you, so that the fear of God will be with you to keep you from sinning" (Exodus 20:20).

God's Ten Commandments for all people:

1. Don't let anything or anyone become a god to you
2. Don't make images of anything in heaven or on earth to worship
3. Don't misuse my name, making it a curse or a joke
4. Don't work without rest. Take time to reflect and worship every seventh day
5. Don't disrespect your father and your mother (so it will go well with you)
6. Don't murder
7. Don't commit adultery, i.e., have sex with anyone not your spouse
8. Don't steal
9. Don't lie about anyone or anything
10. Don't covet what others have

Why do you think these rules for life have been removed from schools and courthouses?

DAY THREE HUNDRED & SIXTEEN

Believe like me
Matthew 28:16-20

When you experience something wonderful, you want to share it with others. Referrals are the best way to build a business or a movement. Christianity spread throughout the world and grew from a handful of establishment-hated, itinerant Jews to become ten percent of the thoroughly pagan Roman empire in less than 300 years because the truth of what people saw and experienced in their own lives was so powerful, they could not contain it. Once the emperor Constantine converted, the church expanded rapidly. Today, Rome is still best known for the Vatican.

Skeptical historians asked, how could it be? How could those original Greek and Jewish followers of Jesus have survived in such a hostile environment?

Aside from the fact that God's plans always prevail, the answer is found in how those early Christians lived their lives. The instructions remain today in the New Testament letters from the Apostle Paul, Peter, John, James, Luke, and the others. They went about being good citizens - pulling discarded infants from the trash heap, feeding widows, providing good products and services.

In Jesus' great commission, he says, "Therefore go and make disciples of all nations, baptizing them in the name of the Father and of the Son and of the Holy Spirit, and teaching them to obey everything I have commanded you. And surely I am with you always, to the very end of the age" (Matthew 28: 19 - 20).

Sometimes we get focused on the making and teaching parts of Jesus' commission. The most powerful "disciples" of Christ live in such a way that people around them are provoked to ask questions that lead to a simple answer - There is a God and Jesus is his son.

Trust God with whatever is to happen next. You may or may not be a part of converting that person to a particular faith path. Jesus met people where they were. You can too.

DAY THREE HUNDRED & SEVENTEEN

Predestination
Ephesians 1:4-6, 11, Romans 8:28-30, Acts 13:48

Predestination is a topic that divides some Christians. God uses the Holy Spirit to draw people to him. You get to decide whether or not you follow his leadings. Too much focus on predestination can dampen your hope, make you lazy, or engender pride. How you act, what you say, and your life choices do matter. You will find evidence of cause and effect everywhere you look.

Jesus said that even he didn't know when the end would come. You can't know the end of your own story. While God knows everything, he's given you a life race to run and freewill day-by-day. He will not be surprised by your bad choices. He will forgive any and all sin you confess.

God's ultimate plan for every person who will submit to Christ's authority is eternity with him. Not all will join us with him. It's not our job to decide. We are given opportunities to speak or act in ways that point toward Christ. In and through those opportunities your character is shaped, and your soul is prepared for something much, much bigger than what we know here.

If you've accepted Christ, you are destined for heaven. While here on earth, you are destined for use by God. He will work everything together for your good. Trust him and obey the urgings of the Holy Spirit.

DAY THREE HUNDRED & EIGHTEEN

Anatomy of forgiveness
Exodus 34:7, Psalm 32

Forgiveness is a meaningless concept if you don't believe right and wrong exists. If it's "all good," why say you're sorry, for anything?

Implied in forgiveness is a wrong committed, either by accident or intentionally, and then erased as the result of some payment. For this sort of "transaction" to take place, you must accept that there's an order or legitimacy of things.

If you break a law enacted by duly elected representatives, a judge appointed by those people you elected can determine the "cost" of your "sin." It may involve paying a fine, doing community service, or even jail time.

Within relationships there's an unwritten expectation that feelings, honesty, and fairness have legitimacy. When trust is broken in some fashion, the "cost" takes the form of the injured person's willingness to let it go, forget the transgression, not hold it against you. Forgiveness is necessary for restoration, a return to good standing, or peace between individuals as well as people and society or organizations.

The ultimate forgiveness transaction came when Christ picked up the tab for every human sin past, present, and future. He set the example to follow. For Christians, forgiveness is a major component of faith that entails accepting these tenets:

1. There is a one, true sovereign God. He is compassionate and forgiving. He holds all people accountable for their actions (Exodus 24:7).
2. You have sinful tendencies.
3. When you sin in thought, word, or deed it is rebellion against God.
4. Confession of sin means you agree that God has a right to declare that what you have done is wrong. You are also affirming the intention to stop the sin.
5. Once a sin is acknowledged and sincerely confessed, it is forgiven forever because of Christ's blood sacrifice. His submission, death, and resurrection enabled the payment for all sin, for all people.

Forgiveness is not something to withhold from others or avoid asking for as needed. Every wrong must be paid for by someone eventually. Yours is covered by Christ. Pay it forward to others.

DAY THREE HUNDRED & NINETEEN

Your gifts will develop out of sight
Luke 2:52

We all want to be sought after for something, desired, included. The attributes that God will use in and through you are always developed out of sight just like most of the iceberg is underwater and fruit appears on the tree after many months of development and nurturing that begins with the roots.

Jesus spent most of his life in obscurity. His public ministry lasted only three years.

If you want to be great at anything - teacher, painter, writer, carpenter, physician, musician, athlete, leader - the becoming will happen mostly alone. People who excel at anything learn to say yes to what develops skill or craft and no to the unnecessary distractions of life.

Your gifts will be noticed and sought after when you are using them versus when you are promoting your gifts. Isaiah 50:11 speaks of the people lighting their own fires instead of waiting on God. He promises that they will walk in their own light, not his.

This is a warning to those who want the harvest without the labor, those who want to take shortcuts. God has placed something unique in you that will be useful to him and your fellowman. Seek to know your gift and then seek to refine and build it. God will ensure you are placed where those gifts will shine brightest.

DAY THREE HUNDRED & TWENTY

Be thoughtful about your personal brand
Proverbs 15:26, 16:21, 24

Everything you do and say is noticed by someone. Everything you do and say, buy, and attend is forming your brand. You are co-marketing with actors, artists, companies, causes with every purchase and shared post.

Think for a moment about what someone looking at your life in real time and on social media might conclude about your brand.

Consider these questions about your own personal brand:

- What words would people use to describe you?
- What do your social media posts highlight?
- Do the artists playing on your devices sing of good things without using profanity?
- Do the movies and shows you watch reflect hope or horror, wholesomeness or worldliness?

Brand symbolizes the promise of a company, product, or individual. You represent the best and most enduring brand ever. How are you doing?

DAY THREE HUNDRED & TWENTY-ONE

Enemies often appear nice and well-meaning
Acts 20:28-31

Enemies come in the form of people, habits, beliefs, attitudes, and substances. An enemy is anything or anyone that tests your will to remain a person free to pursue God's plan for your life.

The majority of enemies you will encounter in life will seem neutral or even pleasant at first. Here are a few examples of things that can become your enemy.

- Relationships that require pretending or silence in certain areas
- People who never acknowledge a wrong or hurt
- Substances such as nicotine, caffeine, alcohol, marijuana, cocaine, prescription pain or anti-depression medicine
- Repetitive behaviors that disfigure or diminish you such as excessive online time, cutting or pulling at parts of yourself, over or undereating
- Rules for thinking and behaving that limit personal accountability and thinking for oneself

God intends for every person to love themselves and others. Love can be tough at times because it can require you to say no, to see and speak unpleasant truth, and sometimes even remove yourself from situations and people.

God also has a unique and specific plan for each individual. A person emotionally or physically enslaved by anyone or anything cannot live out God's plans.

DAY THREE HUNDRED & TWENTY-TWO

How to be a Christian in a non-Christian culture
Galatians 2:11-21

Compromise is important to getting along and is often a first step toward introducing faith to someone. But never compromise the truth of God's Word when confronted with questions or those who twist God's truth. Proverbs 29:25 says that fear of man will prove to be a snare.

Christians can't expect those who don't believe to come to church and immediately begin practicing the faith and adhering to moral teachings. Many of those who need the love of Christ reflected through you will not even be familiar with God's Ten Commandments. A generation has grown up knowing nothing more than a moment of silence. The cultural expression and teaching of America's history has been scrubbed of the stories and unique characters that make it exciting and real across time and culture. This means a majority of people no longer understand that what made the American brand strong and America a leader throughout the world was a firm belief in and reliance on Judeo-Christian values and principles.

So, treat the friend or acquaintance that might be open to speaking about faith or coming to church like you would a guest in your home. You would not expect a guest to clean the house, help pay the mortgage, or discipline the kids.

Hospitality comes first in your home. With Christ and the church, love should come first and prevail. Next, as with any meaningful relationship, somewhere along the way love includes boundaries and some ground rules.

Too often churches today err on the extremes. It's either anything goes because Christ's salvation is "free," or follow this long list of rules and adhere to our doctrine or be an outsider. Start with a conversation and meeting people where they are in life.

DAY THREE HUNDRED & TWENTY-THREE

Jesus' call to big, tough love
Mark 10:42-45, John 13:34-35

Jesus was always talking about and modeling love. Love is an attitude revealed in your actions. In John 13, he made a new command. He told them to love each other, just like he'd loved them. And if they would do this, he said, "Everyone will know that you are my disciples" (13:35).

What kind of love had they witnessed Jesus expressing?

- Washing their dirty feet
- Making time for little children, sick and hurt people, difficult people
- Providing healing to dying and sick people
- Protecting scorned women
- Calling wrong out in no uncertain terms
- Urging people to stop sinning
- Teaching in terms even the unlearned could relate to their own lives
- Associating with socially unacceptable people and listening to them
- Meeting needs and then calling those very same people to follow God's law
- Upholding God's law with compassion and without wavering

The kind of love Jesus calls for is never "about" you. He calls himself a servant and a slave in Mark 10: 44-45.

Jesus' big love makes no room for pride or being delicate or pretending what is wrong is right. It presses you to help when it's not convenient, to give when it hurts, to let go of offenses and stop complaining. Jesus expects you to never go soft on God's truth and his commands but to always be gentle with individuals.

This is hard love. But this is why people take notice when you live this way. It's so very radical. You disappear behind Jesus' supernatural light shining through. They see Jesus. Some will come closer, some will run, others will attempt to kill the light. Trust God with them all and with yourself.

DAY THREE HUNDRED & TWENTY-FOUR

Words as weapons
Ephesians 4:20-32

Words have just as much power to destroy as any fist. Fits of rage that proclaim hate, call out ugly names and curse words, belittle others, and assert dominance destroy the speaker as well as the recipient. If you indulge in this behavior or receive it from someone, you can stop it.

This behavior is of darkness and it destroys people's spirit and dampens their potential.

You may feel powerless to stop it, but you are not. When asked, God will bring all manner of assistance and forces to bear on helping you. If you are the one who rages, pray for self-control and the ability to see the damage you do to yourself and others fully. If you receive rage from someone, pray for help in setting boundaries and learning to love yourself enough and the other person to work toward an end to this behavior.

Ephesians 4: 23 speaks of being made new in the attitude of your mind. Changing your mind and therefore behaviors is possible with Christ's help. It may be very hard, but it begins with awareness of a need to change and then an attitude of willingness.

The next time hateful words are coming out of you or at you stop, literally freeze, take a deep breath, and then pray for God's guidance. Do not rationalize abusive talk. Correction should be firm but yelling, name calling, cursing, and intimidation are never okay.

See James 3 for more about the power of the tongue.

DAY THREE HUNDRED & TWENTY-FIVE

Faith like Mary
Luke 1

Have you ever thought about Mary from a regular girl, human standpoint? She was very young, not of any great wealth or position in society, engaged to a seemingly average guy, and living with her parents in a backwater village. Yet, she set a powerful example of how to deal with life that is relevant to you.

One day she's just minding her own business and the angel Gabriel shows up. He's not an average angel. Imagine a Navy Seal or Green Beret and you will get a sense of Gabe. He's special forces. He says, "Greetings, you who are highly favored! The Lord is with you" (Luke 1: 28).

Luke 29 tells us she was scared and confused. Gabriel responds: "Do not be afraid, Mary; you have found favor with God. You will conceive and give birth to a son, and you are to call him Jesus. He will be great and will be called the Son of the Most High. The Lord God will give him the throne of his father David, and he will reign over Jacob's descendants forever; his kingdom will never end" (1: 30 - 33).

Pause and ponder Mary's first response. Like most of us, she's thinking in literal, practical terms. "How will this be," Mary asked the angel, "since I am a virgin" (1: 34)?

Gabriel's answer is simple. He tells her the Holy Spirit and God himself will handle everything. Note that she's given no explicit instructions. He doesn't tell her to craft an explanation or to cut her hair or to begin a ministry or anything.

Mary says, "I am the Lord's servant…May your word to me be fulfilled" (1:38).

Gabriel may not have shown up with instructions for you, but everything you need to live like Mary is found in God's Word. Read and study it and then believe and act like you trust God has got it all covered and you are his servant.

DAY THREE HUNDRED & TWENTY-SIX

Consequences of faith like Mary
Luke 2

After Mary's amazing encounter with the angel Gabriel and being told God chose her for a special mission, she was given a place of high honor in her community and told to take the next nine months off and relax.

No, that is not at all what happened.

Mary likely went through hell right up to the birth of Jesus on a cold winter's night in a borrowed barn.

In Mary's day, if you were engaged and turned up pregnant, you could get stoned to death or at the least ditched by your fiancé. Joseph had his own encounter with an angel, so he stuck with Mary. But life didn't get easy for either of them. In fact, it got worse in many ways. Ultimately, Joseph is no longer in the picture by the time of Jesus' crucifixion.

From her young days as the virgin who becomes the mother of God's son to the very end, she's portrayed as a humble servant to God. After Jesus' birth when all the shepherds and wise men are coming to see the child all have awaited, "Mary treasured up all these things and pondered them in her heart" (2:19).

It's hard to wait and trust God whether you feel he's called you to something special or not. Yet, if you are alive and know Jesus Christ as the one who saved you, there's a special plan for you. It may not be on a stage, but it is your role on God's stage called history. Be like Mary. Don't attempt to write your script and help God use you. Treasure up and ponder what he whispers into your heart. Trust him to work out all the details, even when you are standing in a Tsunami of trouble.

DAY THREE HUNDRED & TWENTY-SEVEN

Responsibility for those around you
1 Thessalonians 5:12-15

It's so much easier to talk about someone than to talk to them when they are not like you or have an obvious problem. Many of Paul's letters urge the budding Christian communities to act in what seems like two conflicting ways.

The Thessalonians are told to "live in peace with each" other (5:13), and to "warn those who are idle and disruptive, encourage the disheartened, help the weak, be patient with everyone. Make sure that nobody pays back wrong for wrong, but always strive to do what is good for each other and for everyone else (5:14 - 15).

Most would think that to live in peace with each other means to leave people alone, not tell them what to do or not do.

Whether in a community of people or a one-on-one relationship, to warn, encourage, be patient with, avoid revenge, and strive to do the right thing takes energy. It can be exhausting. But it begins with a willingness to be present and to be real. Don't expect a medal or fanfare. Living as someone "keeping it real" will for sure cause many to look the other way. Some will even attempt to eliminate you.

Wherever you are in life with situations, it's about the people and relationships. Whatever you are working toward, God's outcome has to do with bearing up with and loving people, including you.

DAY THREE HUNDRED & TWENTY-EIGHT

"I have had enough, Lord"
1 Kings 19

The bigger your feat or conquest for God, the greater the low that will follow. Think on a time when you felt defeated and weary. Maybe you, like Elijah in 1 Kings 19:4, told the Lord you'd had enough. You'd had a win, done your best, and things just seemed to get worse.

Whenever you take a step toward doing something tough that you know is right, that God is leading you to do, it will always be followed by an opposing force that feels stronger than you. Joyce Meyer says, "New level, new devil."

Do not let this shake your faith. Do not give up. 1 Kings 19 tells the story of how Elijah experienced fear, fatigue, and depression after being used by God to accomplish two amazing feats. Read 1 Kings 18 for the story of how Elijah revealed the falseness of the evil Jezebel and her husband, King Ahab. As a result, the people killed Jezebel's false prophets. Her response was a promise to kill Elijah.

Jezebel had a lot of power. She had invested a lot in her "prophets" to keep the people beholden to her power. Only great leaders willingly relinquish power. Jezebel and Ahab were only about expanding their power. Elijah knew the truth, and God used him to limit their evil. He threatened their pride, authority, and control over the people.

Anything that shines the light of truth into dark places will meet with resistance. Resistance to efforts that will help make things better for people creates an opportunity for you to grow your faith and usefulness to God.

Elijah was human, just like you. He was afraid and ran for his life (19:3). He prayed to God, "'I have had enough, Lord…Take my life; I am no better than my ancestors.' Then he lay down under the bush and fell asleep" (19: 4 - 5).

God's response was to send an angel to feed Elijah. After resting and eating, God called Elijah to meet him on a mountain. He then encouraged Elijah and gave him instructions for next steps in his work. If you are still here, your mission is not over. If you feel weary and defeated, pray, eat, and rest. Seek God for the next steps in your mission.

DAY THREE HUNDRED & TWENTY-NINE

"Everything is possible for one who believes"
Mark 9:14-29

Mark 9 relays a story where Jesus encounters a father whose son is mute and often has convulsions. The father says, "But if you can do anything, take pity on us and help us" (9:22). Jesus responds to the man, and to us all, with an incredulous question followed by a life changing statement.

"If you can?' said Jesus. 'Everything is possible for one who believes" (9:23).

Imagine how breathless you would feel if Jesus said those words to you after all the years, all the times you have suffered, after all the times you've given up hope on healing change. Your life and issues are so huge to you. Those persistent problems that don't change no matter how hard you try or pray seem like mountains of granite.

Then you meet Jesus face-to-face and he asks about your enormous problem. His response is a slight shrug and loving laugh. He says, "This is nothing. Just believe and anything is possible."

Are the tears welling up in your eyes? Stay in your scene with Jesus for a few moments. Let his words sink into your heart because they are true, and he's saying them to you. We are often like the boy's father who exclaimed, "I do believe; help me overcome my unbelief" (9:24)!

You so want to believe, but seriously, it's been too long, it's too enormous, and you're just too hurt. Part of the reason you can't overcome the unbelief is because you believe lies that the enemy has whispered in your ear for years. The other part of why you don't believe is that you have not remained intimate with Jesus. Even as you make mistakes and as things seem to get harder and your disappointment mounts, stay with him. Take hold of his hand like a little child and refuse to let go.

Here's why that's so important - if you are holding onto Jesus, it's much harder to rationalize doing the things that separate you from him. It's not the big, nasty sins that keep us from Jesus. It's the sins we think are inconsequential. For example, over spending, indulgence, getting offended, laziness, bad attitude, selfishness, etc.

DAY THREE HUNDRED & THIRTY

A little evil does a lot of harm
Matthew 16:1-6

In Jesus' day there were two main religious groups among the Jews - the Sadducees and Pharisees. They had a lot of power, and while they both believed in the one true God, much of what they taught and believed was false. All the people suffered because the Sadducees and Pharisees loved power more than truth.

Jesus came and began teaching truth that revealed their lies and challenged their authority over the people. In him, the two parties found something to agree upon. They both hated Jesus and together they plotted to kill him.

Jesus told his disciples, "Be careful…Be on your guard against the yeast of the Pharisees and Sadducees" (Matthew 16:6).

He was telling them that a little bit of evil, like yeast spreading throughout dough to make it rise, can do much harm. Listen very carefully to what those in power are saying. Is it true? You often know deep in your gut what is true and what is false. Words, actions, and ideas that are false make you feel unwell, a bit nervous. If you pay attention, you will come to learn how lies affect you physically, whether they are lies you are telling or those coming from someone else.

Human nature is to seek power and hold on to power, at all costs. The mark of great leaders is an ability to share power with those under them. The first American president, George Washington, set a precedent and great example when he stepped down from power at a time when he could have easily become a king.

Are your leaders speaking truth and honoring the individual or are they spreading evil?

DAY THREE HUNDRED & THIRTY-ONE

Wise people have three things in common
Isaiah 50:10-11

Some say wisdom comes with age. Maybe it's because with age you come to realize how very little you know. Calendar years do not always predict wisdom or immaturity. People with understanding and an ability to lead others well have three things in common:

1. Wise people place a high value on the individual, and the importance of individual freedom to succeed or fail in their endeavors
2. Wise people appreciate history and historical context, even if just their own. This means they have at least a vague sense that history is a teacher, and it will repeat itself for better or worse when conditions are right
3. Wise people know that they can't really accomplish anything of lasting value without others and without God

Isaiah 50: 10 - 11 speaks to the consequences of arrogance, a sense of self-sufficiency, confidence in one's own intelligence and accomplishment. No matter how wealthy, smart, or beautiful you become, there's no pathway to salvation, sanctification, grace, mercy, and forgiveness without God.

DAY THREE HUNDRED & THIRTY-TWO

Was Jesus against wealth?
Matthew 19:19-24

Some will attempt to confuse you and lead you to believing that Jesus was against wealth. Remember that Satan knows God's Word, and he always inserts bits of truth into his traps. Jesus' call to care for the poor, to love one another, and to take up our cross and follow him were not calls to a society built around Socialism.

The success of America, in large part rests on an understanding of the importance of property rights: land, money, one's body and mind. James Madison, Father of the American Constitution, asserted that people not only have a right to their tangible property but that their intangible right to think and do as guided by conscience is a sort of property to which they have a right also.

In Matthew 19: 19 -24, Jesus responds to the wealthy young man who asks how he might be perfect by telling him to sell his possessions and give to the poor and then come follow him. After the young man goes away sad, Jesus says to his disciples, "Truly I tell you, it is hard for someone who is rich to enter the kingdom of heaven. Again I tell you, it is easier for a camel to go through the eye of a needle than for someone who is rich to enter the kingdom of God" (19:23 -24).

Jesus is not making a statement against money or material wealth or people with great wealth.

His message is about trusting in God to care for you and to direct your steps. It is about relinquishing your power to him. When government is in charge of taking the wealth you produce with your mind and body and distributing it to others that is a perversion of God's order of nature and of human beings. While not perfect, Capitalism is the best method for distributing wealth because it rests with individuals creating and trading among themselves, often never knowing each other yet still serving each other's needs and wants.

If you have no wealth to give, then how can you sacrifice for the widow and orphan?

Giving and serving is as much about you as it is about the receiver. You will be poor in spirit if prevented from exercising your free will to sacrificially give of yourself. A surrogate, like government or any other coercion, cannot do this for you.

DAY THREE HUNDRED & THIRTY-THREE

Individual rights and collective good
John 5:1-15, 2 Corinthians 3:17

First among all nations, America clearly defined individual rights. They rest on freedom of choice. This reflects Jesus' life and message. He came so each and every person, male or female, all nationalities, races, creeds, might be free (Galatians 5:1). In the New Testament stories about his ministry and life, you find Jesus showing compassion and being inclusive of those often excluded from places of honor in society - widows, children, women in general, sick, poor, weak, tax collectors, etc.

You always find Jesus empathetic toward all but never coddling or condoning bad behavior. Even Jesus never assumed that his kindness, miracles, or positive words would change a person's heart and mind. Look at a few examples:

- Man whose son had some form of epilepsy (Mark 9: 14 - 29)
- Bleeding woman (Matthew 9:20)
- Woman at the well (John 4: 1 -26)
- Cripple by the pool of Bethesda (John 5: 1 - 15)
- Zacchaeus, the tax collector (Luke 19: 1 - 10)
- Peter, the disciple who Jesus called the rock upon which the church was established (Matthew 16:18)

In every example of Jesus interacting with someone, even up to his mock trial and confrontation with Pontius Pilot before the nasty mob calling for his crucifixion, he speaks the truth. At times, he spoke in parables and metaphor. Sometimes he spoke the truth plainly. But he always leaves the decision of what to do with the truth in the hands of the individual. Jesus never fudged on the facts so people might not feel uncomfortable or have to do inner work to change. He readily healed physical ailments out of the individual's control but never attitudes and actions, all within the individual's control.

How then should governments balance the individual rights of a terrorist with the safety of society or the parent whose child has an addiction that leads them to steal from and threaten the family?

Rules based on principles of right and wrong are invaluable in these situations. Choices have consequences. Individuals forfeit their right to certain freedoms when their choices harm others.

DAY THREE HUNDRED & THIRTY-FOUR

Where Jesus is, demons can't stay for long
Luke 4:31-37

In the New Testament whenever Jesus showed up the "demons" in people would get nervous. They usually acted out, cried out, or begged Jesus to leave them alone. They always put on a show by causing people to do dangerous or stupid things. Wherever Jesus is present, demons can't stay. They never leave without some sort of fight or drama. Why would they?

You have the authority of Jesus at your beck and call 24/7. If you've committed yourself to him in your heart, he's there for you and for those you bring to him in prayer.

Don't be fooled or intimidated by demons. As soon as you bring Jesus in, they will use everything from flattery to downright threats to get you to back off. Be careful also not to confuse the person with the demon influencing them. Your battle is not with the person (Ephesians 6:12). It's likely that the demon is using someone you love very, very much and watching them suffer is excruciating.

The cruelest thing you can do is leave yourself or the other person to the demon, especially when you have the most potent weapon available.

What do demons look like?

They take many shapes and forms, such as addiction, rage, gossip, hurting the helpless, comparison, laziness, compulsions, fear, self-loathing, spending, phobias, lying, unforgiven wrongs and hurts, back talk, hitting, biting, cutting, burning, and so on. The list is endless.

A demon is an unseen agent of your enemy. They often initiate actions and/or attitudes that keeps a person from fully experiencing peace, joy, relationships, and the life path God planned for them.

Don't forget, when Jesus' authority is called in demons can't stay. However, some people will choose their demons over Jesus. People must want help before they can fully receive help. Never stop praying for those you love who have allowed demons to remain in their life. You may also need to use firm, loving words and actions with those who are being taken advantage of by demons.

DAY THREE HUNDRED & THIRTY-FIVE

Have goals and a schedule
Proverbs 16:9

Depending on your personality and habits you developed from a young age, having goals and a schedule may be hard. Balance is the key. Living by percentages applies to your money and your life as a whole.

Your life is meant to be invested, not just spent or thrown away. Even if you've endured tragedy, your life is meant to be invested wisely. No one is a waste in God's eyes.

God gives each of us a set time on earth to learn certain lessons and to play a role in his plans. Extreme obedience is required to follow his schedule and plan. Thoughtfulness and prayer will enable you to set God-given goals and a daily schedule that contributes to your health, wealth, and relationships appropriately.

God will never ask you to work without ceasing for extended periods of time. He's clear about the need for a Sabbath day once a week. God does not want you to be lazy. He may create times of quiet and rest, but in general a balanced life requires some shape and structure. God will not lead you to set goals intended to glorify you. Often goals you are led to set are about preparing you for his use in something that may or may not be related to what you have in mind.

Like a good parent, he delights in you. He wants the best for you, no matter what kind of burdens you have physically, emotionally, or relationally.

The consequences of obedience to God in the use of your time each day are beyond your imagination. Don't rationalize your way out of obedience. Do what you know in your gut and heart is right for you day in and day out.

Take inventory of your daily and weekly schedule. Where do you need to adjust?

DAY THREE HUNDRED & THIRTY-SIX

That nagging, lonely, "what am I doing" feeling
Psalm 139

At some point along the way, most people evaluate themselves and their life. They look at those around them or in the media and compare themselves. Unmet goals, unrealized dreams begin to look like exit ramps in the rearview mirror. Relationships are not easy or fulfilling, maybe none have substance beyond the superficial and perfunctory.

The question nags: "What's the point, does God really have a plan for me?"

Whether you've been lacking in obedience or are on course, if you're still here, God has a plan.

King David's Psalm 139 reveals truth that guides and comforts:

No matter where you are God's right hand will hold you fast (10). When darkness surrounds you, God will bring light in the form of comfort, wisdom, or help (11-12). God knows you intimately because he created you, he knit you together in your mother's womb (13). God knew before you were born everything about your life from beginning to end (16). Praise him because you were made in such a miraculous way by a God who knows and loves each soul (14).

Knowing who God is, how he views you, and what he expects of you as one of his people is the root of wisdom and the wellspring of prosperity. Wisdom is not about amassing knowledge or experience alone. Prosperity is not about a bank account only. God's Word in your heart and mind enable you to be used by him for creating value.

DAY THREE HUNDRED & THIRTY-SEVEN

The meaning of citizenship
Philippians 3:13-15

Becoming an American citizen in some ways parallels becoming a Christian - renewal, shedding the old, free, pledging allegiance to an idea, commitment to a way of life, and respect for the laws. The citizen and Christian alike must be willing, on a figurative level at least, to die for the ideas to which they pledge.

The first immigrants to form lasting communities on the continent that would become America were Europeans, mostly British. They brought their language, Christian faith, and customs. They brought a shared way of thinking based on British Common Law, Greek and Roman philosophy. They came to stay, to be free of war, famine, and religious persecution. The British colonists did not come to conquer. They had economic goals. Early interactions and relationships with the Native Americans were mostly peaceful and friendly. However, things changed when the newcomers began competing for scarce food during droughts and taking up space on land that natives had used for other purposes. Ultimately, as Spaniards, French, Dutch, and more English came, fighting began and then wars. The sheer numbers would overcome the natives along with contagious diseases, like smallpox. Africans would come mostly unwillingly as slaves between roughly 1619 and early 1800s.

Beginning with the settling of Jamestown, Virginia in 1607 and the landing of the Mayflower in 1620 at present day Cape Cod, Massachusetts, immigrants from Ireland, Italy, Greece, and France as well as other countries across Eastern and Western Europe came to America for the idea she represented.

Immigration through most of American history meant starting a new life, without governmental programs. People may have tended to live in neighborhoods with immigrants from their nation of origin, but they learned the language, pledged allegiance to the flag, and integrated into the idea of America, followed the laws, and helped affirm respectable social mores.

Becoming an American, like becoming a Christian means something. It is costly, but the rewards are great. It does not help anyone to lower standards for becoming a Christian or an American. When we elevate those who come not to integrate but to undermine our country or faith, we do great harm to the good of the whole.

DAY THREE HUNDRED & THIRTY-EIGHT

Distinctions between ceremonial, civil, and moral law
Matthew 5:17-20

Every society has ceremonial and civil law created by the men and women in leadership positions. Moral law comes direct from God, e.g., The Ten Commandments. It is unchanging across time. It trumps all manmade law.

Our society today is secular. Ceremonial law is not a part of our culture. For the Israelites, it was an enormous part of life. Sacrifice in the form of beverages, grains, animals, and other personal actions was at the heart of their ceremonial law. Many of those ceremonies foreshadowed the arrival of Jesus.

Civil law is what enables society to remain intact. It involves daily principles of living that guide conduct. America is based on the rule of law, which makes her a Republic. Our constitution was established to ensure equal application of the law, regardless of sex, creed, race, or religion. People entrusted with enforcing laws have on occasion fallen short of this premise, but that does not change the fact that this is the ideal Americans put forward in 1776 and codified in 1787.

Upholding moral law is the responsibility of each individual. While you are born with a sin nature passed down by Adam, understanding right and wrong is something you know in your heart to a large extent. The moral law is a reflection of God's nature and his expectation for people.

DAY THREE HUNDRED & THIRTY-NINE

Life is short, have a purpose every day
Psalm 90:12 - 17

You have an expiration date. God knows the time and place, but you do not. God places some desires in you to accomplish something. Too often the enemy snatches godly desires away.

Knowing that your days are numbered means you want to make it count, to be effective and productive. Maybe you get in a hurry, distracted, wounded, or depressed. This is where your enemy thrives.

The desire God places in your heart is real, and if you will love and serve him, trusting all will be revealed in his good time, he will use your life. But you must understand that true satisfaction will only be experienced in eternity. Don't be fooled into thinking that you can author that satisfaction with accomplishment or relationships.

Ask him what it is he'd like for you to accomplish. Take some small step each day toward what you believe is your purpose right now.

DAY THREE HUNDRED & FORTY

The role of angels in your life
Psalm 91:11

Angels are fascinating, mysterious, and ever present throughout the Bible. Angels are mentioned over 300 times in the Bible. Most angels are God's assistants. They work for and worship him in the spiritual realm, just like you do in the earthly realm.

You will find angels bringing food as well as messages of comfort or warning. At times they bring death, destruction, and war. They appear in spirit or human form.

Some angels became demons and fell from heaven. They are your enemies. Revelation 12: 7 - 9 explains: "Then war broke out in heaven. Michael and his angels fought against the dragon, and the dragon and his angels fought back. But he was not strong enough, and they lost their place in heaven. The great dragon was hurled down—that ancient serpent called the devil, or Satan, who leads the whole world astray. He was hurled to the earth, and his angels with him."

If you are ever in trouble, afraid, lonely, scared, or confused, call out with your voice or in your heart to the Lord. He may send an angel. An angel may come even without you calling. However, you cannot control what they do. They are limited by what God has allowed for any given situation.

"For he will command his angels concerning you to guard you in all your ways…" (91:11).

DAY THREE HUNDRED & FORTY-ONE

You must fight, and God will sustain you
Isaiah 46:4

God expects a lot from his people, and he promises even more to those who will stand firm. This means feeling the fear but pressing on, doubting yourself at times but clinging to what God says about you.

The enemy hates the light inside you. He will work through all manner of people and situations to keep you confused, tempted, and defeated. God reserves vast amounts of power for the believer who will fight. In Ephesians 6, Paul analogizes the word of God to battle accoutrements: the sword, helmet, breast plate.

Each element of armor implies taking action. You must pick up your sword and put on the protective gear. If you do not take action to protect yourself, you will be destroyed.

If a train is speeding toward you, jump off the track. If the enemy is speaking through another person to tear you down and intimidate you, draw a line in the sand and correct them respectfully but firmly.

The devil deals in lies, deception. You deal in facts, transparency.

It will feel scary, especially if the person is in authority over you. Say, "It's unproductive and hurtful when you speak to me that way." Follow with a statement of fact about what you are doing or will do.

God speaks clearly to you through the book of Isaiah - "I am he who will sustain you. I have made you and will carry you; I will sustain you and I will rescue you" (46:4).

DAY THREE HUNDRED & FORTY-TWO

Don't trade the truth for a lie
Proverbs 12:19

Your enemy works daily through people and situations to trick you into choosing a lie over the truth. The truth is simple. You were born with God given rights to your heart, soul, and body. There's a lot of responsibility associated with those rights. Jesus died so you could have complete freedom for the trinity that is your personhood, if you choose to accept his sacrifice.

From an early age, the enemy begins attacks aimed at getting you to believe that to be loved, safe, successful, financially secure, popular, calm, or whatever else you need, you must give up some aspect of your rights.

The term boundaries is used to describe the rightful fence you have to set around yourself. Only you can set boundaries and maintain them. God won't do it for you. People won't do it for you.

Someone with authority or influence will show up with a script you must follow to have love, safety, success, etc. As soon as the "script" entails anything you know in your gut to be abuse or a lie, this is where the test begins. Will you choose integrity - to be whole - or will you compromise, make the exchange to keep the others happy, accepting you.

If the enemy can get you to give in once, twice is easy and so it goes. It's never too late to begin laying out your boundaries. You may have had your personal boundaries trampled at a very young age by a parent, teacher, or someone else with control. Those wounds can be healed. Ask God, and he will help you.

DAY THREE HUNDRED & FORTY-THREE

You are a partner not a slave
1 Peter 2

No matter what worldly role you currently play - mother, child, wife, employee, friend, volunteer - you are a partner not a slave.

The difference can be subtle. A slave is only free to do and say what the one in authority allows. A slave is not entitled to their own opinion or thoughts. A slave is not included in real discussions about how to achieve goals. A slave is not always extended basic respect. A slave is expected to do what they are told.

Without a "chain of command" or authority there cannot be order. Do not confuse your right to be a partner versus a slave with rebellion or disrespect. You are under someone's authority and that authority may be an unfair master that you must endure for a season.

Remember that your true freedom always lies in the choice of attitude and response. You can remain free even in the cruelest of conditions. The secret is to never forget that you belong to Christ. You are his servant. He values you unconditionally.

DAY THREE HUNDRED & FORTY-FOUR

Never negotiate with terrorists or bullies
John 19:1-16

Terrorists and bullies deal in fear to control the actions of others. To negotiate or give in to a person or organization that uses any form of threat to get something is a losing proposition, i.e., either you do x, or we will harm you (physically or emotionally).

Normal, peace loving people often find it hard to deal effectively with terrorists and bullies because they don't know how to think in their terms. A normal person never considers violence an option to get what they want. However, when faced with someone who uses violence to get what they want, the normal person must be willing to meet violence with the authority of violence (police, military, governmental organizations, principal, parent, etc.) as a last resort.

Until you draw a line in the proverbial sand and refuse to let the bully cross it, they will control you and often harm many innocent people. The line implies that you will do whatever it takes to protect the territory - people, including yourself - behind that line.

In reality, this is the most loving thing you can do for all involved, especially those who are innocent and cannot defend themselves. Every single person, you included, is looking for the boundary line, which answers the question, "At what point must I stop?"

The reason this is so hard for some people to draw a line of protection is that deep down they are not sure of their own value, competency, and stamina. Unless you understand the principles of the one, true God - the God who covered your sins, has made an eternal provision for your soul, and is in control of your past, present, and future - you will be unable to confidently and effectively stand up to terrorists and bullies.

Will you draw the line, believing that God has your back?

DAY THREE HUNDRED & FORTY-FIVE

Are all religions created equal?
John 8:12-30

A common criticism of Christians is that they are narrow-minded. To say that Christ is the only way to eternal life in heaven seems ignorant and judgmental to them. Yet, that is the truth that all Christians know.

Those who adhere to other belief systems are made and loved by God, just like you. Your job is to live out Jesus' truth through your words and actions and be ready to answer any question. Some will be called to witness in other countries or among groups with different beliefs.

It's important to educate yourself about what different religions and philosophies believe and practice. Here's a brief comparison of the world's primary monotheistic belief systems:

Catholics and Protestants: Believe in Christ as the one true son of God and Savior of all mankind. Today, the two branches of Christianity are not in hostile conflict. Protestants gather in denominations (Baptist, Presbyterian, etc.) and originated as a protest against corruption and harsh rules within the Catholic church.

Jews: Believe in the God of the Old Testament Bible but that Jesus was only a man. They still await a Messiah. They are unique, chosen people of God. Jews make up less than 5% of the world's population but contribute disproportionally to discoveries in medicine and other areas of advances for civilization. For example, from 1901 - 2016, 22% of all Nobel Peace Prize recipients were Jewish.

Muslims: Believe in a deity called Allah that is molded after the one true God. Islam is a political system with strict rules about how adherents worship Allah. There is no separation between "church and state." The state is run by religious leaders. They believe Jesus was a prophet but that their founder, Mohammad, was the ultimate prophet and above Jesus. Muslims make up 22% of the world's population. The Pew Charitable Trust predicts that by 2050 Muslims will grow to 2.76 billion, or 29.7% of world's population.

DAY THREE HUNDRED & FORTY-SIX

Difference between a successful and unsuccessful person
Judges 17 - 18, Job 6:13

Success is a subjective term. You likely use unrealistic or warped measures to define your own success. In the world, success is associated with beauty and wealth. God's will for your success is to have you become a person of character and courage that is obedient to his every call for your life.

He's always looking for people who will use the power he's given every single individual to be successful to join his ranks of kingdom builders.

The difference between those who succeed as God ordained for their individual life and those who spend a lifetime in confusion, emotional pain, and regret comes down to choosing courage over fear and attention to God's will versus your own or those around you.

But what does it mean to be courageous and know God's truth?

In Judges 17 - 18 the story of Micah and the Danites illustrates how easily people create their own god and illusion of success. It takes courage to wait for God to move in your life and then to take steps toward his will, not your own. Often using your skills and talents to fulfill God's will looks as if there's nothing in it for you.

Micah found that once his self-made idols and purchased priest were stolen by the Danites, he was left with nothing. When you work to achieve God's will, you will be left with the only thing that really matters - him.

DAY THREE HUNDRED & FORTY-SEVEN

"Don't be delicate, be vast and brilliant"
Matthew 10:16

In Matthew 10, Jesus lays down some heavy revelations for his disciples. He's about to send them out on their own. "I am sending you out like sheep among wolves. Therefore, be as shrewd as snakes and as innocent as doves," he says (10:16).

Everything that Jesus asked of them, he's asking of you. It's not any easier today than it was in the first century.

A young woman from North Carolina named Erin Phillips died at the age of 32. She'd been born with Cystic-Fibrosis. Her life was extended thanks to a lung transplant. With her new lungs, she climbed mountains, served orphans, and inspired many. Erin told anyone who would listen, "Don't be delicate, be vast and brilliant."

Those who are too delicate to join in God's work with humanity will find their rewards fleeting. Whether born with or without defects, your time here is short. Jesus' parting words to his gang of mostly uneducated, poor fishermen before sending them out to face a cruel and hurting world were sobering: "Whoever finds their life will lose it, and whoever loses their life for my sake will find it" (10:39).

Coming into the world with real limits on what she could and could not physically do heightened Erin's understanding that her treasure [life] resided in a jar [body] made of clay (2 Corinthians 4:7), but she wasted no time worrying over the jar. She busied herself lavishly pouring out the treasure.

DAY THREE HUNDRED & FORTY-EIGHT

Face the present with faith and grace
James 5:10-11

Life comes at you fast. Today, you may be happy and content, but tomorrow may bring adversity.

If you face something hard right now, the pain that is either dull or excruciating at this moment is being allowed by God to get your attention. Step back and look at your situation and how you feel as if Jesus were looking on with you. Don't turn away. Ask him to help you see it honestly, and the next step toward healing and doing the right thing.

If you turn away now, if you listen to the lie one more time, you will just have to walk this path again.

Even if nothing is going right, you feel as if all is lost, or that it's too late for you, there are five attitudes and actions that God will notice and honor:

1. Work, create something, or serve others
2. Live by percentages with time to work, play, and rest as well as with money to give, save, and spend
3. Don't fear the future or dwell on the past
4. Tell yourself that God values you and has a plan for you
5. Look your best each day and smile at those you encounter

DAY THREE HUNDRED & FORTY-NINE

Lows follow the highs
Judges 15, Luke 4:1-2

Anytime you win, accomplish a great task, or rise up against something big in your life, expect a period of sadness or even depression to follow. This flow of things is partly due to a need to physically replenish but it is also psychological. If you take on enormous tasks or battles without God, you may be undone in the aftermath.

Samson was promised to his barren mother by an angel (Judges 13). The angel told her the child would be a Nazirite, set apart for God, and that he would begin the process of delivering Israel from the Philistines. Samson did become a leader and fought against the Philistines in many odd ways (see Judges 14 - 16).

An impetuous nature led Samson to make many mistakes and ultimately to his death, but God used him for the purposes ordained.

To escape capture by the Philistines on one occasion, Samson killed 1,000 men with the jawbone of a donkey. Afterwards, he bragged about the accomplishment and cried out to God that he would die of thirst.

You may have the strength, intellect, and talent to do much, but remember to allow God to set the pace of your progress and to give him the credit. The body and its physical needs for rest, water, and food will remain with you in this life. The heart and mind also need attention. Heed the signs of sadness, exhaustion, and hunger.

DAY THREE HUNDRED & FIFTY

Ask for healing
Jeremiah 17:14, James 5:16

James says, "Confess your sins to one another and pray for one another, that you may be healed" (5:16).

When you ask God for healing, his prescriptions and modalities may look different than what you have in mind. He may use illness or injury in the healing process.

If you've prayed a long time for healing for yourself or on behalf of another, look for subtle signs of change such as loving people easier and understanding of deep truth yet becoming increasingly humble.

In God's healing process, you may lose what you worked for and experience great hurt yet feel no sense of victimization or entitlement. Farther along the healing path, you may assess your most valuable treasures and comforts and find their presence in your life bordering on the miraculous, such as a child, husband, friends, home, or job.

Even if you feel old and that your healing is incomplete, don't stop praying, as Jeremiah the prophet did, "Heal me, Lord, and I will be healed; save me and I will be saved, for you are the one I praise" (17:14).

DAY THREE HUNDRED & FIFTY-ONE

Created to serve
1 Samuel 18:14

You were created to serve. Every single person is created to serve God's purposes in some form or fashion. This truth can anger or comfort you but will not change.

Often people limit their ability to serve by allowing pride to settle into their heart and mind. King Saul, the first appointed king over the Jews by God, became prideful. David, who would become the greatest king ever, had everything that leads to pride. He was handsome, talented, and a natural leader. He had a likable personality, and "In everything he did he had great success, because the Lord was with him" (18:14).

David made mistakes that cost him greatly, but he always returned to humility and a dependence on God. He never forgot that he was created to serve God and that all of his blessings and success came from God.

You will serve. You can choose to work with God and follow his plan or strike out on your own. It's much easier to stick close to God. Ask him to help you remain humble, in good times and bad.

DAY THREE HUNDRED & FIFTY-TWO

Recognizing the devil's voice
Luke 4:1-13

The devil's voice is the one that encourages you to do something and then condemns you after you do it.

He deals in vicious cycles. Those cycles that begin with your desires for things that might not necessarily be wrong in the right context. You give in, hate yourself later, and then give in again to salve the pain. You might find yourself saying things like "everybody does it," "who cares," "why bother," "just one more time," "I've already done it once," or "it's too late now."

The devil taunts and tempts you in an attempt to find where pride resides within you, because all sin is rooted there. He only needs to make you question God's authority or commands.

The devil tempted Jesus in the wilderness with the same ole tricks he uses on you: doubt God's Word and trade God's promises for less than best or lies. Jesus overcame his enemy with resolve and the Word of God.

Sin is often not in the act but in the reason for the act. The path laid out to lure you away from God is full of short cuts and rationalizations. The enemy tempts you to fulfill legitimate needs but outside of God's timing or his plan for your life.

Temptation begins as pressure leading to discomfort. Pressure mounts. Human nature is to look for relief in some form. The devil will appear with suggestions for alleviating the pressure sometimes through your strengths and sometimes through your weaknesses.

At times you will know that you can do this or that, but God is not giving you permission or a leading to do it. Defeating temptation and outwitting the devil is an ongoing challenge.

Take stock of your temptations. How are you guarding yourself? You must have a plan. "He will always provide a way out so that you can endure it" (1 Corinthians 10:13). God's Word is a defense against all manner of temptations. Memorize a few lines to help you when in midst of temptation.

DAY THREE HUNDRED & FIFTY-THREE

Pay close attention to your heart
Jeremiah 17:9-13, Proverbs 13:12, 14:10

The heart is mentioned over 700 times in the Bible and 150 times in this book. Jeremiah writes, "The heart is deceitful above all things and beyond cure. Who can understand it?" (17:9).

No one knows what's in your heart. At times you may not even be aware of what your own heart is up to. Your heart can be broken, proud, sick, bitter, brave, conniving, determined, faithful, pulled at, sincere, joyful, light. There's no end to descriptions of the heart because it is the essence of every human, both literally and figuratively.

Hearts yearning for too long make for an unhappy person (Proverbs 13:12). Hearts broken can mend and the scars left behind can make you stronger and more loving or weak and bitter (Proverbs 14:10).

God searches and examines your heart and mind (17:10). He's speaking to your heart right now. The world too is pulling at your heart. In your heart, you know there is right and wrong. God uses Scripture and the Holy Spirit to help you know truth from fiction. God wants to lead your heart to love.

DAY THREE HUNDRED & FIFTY-FOUR

Have mercy
Hosea 6, Matthew 9:13 and 12:7

In Hebrew, the word rechem means womb. Rechem is the root of racham, which means protection from harm, and shares a root word for compassion and mercy. God is merciful. He protects you from the full extent of harm that could fall upon you and he withholds the punishment you often deserve. You need mercy and so does everyone you know.

Do you give to others the mercy you desire?

To have mercy connotes to go easy, give a break, bear up with, protect from embarrassment or ridicule.

In Hosea 6:6, God speaks to his people through the prophet Hosea. "For I desire mercy, not sacrifice, and acknowledgment of God rather than burnt offerings." Jesus repeats the statement "I desire mercy, not sacrifice" in Matthew 9:13 and 12:7.

More than any amount of time, money, church attendance, or any other form of sacrifice, God wants you to be merciful to others and yourself. This does not mean that you should ignore wrongdoing or harmful thinking. It means that you should consider context and perhaps what you do not know about someone.

Maybe the absent-minded cashier or slow driver has experienced a loss. The annoying person may be desperate for a friend. Your insistence on pressing for some wrong to be made right just might cause someone to lose their job or fall further into debt.

Walk in the shoes of others. Have mercy. Thank God for the mercy he has shown you today.

DAY THREE HUNDRED & FIFTY-FIVE

The scapegoat
Leviticus 16, Hebrews 9:11-12, Isaiah 53:1-6

Have you ever felt like the scapegoat? It's the one who takes the fall or the hit for the group, the one who takes the blame for the misfortunes and failings of others.

The scapegoat was a goat and powerful part of God's system of atonement given to the Israelites as well as a symbol of the role Christ would play on behalf of all mankind. The sending out of the scapegoat remains a symbolic part of the Jewish Yom Kippur service today.

Leviticus 16 describes the elaborate atonement ceremony God required of his people. As part of the process, two goats were sacrificed. One goat's blood was shed, and one was sent away into the wilderness alone.

The scapegoat was not sacrificed. Instead, this goat was sent away from the community and the presence of God. Exile is an experience much worse than death. This animal served as a reminder of sin, the need to banish all impurity and perversity from a community, and the extreme darkness of being put outside the group.

"When Aaron has finished making atonement for the Most Holy Place, the tent of meeting and the altar, he shall bring forward the live goat. He is to lay both hands on the head of the live goat and confess over it all the wickedness and rebellion of the Israelites—all their sins—and put them on the goat's head. He shall send the goat away into the wilderness in the care of someone appointed for the task. The goat will carry on itself all their sins to a remote place; and the man shall release it in the wilderness" (Leviticus 16: 20 - 22)

Jesus became both goats, the sacrificed goat and the one sent away, separated from God on our behalf. Unlike the ceremonial scapegoat, Jesus came back and was reunited with God and lives forever as the last sacrifice for us all.

DAY THREE HUNDRED & FIFTY-SIX

Prayer can change God's mind
2 Kings 20

God never changes but prayer can move him to compassion. Prayer is always the answer to everything in life. When good things happen offer up praise. When bad things happen pray for mercy and forgiveness. When all feels lost and there seems no way out, pray like Hezekiah.

Hezekiah was king of Judah (715 - 686 BC). Second Kings 20 records that he became ill and was about to die. The prophet Isaiah took word to him from God affirming that his death was impending. "Hezekiah turned his face to the wall and prayed to the Lord… 'Remember, Lord, how I have walked before you faithfully and with wholehearted devotion and have done what is good in your eyes.' And Hezekiah wept bitterly" (20: 2 - 3).

Isaiah had not even left the palace before the Lord said, "Go back and tell Hezekiah, the ruler of my people, 'This is what the Lord, the God of your father David, says: I have heard your prayer and seen your tears; I will heal you. On the third day from now you will go up to the temple of the Lord. I will add fifteen years to your life. And I will deliver you and this city from the hand of the king of Assyria. I will defend this city for my sake and for the sake of my servant David'" (20: 5 - 6).

You never know how God will respond to your prayers. There's nothing to lose by sincerely asking. Don't forego praying because you don't believe God will change a situation. Anything is possible. Start and finish with prayer.

DAY THREE HUNDRED & FIFTY-SEVEN

Don't ask God to follow you, follow him
Nehemiah 8:10, Deuteronomy 31:6, Psalm 9:10

God promises to never leave or forsake his children. He'll follow you wherever you go. However, you will be better served to follow him rather than attempting to drag him along for your escapades.

You have dreams and plans, most of them are good, well-meaning ideas. Some are self-centered and rooted in pride. Human nature is to get fixated on what you want like a hound following his nose. Once you are invested in getting that thing, whatever it is, you forget to stop and wait for God's directions and his timing. You might throw out quick prayers that are just invitations for God to come along with you.

What you are after in every pursuit is joy. You might think you are after revenge, fame, a job, support, fun, and a host of other ideas. Deep down, what you want is relief. You want to feel peace and joy.

You will never find it for more than a moment running along your own path. The joy of the Lord is your strength. Until you accept his joy as enough, you will never find lasting joy or peace.

Begin praying, "God, where will we go today? I'm ready to follow wherever you lead."

DAY THREE HUNDRED & FIFTY-EIGHT

Embracing challenging seasons
Luke 17:1-10

There are challenges in life that require focus, tenacity, and often great sacrifice for a season. Most of these opportunities are time sensitive, meaning you have a window of time to achieve the maximum impact.

High school, parenting, and training for tests or events are such seasons. You can't get such times back or redo them. They are times that if you do the hard work in season, the pay-off can last well into the future.

There's a certain amount of solitariness and personal risk that goes along with achieving something big. You will feel weak and tempted to give up. You will look around and see people seemingly having fun and enjoying things you want. Keep your eyes on God and attention on the tasks at hand.

Allow God to end the season, not you. Don't let up or give up prematurely. Many times, people get within close range of a big goal and quit, forfeiting all the hard work, all the investment they made. Don't let that be you. Let the outcomes be God's. Don't prejudge.

He's always got the long view in mind. He sees what's over the horizon that you cannot.

DAY THREE HUNDRED & FIFTY-NINE

There's no defense against kindness
Isaiah 61:3, Romans 2:4

William P. Young, author of *The Shack*, once said, "God wins people over with kindness, with grace. You can only accept it or run away. This is the kind of God that leads to repentance."

As an agent of God, he does not need you to defend him. He needs you to point the way with your life and to love others as he guides you day-by-day. He's already given you "a crown of beauty instead of ashes, the oil of joy instead of mourning, and a garment of praise instead of a spirit of despair…" (Isaiah 61:3).

Please do not mistake God's call to kindness for one to be a doormat, or a punching bag, or a lemming or blind, deaf, and dumb. You might get treated like a doormat, punching bag, or disabled person. Respond like Christ - speak the truth in love, go about your calling and living a godly life.

Be kind. Then when God prepares the hearts of the angry, hurt people for his love, you will be the one they remember.

DAY THREE HUNDRED & SIXTY

Beware your personal Sirens
1 Kings 12:25-33, Exodus 33:1-6

The Sirens are the mythological half bird, half woman creatures described in Homer's Odyssey that lured sailors to destruction by the sweetness of their song.

Sirens are metaphors for those people and things that distract you from a mission, your God-given mission. They always appear after a tough battle or when the journey is simply taking longer than you'd anticipated.

The longer you stay with the Sirens, the harder it is to leave. The Sirens become like golden handcuffs. You are imprisoned, but it's easy to forget that fact because the money is good, you're having fun, or it's just easy.

Your mind must be free to achieve the ultimate end of your God-given mission. If you are not self-aware and diligent, you will live an entire lifetime in the chains forged by your own unwillingness to resist the Sirens.

Don't stay in whatever place where Sirens have lured you. It's inevitable that you will visit. But keep it short. Pray for God's help.

DAY THREE HUNDRED & SIXTY-ONE

Know the look, feel, and smell of truth versus fiction
Proverbs 8:7-9

Barring some form of handicap or aberration, people are born with a basic sense of right and wrong, sincerity versus duplicity. Little children are often great character judges. People hide things when they know on some deep level that what they are doing is wrong. It's important to retain your sense of truth into adulthood.

The only way to know the truth about yourself and others is to remain close to God. If you will seek him through prayer, Bible reading, and listening, he will give you discernment. God directs every step and gives the person who follows him a sense of what is true and what is not, exactly when you need to know these things.

The truth about things and people eludes you when the desire to be important, popular, wealthy, and beautiful dominates your heart and mind.

Be truthful with yourself and others.

DAY THREE HUNDRED & SIXTY-TWO

Making everything new
Revelation 21

Genesis begins with the creation of everything by God. The first book of the Bible relays stories of people's lives to illustrate how God operates and the nature of humans. Christ came for the purpose of redemption, giving all people the chance to be forgiven and live forever in heaven. In the end, the Trinity (God as father, Jesus as son, and Holy Spirit as counselor) will usher in "a new heaven and a new earth" (21:1).

God will live with his people in this new heaven and earth (21:3). "He will wipe every tear from their eyes…" (21:4).

The Disciple John is receiving the revelation from Jesus who says, … "I am making everything new!" Then he said, "Write this down, for these words are trustworthy and true."

He said to me: "It is done. I am the Alpha and the Omega, the Beginning and the End. To the thirsty I will give water without cost from the spring of the water of life. Those who are victorious will inherit all this, and I will be their God and they will be my children. But the cowardly, the unbelieving, the vile, the murderers, the sexually immoral, those who practice magic arts, the idolaters and all liars—they will be consigned to the fiery lake of burning sulfur. This is the second death" (21: 5 -8).

What to make of these exclusive and definitive words? Life on earth is a time of testing. You get to choose whether you will prevail against the evil that comes at you and remain faithful or not. Remember Jesus' words in Matthew 11:30, "For my yoke is easy and my burden is light."

DAY THREE HUNDRED & SIXTY-THREE

What to do about your mistakes
Genesis 4:6-7, Proverbs 28:13

"Everybody makes mistakes, but only fools repeat them" (NIV notes pg. 1340). If you are wise, you will assess, correct, and remember mistakes so as not to repeat them. If someone points out a mistake, wrong, or sin, take their words into consideration, especially if it comes from someone in authority over you.

Cain is the archetypal example of what happens to those who will not correct mistakes in action and attitude.

"Then the Lord said to Cain, "Why are you angry? Why is your face downcast? If you do what is right, will you not be accepted? But if you do not do what is right, sin is crouching at your door; it desires to have you, but you must rule over it" (Genesis 4:6 – 7).

Instead of attempting to make a better sacrifice, he killed his brother who in this story represents the ideal, the one who made a sacrifice pleasing to God. Your conscience knows when you've done wrong or right. Listening to it will lead to correction. Ignoring it will lead to death, literal or figurative, but one is as bad as the other.

DAY THREE HUNDRED & SIXTY-FOUR

Endure hardship as discipline
Hebrews 12:4-17

"Afterward, as you know, when he wanted to inherit this blessing, he was rejected. Even though he sought the blessing with tears, he could not change what he had done" (12:17).

Esau is the one who cried about the blessing he'd given up for a cup of soup (Genesis 25: 29-34). His brother Jacob tricked him, which was a terrible betrayal. But Esau lived recklessly and resisted the discipline associated with his position and responsibility. So, in a moment of thoughtlessness he traded his birthright for the soup. He was tired and hungry. Esau had no experience with self-discipline. He had to live with regret.

No one likes discipline. It comes in the form of hardship and discomfort, not getting your way, being put in your place. But it must and will come. It will come from God as well as your parents, teachers, and friends, if you will accept it. If you refuse, it will come from the world.

"My [child], do not make light of the Lord's discipline, and do not lose heart when he rebukes you, because the Lord disciplines the one he loves, and he chastens everyone he accepts as his [child]" (12: 5-6).

Discipline can harden you and cause bitterness, or it can mature you. You get to choose the response but not the form or type of discipline. Don't waste your energy fighting discipline. Use the lessons to build up your ability to have peace and enjoy your life.

DAY THREE HUNDRED & SIXTY-FIVE

Encouragement to go on
Philippians 4:4-9

If you've come to the end, it's time to begin again. That holds true for whatever end you've come to – the end of this devotional, a program, a job, a marriage, your wits, your faith, yourself. You will be faced with endings and there's always two choices. Give up or get up.

I began writing these short devotionals in 2012. My daughter was twelve. I'd just finished a year of dealing with breast cancer. We'd moved from the farm to the city. I had so much hope for new beginnings. It turned out to be the hardest stretch of my life. That stretch continues to this day (November 2019).

My disappointment in the outcomes of about everything have made me want to forget about this book and all else I've sacrificed for, dreamed of, and pursued. But I do not allow myself to give up. With God's grace and mercy, I will continue on as long as I have breath.

No matter what is happening in your life today, don't give up or stop believing. Those who give up eventually slip into darker and darker places. God has you here for a reason. Choose him. Reach for the light.

Make a note of these anchor verses from the Apostle Paul (Philippians 4: 4 – 9):

Rejoice in the Lord always. I will say it again: Rejoice! Let your gentleness be evident to all. The Lord is near. Do not be anxious about anything, but in every situation, by prayer and petition, with thanksgiving, present your requests to God. And the peace of God, which transcends all understanding, will guard your hearts and your minds in Christ Jesus.

Finally, brothers and sisters, whatever is true, whatever is noble, whatever is right, whatever is pure, whatever is lovely, whatever is admirable—if anything is excellent or praiseworthy—think about such things. Whatever you have learned or received or heard from me, or seen in me—put it into practice. And the God of peace will be with you.

NOTES, PRAYERS, DOODLES

ABOUT THE AUTHOR

Carla Harper is an author and publisher living in North Carolina. Her first novel, WORTHY, released in 2016. *The Worthy Girl's Guide to Life* is a companion to the novel.

Conquistor Veritas (carlagharper.com) is a publisher and distributor of books nationally and internationally. Carla helps writers get their work published and distributed in a professional manner.

Missionstatements.com offers writing services and inspirational leadership quotes to individuals and businesses all over the world.

West65inc.com offers marketing and branding services to small and mid-sized organizations and businesses.

Contact Carla to order books or get help publishing your work at carlamgarrison@gmail.com

www.ingramcontent.com/pod-product-compliance
Lightning Source LLC
Chambersburg PA
CBHW060457010526
44118CB00018B/2441